PRAISE FOR *WHITE ESTATE FRAUD*

I0617837

"Steve Daily strikes again. In *White Estate Fraud*, he and Nancy Paige present an ethical, moral, and probably legal challenge to the Seventh-day Adventist Church. They advance what they consider to be a trajectory of lies, dishonesty, and deceit within one of the most successful organizations in the world. The claims presented should not go unanswered by the church."

Clinton Baldwin Ph.D., author of four books including,
***Justification by Faith: More than a Concept-a Person,* and**
former director of Christian Scholar's Forum International

———

"*White Estate Fraud* is just another classic example of the dishonesty that can be found in Ellen White, the White Estate, and Adventist history from its very inception to modern times. An eye-opening account of the highly deceitful role that Arthur White played in this process."

Dale Ratzlaff, author of *The Cultic Doctrine of*
***Seventh-day Adventists,* founder of Life Assurance Ministries,**
***Proclamation magazine,* and LAM Publications, LLC**

———

"Steve Daily demonstrates unequivocally that Carrie Johnson was never Canright's secretary, and the story of him recanting was a pious fraud. Moreover, Daily reveals the shocking inner workings of the White Estate, which would make any Christian with an ounce of integrity recoil in horror."

Dirk Anderson, author of *White Out* (2001) and *Prophet or Pretender*
(2021) and founder and host of www.nonsda.org/www.nonegw.org

———

"*White Estate Fraud* is a gripping read with profound truths of an espionage tale put forth to destroy and ruin the character and personality of an innocent, God-fearing man, a man who found the gospel among the ruins of strange doctrines. You see, knowledge has increased and with the help of social media there is nothing left hidden. The evidence is powerful and convicting that Mr. Canright was a sincere seeker of truth as it is in Christ Jesus. He trusted in the old resource that detects truth from error, the Bible, and for that he was discredited. The lights are out for Ellen, Arthur, and Carrie while Canright's light shines brighter. The Bible is true, all that claim the name of Jesus will suffer persecution. But the path of the just shines brighter and brighter until the perfect day. So, stand strong and be faithful to the truth, no matter the cost let your light shine."

Esmie G. Branner. Ph.D., cognitive neuropsychologist and author of
Beyond the Veil of Darkness

———

"Steve Daily's ability to captivate readers from the very first page is unmatched. The depth of his research and his skillful storytelling combine to create an immersive experience that tests our preconceptions and leaves us questioning the motives of those involved. With each turn of the page, the author (along with some wonderful insights from contributor Nancy Paige) deftly exposes previously unknown information, leading readers through a complex web of truths and half-truths. The confrontational nature of Daily's work is apparent as he shines a light on the shadows of Canright's mistreatment. This confrontation with uncomfortable truths challenges readers to reconsider long-held notions and compels them to reevaluate the impact of the decisions made by those in positions of authority. Steve Daily's exposé of the underhanded treatment of Dudley M. Canright stands as a triumph of academic research and scholarly investigation.

Peter Dixon, founder and host of the YouTube channel SDAQ&A—
A Former Adventist Looking in from the Outside

———

"Steve Daily and I have known each other for almost four decades. I have been persistently struck by his intellectual energy, breadth, and productivity and by his dedication to the Gospel. His coauthor, Nancy Paige, has made clear her commitment to truth and to righting past wrongs by providing evidence drawn from both her experience and her research that her grandmother, Carrie Johnson, profoundly misrepresented D. M. Canright in *I Was Canright's Secretary* and in lurid public lectures; her testimony deserves the careful attention of anyone who has encountered Johnson's widely circulated narratives. In this book, Daily and Paige have continued the important earlier work of Norman F. Douty, helping to ensure that Canright is not seen, because of Johnson's fabrications, as a broken, lost, indigent, demon-possessed apostate but that he receives the respect he deserves as a capable, effective Christian minister."

Gary Chartier Ph.D., associate dean,
distinguished professor of law and usiness ethics at the Tom and
Vi Zapara School of Business, La Sierra University

————

"*White Estate Fraud* is a breakthrough in SDA history. It reveals never before published revelations of the extreme deception that Arthur White, the White Estate, Carrie Johnson, and the Adventist Church were willing to engage in to try to destroy the reputation and character of their most effective critic, D. M. Canright, a humble godly minister of the gospel! Adventism's most infamous critic was castigated in the book *I Was Canright's Secretary*, required reading for serious students of SDA history. Actually, author Carrie Johnson never worked for Canright—and may have never even met him. This is according to Carrie's own granddaughter, who in this great work has collaborated with psychologist Steve Daily to expose what might be the most embarrassing scandal in Adventist history."

Martin Weber, author of *Adventist Hot Potatoes*,
***More Adventist Hot Potatoes,* and the soon coming**
Idolatry of Ellen White

the
WHITE ESTATE
FRAUD

Seventh-day Adventism's Scandalous Untold Story

STEVE DAILY, PH.D.

WITH NANCY PAIGE

MEDIA.COM

Published by

Illumify Media Global

www.IllumifyMedia.com

"Let's bring your book to life!"

Paperback ISBN: 978-1-959099-49-9

Cover design by Debbie Lewis

Printed in the United States of America

To:

Nancy Paige and Norman Douty,
who made the book possible, and
to my Facebook reading group

CONTENTS

ABBREVIATIONS

EGW	Ellen G. White
SM 1	Ellen G. White. *Selected Messages*. Bk. 1. Hagerstown, MD: Review and Herald, 2006.
SM 2	Ellen G. White. *Selected Messages*. Bk. 2.
SM 3	Ellen G. White. *Selected Messages*. Bk. 3. Hagerstown, MD: Review and Herald, 2006.
Testimonies 3	Ellen G. White. *Testimonies for the Church*. Vol. 3.
Testimonies 4	Ellen G. White. *Testimonies for the Church*. Vol. 4.
Testimonies 5	Ellen G. White. *Testimonies for the Church*. Vol. 5. Mountain View, CA: Pacific Press, 1948.
Testimonies 8	Ellen G. White. *Testimonies for the Church*. Vol. 8.
Testimonies 9	Ellen G. White. *Testimonies for the Church*. Vol. 9.

FOREWORD

Few Adventists were as zealous for Ellen White as I was in 1998. I operated the most-frequented apologetic website defending her. Based on the *partial* information supplied to me by the SDA sect, I was convinced she was a true prophet of God. That momentous year, a man named Dale Ratzlaff called me and challenged me to read a book called *Life of Mrs. E. G. White, Seventh-day Adventist Prophet, Her False Claims Refuted*, by D. M. Canright. I had heard he was a critic of Ellen White, but I had never read his book. Like many Adventists, I believed the buzz in SDA circles that he was an apostate former SDA who was led by Satan to criticize God's true prophetess. When Ratzlaff sent me the book, I opened it with a healthy dose of skepticism, but also with anticipation, looking forward to exposing Canright as a liar and a fraud. As I read page after page, I could hardly put the book down. When I finished, I was in a state of shock and denial. I kept telling myself, "This can't possibly be true." Determined to prove it false, I went to the local SDA university and spent weeks reading F. D. Nichols's book and trying to find any material to prove what Canright wrote to be false. To my utter astonishment, everything I researched turned out to prove that Canright was correct. To call his book life-changing would be an understatement.

One of the greatest sins a church can make is the sin of omission—hiding or squelching critical information about the denomination instead of dealing with it in a transparent manner. I realized that many people, like me, were making the decision to believe Ellen White and follow her teachings based up *partial* information—flattering historical accounts written by her most ardent admirers. If people knew the *omitted* stories about Ellen White, such as the one told by Canright, I believed that many, like me, would walk out of the sect and never return. Thus, I determined to make *omitted* information about Mrs. White available on the internet so others could make an informed decision about her.

As soon as I put Canright's book on my web page, I had SDAs writing to me, telling me I was delusional because Canright had recanted. In fact, his own secretary reported it. Their logic was, *Why should I bother reading this book if the author himself recanted?* This is why the book you are holding in your hand or reading on an electronic device is so important. Steve Daily demonstrates unequivocally that Carrie Johnson was never Canright's secretary, and the story of him recanting was a pious fraud. Moreover, Daily reveals the shocking inner workings of the White Estate, which would make any Christian with an ounce of integrity recoil in horror.

One of the saddest and most disturbing legacies of Adventism is their shameful historical record of assaulting the character of those who challenge the validity of the sect's teachings or prophetess. This practice started with Ellen White, as documented on our web site. As Daily reveals in this book and *Ellen G. White: A Psychobiography*, those who have humbly stood up for honesty, integrity, and transparency in the SDA sect have been maligned. Like Canright, Walter Rea was also victimized. I remember the day in 2004 when I spoke with him on the phone. Numerous Adventists had told me he had recanted, so I wanted to get the facts straight from the source. He told me he had *not* recanted, nor would he ever recant.

If you are a Seventh-day Adventist, you may be surprised to hear that the *facts* may differ widely from what you heard. I encourage you to read this book with an open mind and heart. One of the most difficult things you can do is read a book that differs from your preconceived opinions. We all naturally want to read material that agrees with what we already believe. I would ask you to please lay aside all your preconceived ideas about Canright and his secretary and allow the facts and the evidence to speak to your heart. After you get to the end of this book, ask yourself this one question: Is this how a church led by God operates?

God bless,
Brother Anderson
www.nonsda.org / www.nonegw.org

PREFACE

There are way too many forms of religious abuse in our world today, but this volume is committed to exposing one of the most scandalous and unknown case studies I have ever come across in this regard. I uncovered the fraud by accident while receiving feedback from my reader's group on my Facebook page. A relative of one of the perpetrators of the fraud shared some information I had never heard before, and as I researched her comments, I realized that this untold story deserved to be exposed.

The White Estate was established in 1915, shortly after the death of the "prophet"/founder of the Seventh-day Adventist Church, Ellen G. White. The purpose of the estate was to organize, distribute, and compile additional books from Ellen's writings—and unofficially, to protect and promote Ellen's name and works into the future. The two primary leaders of the White Estate in the decades after its founding were Ellen's son Willie, who was in charge until his death in 1937, and Ellen's grandson Arthur, who succeeded his father. The hidden work of Arthur White will play a very prominent role in this book.

In his monumental six-volume biography of Ellen White, which Adventists consider to be "definitive," Arthur stated in volume 1 that one of his goals was to write with "such detail and with such documentation as will meet the expectations of the scholar." After wading through this laborious apologetic work, I found it interesting that the author failed to mention little details such as Ellen's lifetime pattern of dishonesty; lying about "visions"; making up "visions" that falsely condemned others; controlling, manipulating, and financially exploiting her own church members' plagiarizing other authors and demanding the highest royalties from books she stole from them; falsely attributing all kinds of inaccurate, harmful, and racist views to God; and making blasphemous claims for herself.

In 2020, I published a psychobiography of Ellen White, a major religious icon who engaged in significant religious abuse that was largely unknown to the general population, as well as to the vast majority of the 20 million-plus membership of the denomination of which she was the "prophet"/founder. In the wake of this publication, I heard from literally thousands of individuals who felt they had experienced some form of religious abuse at the hands of this "prophet" or the movement she launched through her claimed "visions" and allegedly God-given authority and revelations.

One of the abuse victims I got to know through this process was a wonderful woman named Nancy Paige, whose grandmother Carrie Johnson had colluded with Arthur White to fabricate an entire book, *I Was Canright's Secretary,* to try to destroy Ellen's most threatening critic, D. M. Canright. My book, written with Nancy's help, exposes this scandalous fraud for the first time. The evidence that Carrie Johnson never even met D. M. Canright is overwhelming, as you will see in the following pages. Yet that did not prevent Carrie, Arthur White (a professed historian and scholar), and the Adventist Church, which aggressively marketed this book, from committing character assassination of the highest order. Fasten your seat belts as we embark on a well-documented story that is hard to believe.

But first, I will briefly share my credentials and life experience, which I hope qualify me to tackle this difficult, powerful, and relevant subject. I am currently the author of twenty-seven books, with this being the twenty-eighth. Ten of my books deal directly with Ellen White and Seventh-day Adventism and all deal with religion, psychology, and history, the three disciplines I taught at the university level during my twenty-four years on the faculty of Loma Linda University and La Sierra University in Southern California. I was also a campus chaplain and pastor during that period, involved in a great deal of counseling. I have been a licensed psychologist since 1992 and have a PhD in psychology as well as an MA in history and a doctorate in religion from Claremont School of Theology, where my dissertation integrated history and religion related to Ellen White and Adventism. I did ten years of postdoctoral work at UCLA, where I worked in the field of addiction research and treatment, before retiring in 2020 to concentrate on my writing. It is our hope as authors that this work will be helpful to many who have struggled with religious abuse at the hands of cultic and deceptive religion. We also hope it will make a significant contribution to the literature on Ellen White, the White Estate, and Seventh-day Adventism.

Preface by
Nancy Paige, Granddaughter of
Carrie Johnson

When I first read Grandma's book, *I Was Canright's Secretary*, I was twenty and still an Adventist who believed the church was the only true church, and, of course, that Ellen White was God's messenger. Carrie Johnson fancied herself an expert on D. M. Canright, assisted by Arthur White. She received kudos from bigwigs from the General Conference, which made her a star.

For fifteen years I had watched Arthur White visit Grandma in her home, first in Niles, Michigan, and then in Berrien Springs, Michigan. He would turn in to the driveway of her Berrien Springs home in his shiny black Lincoln Continental with suicide doors, dressed in a starched white shirt, black suit, and shiny black shoes. He would sit at Grandma's kitchen table and chat about her book a bit, and then he would start pointing out what he wanted her to fix. His demeanor was larger-than-life, and it was always his way or the highway. (Incidentally, he hated kids. We were in his way.)

Carrie, as far as we know, had never spoken to anyone about her goal to write a book about D. M. Canright. Our family had never heard her story. We did not hear her siblings speak of her working for Canright. There are no documents or photos at all, no mentions of her in any SDA books until at least fifty years after Canwright's death. Canright's letters and books in 1913 never stated that he had a secretary.

When Carrie left Battle Creek, Michigan, in the summer of 1913, she wrote in her book that the new Southern Illinois Conference president had hired her to be his secretary, starting in 1914. Though there is no evidence that she ever worked for him, we know she was in the area because she met Frank Johnson, my grandpa, while he was the treasurer of the Conference for two years. They got married and then moved several times before my dad was born.

In this book, we will question the roles of both Arthur White and Carrie Johnson to separate the truth from the lies by answering the following questions:

1. Why did Carrie take so long to begin her research?
2. Did Arthur write most of Carrie's book? If not, who did?
3. Why did Carrie refuse to give Canright's diary back to the Canright family?
4. Was Carrie's manuscript ever validated?
5. Did Arthur know that Frank and Carrie had been disfellowshipped from the Niles, Michigan, Adventist church?
6. Why does the foreword of Carrie's book claim that she and Frank were Adventists in good standing?
7. Why was Canright's diary so valuable that the White Estate is not willing to publish it?

Introduction:
THE GOD FRAUD

In 1971, the Seventh-day Adventist Review & Herald Publishing Association issued the first copy of Carrie Johnson's book, *I Was Canright's Secretary*. This book was heavily marketed by the Adventist Church and used to besmirch the character of Ellen White and the SDA Church's most effective critic for more than a century, D. M. Canright. The author claimed she had been sworn to secrecy by Canright, so the following disclaimer was issued with the book: "Sworn to secrecy when employed to assist D. M. Canright, Mrs. Johnson, now many years after his death, feels that she is no longer bound to this pledge to keep in strict confidence what she heard and saw during the period of time she served as his secretary." That disclaimer—issued by the author; the secret coauthor, Arthur White, head of the White Estate; the publisher; and the Adventist Church, which tirelessly promoted the book—should have read, "The material contained in this book has been fully fabricated by the author, with the extensive help of Arthur White. The overwhelming historical evidence demonstrates that the author never even met D. M. Canright, much less worked for him, and yet, White and Johnson colluded for years to publish this premeditated assault on and destruction of a good and innocent man's name after his death." This volume will substantiate these claims.

Arthur White was born into Seventh-day Adventist privilege. He was one of seven siblings born to William C. and Ethel May White, and one of seven grandchildren born to Ellen G. White, founder of the SDA Church, and her co-founding husband, James White. This is a book about the incredible dishonesty and unbelievable arrogance of Arthur White and his circle. What motivates a person—especially one who heads a prestigious institute and claims to be an objective historian and scholar—to engage in such immoral behavior? Why would a person of such status collude with a woman known for her dishonesty, who had been disfellowshipped from the SDA Church for stealing funds as a church employee, when doing so involved such obvious risks? Clearly, Arthur was aware of the risks, given that he tried to keep his repeated meetings with the author secret and his participation in the authorship hidden.

In my last book, *Ellen G. White: A Psychobiography*, I explored whether the repeated accusations of fraud and pathology leveled against Ellen White both during and after her lifetime stand up to historical and psychological scrutiny. After extensive research, I was forced to conclude from the source documentation and overwhelming historical evidence that this religious icon was indeed a fraud and a woman troubled by extreme pathology. What I found most striking in my research was that despite her lifetime patterns of dishonesty, deception, fraud, plagiarism, financial exploitation, falsely condemning people in the name of God through bogus "visions," absolute claims of authority, and gross misrepresentation of God through visionary claims, this woman still managed to survive all her critics and to be elevated by the SDA Church as a religious icon. Part of the reason for this was that Ellen made it a point to isolate herself and her church from mainline culture and to unmercifully destroy those who questioned her "visions" by condemning them via new "visions."

The other reason, as I see it, is that Ellen's initial followers had all embraced the Millerite message of the 1840s: that Jesus Christ would return to earth and the world would end on October 22, 1844. They were so invested in this false teaching that when it failed, they were both profoundly disappointed and desperate for something else to believe in.

Seventeen-year-old visionary Ellen Harmon (later to be White) met that desperate need by claiming to have had a vision (which she largely plagiarized from Joseph Turner, author of the ludicrous 1800s volume *The Hope of Israel*) indicating that they had been right in believing the October 1844 date, that probation had closed for the whole "wicked world" on that date, and that they alone would be saved as long as they didn't leave this little group. After seven years of false prophecies along these lines, Ellen and her husband deleted her unfulfilled prophecies from her writings and focused on her "visions," which attracted new people who wanted to feel special. The small group of, by this time, approximately 150 began to grow quite rapidly. Converts were told that they comprised the true, last-day "Remnant Church of God" and that all the other churches, Protestant and Catholic, constituted "Babylon."

Human nature is such that people want to feel special. They want to believe that they are in the "in group" and that others are on the outside, looking in. So, when you can convince them that God has shown you "visions" proving this to be true, a certain portion will be highly motivated to embrace such teachings; hence, the appeal of cults. It was this environment that allowed Ellen White to annihilate her detractors by condemning them through "visions" supported by her followers. She thus gained increasing authority, entitlement, wealth, power, influence, privilege (White privilege), and honor, despite increasing dishonesty and hypocrisy in her own behavior. This matriarchal privilege was witnessed by her son Willie and her grandson Arthur, who, as noted earlier, would become the keepers of the "prophet's" status and authority after her death through their respective positions as leaders of the White Estate for the first six decades of its existence (1915–1977). This has everything to do with the presumption and entitlement we see in the life of Arthur White once he succeeded his father, Willie, as head of the estate in 1937.

Ellen White had been successful at manipulating and exploiting her followers through a pious fraud and false visions throughout her lifetime, so, it is not surprising that Arthur, emboldened by his grandmother's success, adopted a similar, ends-justifies-the-means approach to life. He was so invested in perpetuating the prophetess's "successful myth" that he could not envision being exposed any more than he could envision his grandmother being exposed. This explains his arrogance and presumption as he engaged in risky and reckless behaviors that would cause normal people to shudder, or at least to contemplate the potential consequences of their careless actions. But Arthur went to his grave claiming he had written the ultimate multivolume biography of his grandmother and secretly believing he had effectively protected her vulnerable reputation through his evil and deceptive dealings with Carrie Johnson. This book is committed to setting the record straight and allowing objective readers to see and weigh the historical evidence for themselves.

Chapter 1 will discuss the concept of the "Big Lie" and how it applies to Adventism, Ellen White, Carrie Johnson, and Arthur White. Chapter 2 will consider why Dudley Canright was such a threat to Ellen and look back on the close relationship they had once enjoyed before Ellen turned against him, the church attacked him, and he responded. Chapter 3 will unpack the deeply dishonest character and actions of Carrie Johnson, long before her book was published. Chapter 4 will explore the fascinating saga of how Carrie plotted and carried out a premeditated plan to steal Canright's diary from his family under false pretenses and to ensure that they would never be able to recover it, while attributing all kinds of insidious and false accusations against Canright that were supposedly based on it. Chapter 5 will explore the role of Norman Douty, author of Canright's true biography, *The Case of D. M. Canright*, and how he was mistreated and threatened by Arthur White and the White Estate. This chapter more than any other provides the evidence that Johnson never met Canright. In chapter 6, we will examine the hidden relationship between Arthur White and Carrie Johnson in the roles they played as desperate colluders against the truth.

In chapter 7, we will look at the convincing evidence that demonstrates that Carrie Johnson's book was in fact a total fabrication and that she never even met D. M. Canright, much less knew or worked for him. Chapter 8 will explore the deliberate negligence on the part of SDA leadership and the Review & Herald in their failure to vet the book, as well as the willingness of the SDA membership in general to embrace it as if it were absolute truth. In chapter 9, I will try to do a psychological analysis of Carrie Johnson based on the historical evidence and her family testimony. In chapter 10, I will attempt a mini-psychobiography of Arthur White, comparing him to his grandmother. Chapter 11 will take an objective look at D. M. Canright, in contrast to the travesty that was offered by Carrie Johnson and Arthur White. And finally, chapter 12 will discuss the importance and need for this book by summarizing its major points and offering my conclusions.

We hope this will be an enlightening read and a God-ordained exercise in seeking the truth. God bless you on this journey!

1

THE BIG LIE

The "big lie," is a term that is credited to Adolf Hitler in his book *Mein Kampf*, in which he accused the Jews of telling a big lie to blame the Germans for World War I and to plot a war of extermination against Germany.[1] Ironically, this was a clear case of projection: the Nazis used this propaganda to justify their very own campaign of extermination against the Jews in the Holocaust.[2] Of course, the term "Big Lie" can apply to all kinds of things that are not as serious as genocide and that are more deliberate than delusional. I have seen it many times in politics and with numerous clients in my clinical practice as a psychologist over the years. In the realm of politics, one of the most heinous examples was the big lie that Harry Reid, Senate majority leader, told about Mitt Romney, then Republican candidate for president, in 2012. Reid asserted to the Senate in no uncertain terms, right before the election, that Romney had not paid any taxes for the past decade. The press ran with the story. Romney then lost the election, though it was proven afterward that he had paid nearly $2 million in taxes in 2011 and over $3 million in taxes in 2010. Now, I am no fan of Mitt Romney, but when Reid has been confronted about his big, deliberate lie, his smug reply has been, "Romney didn't win, did he?"[3]

For a national figure, and the Senate majority leader, to engage in this kind of evil, with no regret or remorse, is so despicable that it deserves to be remembered for a long time. More recently, George Santos, the newly elected congressman from New York, was found to have totally fabricated both his educational and his job experience to get elected to the House of Representatives.[4] And he hasn't had the decency to step down even after these ridiculous lies were exposed. Unfortunately, deception and dishonesty have now become so common in politics that they hardly get the attention they deserve. But as we will see in this book, when it comes to fabrication, Santos had nothing on Arthur White and Carrie Johnson, only they did it in the name of God! This kind of Big Lie demonstrates a total lack of morality and integrity.

But big lies can also occur in interpersonal relationships. The most striking example from my counseling experience was a couple I was trying to help through their decision to get a divorce. Initially, they claimed they were committed to a cordial divorce, but when they lawyered up, things got real nasty. The accusations began to fly and degenerated to such a point that I decided to meet with each of them individually. Out of nowhere the woman had begun accusing her husband of domestic violence and molesting their girls. This seemed completely uncharacteristic both of the man and of his wife, who was making the accusations. So, I asked her about it in private, and she said, "This is completely confidential, but my attorney insisted that I go this route if I want to get the best settlement I possibly can for myself and the kids." The lawyer had opted for a deliberate Big Lie to put the husband and his attorney in the most defensive position possible, with no concern for the character assassination being committed. Which brings us to the subject of this book.

Ellen White and Seventh-day Adventists have certainly never been guilty of genocide, like Hitler, throughout their history, but both learned to use the concept of the Big Lie as an effective propaganda technique. Ellen claimed to have received thousands of "visions" from God that enabled her to pontificate on a massive number of subjects on which she asserted she had infallible authority from the throne of the Almighty. She further claimed that everything she published came directly from God and fit perfectly with biblical truth.

In these letters which I write, in the testimonies I bear, I am presenting to you that which the Lord has presented to me. I do not write one article in the paper expressing merely my own ideas. They are what God has opened before me in vision—the precious rays of light shining from the throne.[5]

If they [Ellen's testimonies] are not heeded, the Holy Spirit is shut away from the soul.[6]

When I send you a testimony of warning and reproof, many of you declare it to be merely the opinion of Sister White. You have thereby insulted the spirit of God.[7]

The testimonies . . . never contradict His Word. . . . There is one straight chain of truth, without one heretical sentence, in that which I have written.[8]

Ellen White not only falsely equated her writings with the Bible and plagiarized extensively from many other authors, but as you can see from the quotes above, she committed blasphemy by claiming that rejecting her writings was an insult to God and would result in a person being "shut away" from the Holy Spirit. Her "Big Lies" have been documented and exposed by numerous researchers and scholars, both during and after her lifetime,[9] including my last major work. However, Ellen's most threatening critic during her lifetime was D. M. Canright, a well-known minister and church leader who knew the prophetess personally and was intimately aware of her flaws. What the White Estate, and particularly its head, Arthur White, did to Canright is the focus of this book. It qualifies as a "Big Lie" in a class of its own.

The White Estate was established in 1915 after Ellen's death (although it was not legally incorporated as a separate legal organization from the SDA Church until 1933), to oversee, protect and promote her writings in perpetuity. Mrs. White handpicked the board for this entity in her will.

Each board member was to hold a lifelong appointment. The mission of the White Estate, according to the *SDA Encyclopedia*, is to circulate Ellen White's writings, translate them to create new compilations from her writings, and to provide resources for helping to better understand her life and ministry. It also includes other duties, such as handling her properties, "conducting the business thereof," "securing the printing of new translations," and the "printing of compilations from my manuscripts."[10] Her will, dated February 9, 1912, named five church administrators to serve as a board of trustees, with A. G. Daniells, the General Conference president, chairing the board, and Willie White (Ellen's son) in charge of day-to-day operations.

For the first sixty-three years of its existence, the White Estate's day-to-day operations were controlled by Ellen White's son Willie and her grandson Arthur. Both men were painfully aware that their positions were the product of nepotism and did their best to put forward a front of objectivity. But it was only a facade. In Willie's case, he was fully aware that the nature of his mother's so-called visions was nothing like what the prophetess had claimed and the church had been taught. As opposed to the detailed content that Mrs. White claimed to see in vision, on almost every conceivable subject, Willie informed Fannie Bolton, much to her surprise when she was hired to become one of Ellen's assistants, that the "visions" were nothing more than general flash-light, panoramic scenes of past or future events,[11] and what he didn't say was that his mother filled in the details herself with her fanciful imagination and extensive plagiarism. Willie knew good and well that the church had been deceived about his mother's "gift," but he was all too willing to participate in the deception for his own benefit.

But Willie's dishonesty fades in comparison to the flagrant and premeditated fraud that was perpetrated by his son Arthur, who was the secretary, or acting head, of the White Estate after his father's death, from 1937 to 1978. One aspect of this fraud will prove that all of Arthur's attempts to present himself as an objective historian and scholar were nothing more than a cover for deliberate dishonesty and one of the greatest Big Lies ever told in Adventist history. In this chapter, we will outline the nature of this Big Lie and spend the rest of the book filling in the details with extensive documentation. To understand the significance of the Big Lie that Arthur White, Carrie Johnson. and the Adventist Church told, fabricating a book about Ellen White's most effective critic to that point, Dudley Canright, and deviously assassinating his character based on false claims, supposedly from his diary, which Johnson "borrowed" from the Canright family, with no intention of returning it, we need to first look at what led up to all this evil.

Typically, those who attempt to tell Big Lies to deceive people have gotten away with a pattern of telling lesser lies to benefit themselves and/ or to hurt others. This was certainly the case with Ellen White, as well as with her grandson Arthur. But let's begin with some of the most prominent examples in Ellen's life before we look at Arthur. There are definite patterns of dishonesty to be found in Ellen Harmon White's life before she founded the Adventist (Sabbatarian) Movement.[12] But for the purposes of this book, we will confine our examples to what Ellen did in the Adventist Movement.

The very first vision Ellen claimed to receive in connection with the group who would later become the Seventh-day Adventist Church was largely plagiarized, based on clear evidence, from a paper that author Joseph Turner had written that was available to Ellen. The day after Ellen presented her "vision," Turner contacted her and asked her to share the vision with him. After hearing her recounted vision, he replied that he had "told out the same" in his paper.[13] The fact, that this "vision" taught that probation was closed for the entire world—unless, of course, they were part of their little group of approximately 150 people—is proof enough that it did not come from God, but Ellen claimed that she *had* received this "vision" from God.

In other words, she started her Adventist ministry with a lie. In the next couple of years, Ellen Harmon, who became Ellen White on August 30, 1846, after taking the position with her husband-to-be that marriage was now forbidden by God,[14] was caught in several more lies. She claimed God had shown her that He would return to earth during very specific seasons of the year, only to see those seasons pass without incident. This became so tiresome to Ellen's best friend, Lucinda Burdick, who traveled with her, that Burdick discontinued her relationship with Ellen and gave the following testimony about her friend's pattern of telling untruths:

> I became acquainted with James White and Ellen Harmon (now Mrs. White) early in 1845. . . . She pretended God showed her things which did not come to pass. At one time she saw that the Lord would come the second time in June 1845. The prophecy was discussed in all the churches, and in a little "shut-door paper" published in Portland, Me. During the summer, after June passed, I heard a friend ask her how she accounted for the vision. She replied that "they told her in the language of Canaan, and she did not understand the language; that it was the next September that the Lord was coming, and the second growth of grass instead of the first in June.[15]

But September would also pass with no Second Coming, so two more false prophecies were added to the list. Some have suggested that Ellen was just an immature teenager at this time, so it is not surprising that she would misunderstand things. But, Miles Grant, who also knew Ellen well in the 1840s and would later write a book exposing her failures, including the concerns of Lucinda Burdick, showed that even in her youth Ellen was quick to condemn those who questioned her "revelations." Picking up where Burdick's letter left off, Grant quoted:

> September passed, and many more have passed since, and we have not seen the Lord yet. It soon became evident to all candid persons, that many things must have been "told her in the language of Canaan," or some other which she did not understand, as there were repeated failures. I could mention many which I knew of myself. Once, when on their way to the eastern part of Maine, she saw that they

would have great trouble with the wicked, be put in prison, etc. This they told in the churches as they passed through. When they came back, they said they had a glorious time. Friends asked if they had seen any trouble with the wicked, or prisons. They replied, "None at all." People in all the churches soon began to get their eyes open, and came out decidedly against her visions; and, just as soon as they did so, she used to see them "with spots on their garments," as she expressed it. I was personally acquainted with several ministers, whom she saw landed in the kingdom with "Oh! such brilliant crowns, FULL of stars." As soon as they took a stand against the visions, she saw them "doomed, damned, and lost forever, without hope."[16]

Suffice it to say that Ellen became well-known for her dishonesty even before she unleashed her Big Lie that the whole world was lost except her circle of 150 and that those who did not accept her shut-door "visions" had committed the unpardonable sin and were in league with the devil.

Following are some quotes from those "visions":

I was shown that the commandments of God, and the testimony of Jesus Christ, relating to the shut door, could not be separated . . . My accompanying angel bade me look for the travail of soul for sinners as used to be. I looked, but could not see it, for the time of their salvation is past.

The sin against the Holy Ghost was to ascribe to Satan what belongs to God or what the Holy Ghost has done. They said the shut door was of the devil and now admit it is against their own lives. They shall die the death.[17]

In a view given June 27, 1850, my accompanying angel said, "Time is almost finished. Do you reflect the lovely image of Jesus as you should?" Then I was pointed to the earth and saw that there would have to be a getting ready among those who have of late embraced the third angel's message. Said the angel, "Get ready, get ready, get ready. Ye will have to die a greater death to the world than ye have ever yet died." I saw that there was a great work to do for them, and but little time in which to do it. . . .

Some of us have had time to get the truth, and to advance step by step, and every step we have taken has given us strength to take the next. But now time is almost finished, and what we have been years learning, they will have to learn in a few months. They will also have much to unlearn, and much to learn again.[18]

I saw that Jesus prayed for his enemies; but that should not cause us to pray for the wicked world, whom God has rejected.

When he prayed for his enemies there was hope for them, and they could be benefited and saved by his prayers, and also after he was a mediator, in the outer apartment for the whole world; but now his spirit and sympathy were withdrawn from the world; and our sympathy must be with Jesus, and must be withdrawn from the ungodly.[19]

These are just a few of Ellen's shut-door "visions," but her big lie was that God had shown her in a vision that the whole world except their little cult was lost, and that even her true believers only had "a few months" to get ready before their probation closed and Christ returned. If this isn't a Big Lie, I don't know what is. You can't be more of a cult leader than to tell your followers that the entire world is lost except for them, and that if they don't believe and follow your visions, they too will be lost for eternity.

After all the false date setting for the second coming of Christ that Ellen had engaged in based on supposed visions, she still managed to insist that Christ was going to return on October 22, 1851. This was the basis of her final shut-door "Testimonies" listed above. When that date also passed in failure, James and Ellen deleted her shut-door visions from their writings, and in the future, Ellen would deny ever having such visions.[20]

The major problem with Ellen White's claimed visions was that she attributed their content to God. So, the Big Lie that Ellen was telling became the Big Lie that God was telling. It was *He* who was claiming that the world—except for Ellen and company—was consigned to hell and that He would return to earth on October 22, 1851—or whenever, since Ellen pinpointed numerous dates. This was a huge problem throughout her "prophetic ministry." When Ellen White says racist things,[21] she makes God a racist; when she writes about God hating children,[22] she makes God a child hater; and when she attributes to visions from God all manner of ridiculous statements based on the thinking of her day,[23] she commits extreme blasphemy, making God out to be a fool.

After Ellen's death in 1915, the top SDA Church leaders and academics, aware of the problems that her writings posed to the church, including her extensive plagiarism, called a conference to address these issues. The gathering was called the 1919 Bible Conference, and all its participants were sworn to secrecy.[24] Realizing that the SDA Church had been guilty of telling a Big Lie to its membership concerning Ellen White, they were now faced with the challenge of trying to reveal the truth about her to the church without causing the whole denomination to collapse. Some Ellen White apologists who attended those meetings believed that Ellen's writings were true and infallible; they were highly disturbed by the tone of the conference. So, when it was over, they immediately broke their vows of silence and led a campaign to oust the current leadership. This caused such controversy and division in the church that the transcripts of the 1919 Bible Conference were buried deep in the General Conference archives, forgotten, and not rediscovered until 1974.[25]

It also meant, when the Ellen White "true believers" won out and had those who were trying to tell the truth at the 1919 Conference put out of office, that the church would become dominated by extremely conservative leaders over the next three decades. These would be Ellen White disciples who believed that her writings were infallible and straight from the throne of God. They accepted as absolute truth the claims of their "prophetess" that all other Christian churches—Protestant and Catholic alike—constituted "Babylon" and that Seventh-day Adventists alone were God's true Remnant Church on earth. This caused other churches to look askance at Adventism and to generally denounce it for the cult that it was. It wasn't until the mid-1950s that a more moderate group of leaders briefly came into power and deceitfully convinced at least one major cult expert, Walter Martin, that SDAs weren't a cult. But even Martin, realizing later that he had been deceived, would contend that Ellen was a false prophet used in a cultic manner by Adventists who had returned to their anti-evangelical views.[26]

For our purposes, in this book, it is important to understand that the more condemning SDAs were of other Christian churches, the more inclined these churches were to be hostile to and look for faults in Adventism and to denounce it as a cult. We will explore the implications of this more in the next chapter, but what I want you to see in the remainder of this chapter is how Arthur White was educated and trained during this most conservative and apologetic period in Adventist history, and how that clearly impacted his writings and actions throughout his lifetime. Willie White, Arthur's father, not only had a firsthand knowledge of how Ellen operated, but he hung out with several other SDA leaders who also knew Ellen very well, both personally and professionally. Willie was well acquainted with the chief SDA administrators and academics who led the 1919 Bible Conference and had close relationships with many of them, so he was not part of the ultraconservative group that started a witch hunt to purge these men from leadership after the conference was over.

But as noted before, things changed dramatically when A. G. Daniells, the longest-serving General Conference president, was removed from office at the next GC session (1922) and those with a similar open mind were put out with him or purged from their academic positions.[27] From this point forward, it became dangerous for anyone in leadership to question not only the inspiration of Ellen White's writings, but their absolute authority in the church as well. The new theological superstar in Adventism was a young man named Francis Nichol, who gained some national fame in his debates with Maynard Shipley over creation and evolution shortly before the Scopes trial attracted much greater national attention to this issue.[28] But when it came to Ellen White, Nichol was the apologist of all apologists. Not only did he write the voluminous and "comprehensive" work, claimed to be definitive by SDAs, against all who could be labeled as critics of Ellen White,[29] but he did so in a very shrewd and dishonest manner that Adventists generally found convincing but any honest, well-informed SDA historian can see was highly deceptive.

For example, the biggest and most obvious deception that Ellen promulgated, for seven years, through her "supposed visions," was the shut-door teaching, which, as noted earlier, claimed that probation had closed for the entire world except her little circle of Adventist believers. Nichol, whose 703-page book was packaged as a "red book"—just like Ellen White's—devoted a full 106 pages to dealing directly with the shut-door question and its relationship to the seven-year theory that Christ would return on October 22, 1851. In addition to this, he wrote two other lengthy books, one supposedly answering every question or criticism one could raise about Adventism (*Answers to Objections*, 895 pages) and one specifically focusing on the history and criticisms related to the 1840s (*The Midnight Cry*, 584 pages), - when Ellen was strongly pushing the shut-door belief based on her "visions."

And in all these apologetic works Nichol dogmatically asserts that his defense of Ellen White's views on the shut door are based on original source documentation. And yet, he fails to discuss or explain any of the crucial original statements Ellen made about the shut door during the actual years 1844–1851 (contained in my book). Instead, he quotes the "prophet's" denials of these "visions/Testimonies" given in 1874 and

1883 with reference to the few that he does mention.[30] Which are you going to believe: Ellen's actual words written between 1844 and 1851, or her denials of these statements written decades later? Arthur White would follow Nichol's same pattern in his writing about the shut door.

> With my brethren and sisters, after the time passed in 1844, I did believe that no more sinners would be converted. But, I never had a vision that no more sinners would be converted.[31]

> For a time after the disappointment in 1844, I did hold, in common with the advent body, that the door of mercy was then forever closed to the world. This position was taken before my first vision was given me. It was the light given me of God that corrected our error, and enabled us to see the true position.[32]

These denials are in direct contradiction to the "visions" Ellen claimed God had given her between 1844 and 1851. This is hardly scholarship, and Nichol made similar denials regarding Ellen White's blatantly racist statements (again, based on professed visions),[33] as well as many of her other false and controversial claims.[34] Much of what Nichol wrote was intended to offset and refute the very damning criticisms that D. M. Canright, had leveled against Ellen, which were gaining a great deal of traction with the churches condemned by Adventism in the five decades after Ellen's death, as we shall see in the next chapter. So, in the eyes of SDAs, Nichol was the primary dragon slayer of these churches and the champion defender of Ellen White during this period.

During his later years, Nichol was also the chairman of the board of the White Estate and worked very closely with Arthur White, who was the secretary in charge of day-to-day operations. For the most part, Arthur simply used the arguments of Nichol to defend his grandmother, while stridently trying to claim historical objectivity, lest he be accused of nepotism.

Arthur was not a trained historian—his education was in accounting and business—but he was given an honorary doctorate from Andrews University and certainly tried to pass himself off as an historian. In reality he was an apologist of the first order, and later an outright deceiver. But he learned a great deal from Francis Nichol. By embracing the continual pattern of lies and cover-ups that characterized the apologetic works of these men, Arthur would be emboldened to graduate to the level of the premeditated Big Lie when the opportunity presented itself—with Carrie Johnson.

2

THE THREAT OF DUDLEY CANRIGHT

There is a paranoia in Adventism that is deeply engraved in the minds of those who are raised in the subculture. This, like so much else in the movement, can be traced directly to Ellen White. The whole world will eventually turn against Seventh-day Adventists, God's true Remnant Church, and persecute them, because they alone keep the commandments of God, and especially the fourth commandment, the seventh-day Sabbath. Even other Christians, both Catholic and Protestant, will receive the mark of the Beast by engaging in Sunday worship. They will also target SDAs through national and worldwide Sunday laws that will make it illegal to worship on Saturday. As absurd as this sounds to a normal person today, it made sense to Ellen in the late 1880s, when the Blair Bill was before Congress and Adventists greatly feared that a national Sunday law was about to be passed. This fear was greatly driven and perpetuated by Ellen White, who claimed to have received "visions" from God showing her this very thing, and then wrote about it in her highly plagiarized book *The Great Controversy*.[1] Once the shut door was discarded by Adventists after 1851, the Sabbath alone became the center of their identity and eschatology (teaching about last-day events). Still to this day, most SDAs continue to believe, and are taught, that these persecuting Sunday Laws are surely coming.

So, it is not surprising that SDAs were not particularly popular with non-Adventist churches during this period and through most of the twentieth century. After all, Adventists were accusing these Christians of being Babylon, in league with the Beast of Revelation, and Ellen White was condemning them as outright devil worshippers.[2] D. M. Canright was an SDA minister known for debating these condemned Christian ministers from other churches and supposedly winning such debates, based on Adventist history. He was an expert on Adventist doctrine and a champion of their cause against all critics. So, one would be right to expect that when he eventually concluded that Adventists were wrong and that Ellen was not a true prophet, then left the SDA Church for good in 1887, Canright and his books would become a popular source of attack against SDAs and their condemning ways.

This was a period of extreme debate and competition between denominations in American history, and Adventists were generally considered to be a cult just as much as Mormons and Jehovah's Witnesses. In fact, Seventh-day Adventists were considered even more condemning, dishonest, and deceptive in their methods than these other cults. SDAs, with their contempt and condemnation for other churches—whom they called Babylon—were especially known for their sheep-stealing tricks, holding evangelistic meetings in public buildings and failing to identity who they were until they had hooked their unsuspecting attendees with their cultic teachings.

In such an environment, Canright and his works became a very welcome weapon for those who felt they had been unfairly attacked and falsely condemned by SDAs. Francis Nichol did his best to try to counter Canright in his books, but Canright's influence was still far too great and effective where SDAs were concerned. So, it became expedient for the White Estate, through Arthur White and a woman of very questionable reputation, Carrie Johnson, to fabricate a book to seek to discredit Canright and destroy his reputation. We will look at the details of this effort in the chapters ahead, but in the remainder of this chapter we will try to determine how and why one minister seemed such a threat to the entire SDA Church.

The last "testimony" Ellen sent to D. M. Canright, was dated April 20, 1888. In it she spoke of an earlier temptation that had come to him "through false and ambitious hopes to become greater away from our people than with them," and warned against the sin of seeking "through disobedience to rise to greater heights, to gain some flattering position."[3] This "testimony" is quite ironic, in that it would be hard to find an example of a person in Adventism seeking for recognition, authority, and power more than Ellen White herself. But Adventists have long argued that Canright was a self-seeking attack dog against the church and that he had left Adventism to build his own reputation by destroying EGW and SDAs in spite of the church supposedly treating him with grace. Norman Douty, in his excellent book *The Case of D. M. Canright*, shows this is false. In chapter 8 he provides overwhelming evidence that Canright wanted to walk away from Adventism peacefully and have nothing to do with it. But it was the church that went back on their agreement and attacked Canright in unprovoked ways, which Douty reveals in chapter 9:

Canright's separation from the Adventists had been marked by peace; at the time and for a short period afterwards, both sides seemed to exert themselves to show friendliness to the other. But the truce, as I stated, was to be short-lived. In a matter of months, a state of hostilities began which continued to the end of Canright's life, over thirty years later. The important question is: Who broke the truce?

We have seen in chapter 8 that about the middle of March 1887, an article appeared in the *Review and Herald* which seemed to be directed against him, though it contained no mention of his name. About a month later—on

April 12th–two items were printed in the same periodical that expressly named him. Both of these were written by men belonging to the Otsego Adventist Church, which Canright had left less than two months before. One was sent by the church clerk, W. W. Shepard; the other, by J. B. Buck, a member.

Mr. Shepard's report contained nothing objectionable. In reference to the one prepared by J. B. Buck, this is what Butler said in an Extra issue of the *Review and Herald*, which was first published in November of 1887: "Bro. Buck's report refers to the fact that he had been laboring with Eld. C. At Pine Grove and Almena just before he left our people. 'This,' he says, 'was Eld. Canright's last work among us; and when the report of his *apostacy* was received, they were much shocked, but their confidence was not shaken in the present truth; for they remembered that in Christ's time there was one [Judas] who saw the miracles he did and heard his preaching, and yet *apostatized* from the present truth of that time. And as the Scriptures plainly state that in the latter time some shall depart from the faith, we see in this only another sign that we are in the last days.'"[4]

This is the typical response to those who question Ellen White or leave the SDA Church. The prophet foretold that some, even bright lights, would apostatize from the faith and leave the truth.[5] So, every person who questions or rejects her prophetic authority becomes a fulfillment of prophecy. While Christians in general reserve the term *apostasy* to mean the sin of rejecting Christ and leaving the Christian faith, Adventists have historically used it to describe the behavior of anyone who leaves their denomination –characteristic of a cult–because they saw themselves as the one true church. Canright rightly believed that for the church to publicly print references to him as a "Judas" and "apostate" in their main church publication was a clear violation of their agreed truce. This seems like a fair conclusion, unless you happen to be trying to convince an SDA steeped in the brainwashing of Adventism. Not only did the Adventists break the truce with Canright; they also secretly disfellowshipped him, without informing him of their action, and then lied about what they had done, claiming they had "quietly dropped" him from their church roll based on his own earnest request. Let us return to Douty's account, as I cannot improve on his description of what happened in this regard.

Buck's report agreed with what Shepard had recorded in the Church Minutes for Feb. 17, 1887. He had stated therein that after Canright, on that fateful evening, had concluded his remarks, J.B. Buck moved that Canright be *excluded* from Adventism because of his *apostacy*. (The italicized words are underscored in the handwritten record). The motion was seconded and carried. It is plain that this took place *after* Canright had left the meeting. It is also plain that, to his dying day, he knew nothing about it. But it is *not* plain that Butler, who presided, was ignorant of the action. Yet all he reports is that Canright's name "was quietly dropped from the church roll" in response to his own earnest request. I now return to the Extra account.

Butler comments: "We have been particular to copy every word said which could be thought to reflect upon the Elder in these reports, and we are sure the candid reader will be surprised that there is so little that could be complained of, when we consider that these words came from the very church which Elder C. Left to join those opposed to us in faith—the very place where there would be likely to be deep feeling on that point, if anywhere."

Now G.I. Butler, though not a man of the schools, was no ignoramus, and so he knew very well that the term "apostate" was a very offensive one. In fact, he employs it in this sense on the very next page of the Extra. He knew, therefore, that "the candid reader," instead of being surprised that there was "so little that could be complained of," would be surprised that such charges could be so described. Accordingly, he felt it necessary to attempt a justification of this description. Here it is: "There is one word, 'apostasy,' used which may seem to some objectionable. Eld. Canright tries to make it appear that our using this word concerning him is very uncharitable. Webster defines *apostate* as follows: 'One who has forsaken the faith, principles, or party to which he before adhered.' We know of no other word which would so exactly describe Eld. Canright's course. What, then, is there uncharitable in its use? It expresses in his case the exact truth. . . . These reports to which I have referred were written by persons holding no positions of responsibility in the denomination, and what they say is mild indeed. . . . yet he claims to have been terribly abused. This claim is utterly without foundation."

Let us examine this defense of Butler's. In the first place, would he have considered it other than objectionable if Canright had spoken of James White as "an apostate Christian minister"? Yet White tells us in *Life Incidents* (p. 104) that he had been ordained, at Palmyra, Maine, as a minister of "The Christian Church" (not to be confused with the one so termed today). But he subsequently left that denomination to become a Seventh-day Adventist.

In the second place, Butler quoted only part of Webster's definition of an "apostate." The whole of it reads thus: "one who has forsaken the faith, principles, or party to which he before adhered; especially, one who has forsaken his religion for another; renegade." Since Webster has been appealed to, Butler must let Webster explain his own terms. What, then, does Webster mean by forsaking one's *faith*? His fifth definition of "faith" is the only one relevant, and it says: "that which is believed; esp. a system of religious beliefs; as, the Jewish or Islamic *faith*." Hence Webster does not use the word apostate in a denominational sense (Presbyterian or Baptist *faith*), but only in relation to radically different religions. This is confirmed by his definition of "renegade," which is: "An apostate from Christianity or from any form of religious faith." It is plain then, that, when Canright was called an apostate, he was branded with a term that meant a forsaker of Christianity itself.

In the third place, Mr. Buck had made it clear that he was not using the word "apostate" in any mild sense, for he wrote of Canright's apostasy as like that of Judas Iscariot's and of the followers of the Antichrist (as Mrs. White interprets 1 Tim. 4:1). Now the devil himself is only one degree worse than these reprobates."[6]

This is so often the SDA way that it is not too surprising that Arthur White would mimic the dishonesty that preceded him to the fraudulent extremes that he did. But Butler, who had tried to be a friend to Canright, clearly went to the opposite extreme in his false defenses of the church. His attempt to minimize the attacks by saying they came from members who held no significant position in the SDA Church is hardly convincing, given that their criticisms were printed worldwide in the official Church paper, the *Review and Herald*, by Uriah Smith, its most influential and well-known editor. Furthermore, Butler, the highest-ranking Adventist–the General Conference president–tried to justify and defend these criticisms himself. He even went so far as to declare that Canright's claim that the Church was first to break their truce was "utterly without foundation."[7] This has to seem like a joke to the objective reader, and it certainly held no credibility with Canright, who wrote, "No less than eight articles appeared in their leading paper, the *Review*, attacking me openly or covertly, calling me an apostate, traitor, unstable, unreliable; comparing me to Balaam, Judas, Demas and other bad men; insinuating that I left them for money or popularity; that I must have been guilty of some secret sin, as adultery or the like."[8] For these reasons he was forced to defend himself in the pulpit and the press.

The irony of this situation is that the SDA Church brought the entire Canright crisis upon themselves. Even though it was the whole denomination, with their "prophet" and lawyers, against one man, the SDA Church clearly broke the truce and could not resist their natural practice of criticizing, attacking, and condemning anyone, especially any high-profile person, whom they felt had made the "terrible mistake" of leaving their denomination (more accurately, their cult). All the controversy surrounding Canright, all his opposition, books and sermons exposing their SDA errors and deceptions, could have been avoided had they quietly allowed Canright to peacefully leave as he proposed. So, the outrageous fraud and fabrication that Arthur White and Carrie Johnson would create only came about because SDAs were stupid enough to make unprovoked attacks on Canright that included vicious and immoral innuendo. Being trained in the Adventist ministry it was my experience, that Canright was compared to Judas Iscariot and spoken of with the most unrestrained disdain. And yet, when I studied his life outside of Adventism, I found him to be a man of very honorable and humble character, who was dearly loved in the churches and communities where he served, and who basically represented the opposite of what SDAs had made him out to be.

Norman Douty's book contains pages of testimonials from individuals who knew Canright very well and who worked closely with him. They considered him to be a man of the highest character who modeled the love and grace of God tremendously during the many years that they were associated with him. The fact that SDAs, through the head of the White Estate (Arthur), would collude with a woman who had demonstrated a clear pattern of dishonesty, to craft a premeditated tale designed to discredit Canright and destroy his reputation is one of the saddest acts ever committed by a denomination claiming to worship Jesus Christ. It is no wonder that White regularly met secretly with Carrie Johnson for years to guide and direct her writings, then denied any relationship with her when questioned about it. We will go into this in detail in the chapters ahead, but for now, understand that the man they intentionally smeared was of the highest character. He had desired and arranged to leave Adventism quietly and without controversy, until the church grossly violated their agreement with him.

Let us look at one more aspect of why Canright was such a threat to Adventism, and why he was particularly targeted by their "prophet," Ellen White.

CANRIGHT'S CLOSE RELATIONSHIP TO ELLEN WHITE

At the height of Canright's evangelistic career in Adventism, the pastor/ evangelist married nineteen-year-old Lucretia Cranson on April 11, 1867. Lucretia and her sisters had been orphaned young when both their parents died prematurely. She was raised by the well-known (in SDA circles) George Amadon family in Battle Creek. The three orphan girls were befriended by Ellen White, and Lucretia in particular became like a daughter to Ellen and lived with the Whites for a significant period. This fact would become important with regard to Ellen's relationship to Canright, who was very much like a son-in-law to the Whites. Dudley's marriage to Lucretia bore them three children, two of which survived infancy, but would be relatively short due to Lucretia contracting tuberculosis and dying of it in 1879. But during their twelve years of marriage, Ellen had some very strong opinions about the Canrights, their marriage, and their child-rearing, and just happened to have "visions" from God intended to set them straight in all of these areas. The Whites had a real sense of entitlement and ownership where Adventism was concerned. James was known for his controlling, oppressive, and dictatorial leadership style in Adventism when Canright was married to Lucretia, and the extreme, monolithic power that he wielded in the movement was typically supported by his wife's "authoritative visions" whenever they were necessary.[9]

It is bad enough to impose a dominating style of leadership in a church, backed up by claimed visions from God, but when this approach is applied to micromanaging the personal lives of family and close friends, you can expect there will be fireworks. Ellen even tried to control her dominating husband through "visions," leading to strong marital tensions,[10] so it is not surprising that her same attempt with Dudley and Lucretia would not be well received. The Whites and Canrights were close enough that they vacationed together, but their friendship took a major turn for the worse after a getaway in Colorado exploded into open conflict. Canright described the experience:

> In July, 1873, myself and wife went to Colorado to spend a few weeks with Elder White and wife, in the mountains. I soon found things very unpleasant living in the family. Now my turn had come to catch it, but instead of knuckling down, as most of the others had, I told the elder my mind freely. That brought us into open rupture. Mrs. White heard it all but said nothing. In a few days she had a long written "testimony" for wife and me. It justified her husband in everything, and placed us as rebels against God, with no hope of heaven only by a full surrender to them. Wife and I read it over many times with tears and prayers; but could see no way to reconcile it with truth. It contained many statements which we knew were false. We saw that it was dictated by a spirit of retaliation, a determination to break our wills or crush us.[11]

Because of the fabricated biography that SDAs have used to discredit Canright, they are inclined to dismiss or reject anything he wrote about Ellen or Adventism as biased and untrue. One purpose of this book is to show that it was Ellen White and Adventists who have treated Canright in an evil manner, rather than the other way around, and that Ellen and James's abusive behaviors toward Canright and many others can be easily documented by very credible sources beyond Canright's testimony.[12] When Canright says it was a long testimony against him and his wife, he is not exaggerating. On August 12, 1873, Ellen sent a testimony, which she repeatedly claimed was based on visions from God, which was published in full in volume 3 of her *Testimonies for the Church*[13] (withholding the Canrights' names). In that testimony Ellen attempted to settle this family squabble by claiming that God had given her more than twenty-five pages of single-spaced print, in vision, accusing the Canrights of multiple character flaws and warning them that their eternal life was at stake unless they submitted to her divinely given warnings. After reading this full testimony again, I was struck by the general nature of her accusations and the total lack of specific wrongs or acts that might elicit such "visions" from God. As a student of Ellen White's life, I have explicitly demonstrated and documented that this was the pattern in the life of this "prophetess": she condemned and demonized those with whom she had a personal issue, using general criticisms that could fit almost anyone and attributing them to having come straight from God.

Let us look at some examples from this protracted "testimony": Ellen starts by writing, "For some months I have felt that it was time to write to you some things which the Lord was pleased to show me in regard to you several years ago."[14] So, God was supposedly "pleased" to show Ellen these negative things about the Canrights years before, but she withheld any mention of them until there was a blowup in the family. Is that what God really told her to do, *"Save these warnings and condemnations until the Canrights really tick you off; then give them a twenty-five-plus page description of My visions to you"*? You can decide for yourself. The Whites felt during this vacation that they were inconvenienced by how the Canrights cared for their children yet failed to show them, the founders of the Church, the proper reverence and respect. So, Ellen writes, "I have been shown that both of you are naturally selfish. . . . Both of you should cultivate reverence and respect for others."[15] Isn't selfishness a general quality of sinful human nature? Is there not great evidence to show that Ellen and James were often extremely selfish in their leadership styles?[16] And are we as human beings to "reverence" other human beings, or only God? Again, you decide. "Among your brethren you have too frequently made it a practice to make arrangements agreeable to yourselves and to take a course to gather attention to yourselves, without considering the convenience or inconvenience of others," Ellen accused. This from a woman who claimed that God had shown her in "vision" that church members were to sell their homes and possessions and give the money to "the cause" of God, which she and James controlled, because the Lord was returning so soon. When He failed to return, Ellen continued to claim visions for years, telling members to at least downsize their homes and give the profits to "the cause," while the Whites themselves greatly increased in wealth, and never sold or downsized their homes.[17] And no one ever demanded attention for themselves more than Ellen White in the Adventist movement.[18]

Ellen continues:

> I was shown that neither of you really know yourselves. If God should let the enemy loose upon you, as He did upon His servant Job, He would not find in you that spirit of steadfast integrity that He found in Job, but a spirit of murmuring and unbelief. Had you been situated at Battle Creek during my husband's illness, at the time of trial of our brethren and sisters there, when Satan had special power upon them, both of you would have drunk deep of their spirit of jealousy and faultfinding. You would have been among the number, as zealous as the rest, to make a diseased, careworn man, a paralytic, an offender for a word.[19]

So, if God can't find anything specific to condemn the Canrights for, He must condemn them for what they *would* have done given the chance. They wouldn't have been as faithful as Job, given his trials, but of course Ellen would have been.

To attribute this kind of stuff to God when it was clearly based on personal baggage Ellen had been harboring against the Canrights speaks for itself. But there is much more. The sanctimonious prophetess had to attack their diet as well: "I was shown that the manner in which you and your wife eat will bring disease, which, when once fastened upon you, will not be easily overcome."[20] For Ellen, diet and works righteousness determined eternal life, as we shall see. And yet, there is no evidence that either of the Canrights violated Ellen's numerous "visions" condemning all kinds of dietary practices to nearly the degree that Ellen herself did. Her attempt to legalistically micromanage the lives of this young couple, while attributing it to God, is all the more revolting given her own hypocrisy.

In fact, a very strong argument can be made that every single criticism, condemnation, and warning that Ellen levels against the Canrights in this twenty-five-plus-page "testimony" can be shown, through source documentation and historical evidence, to apply to her much more than to either of the Canrights.[21] Yet, this does not stop Ellen from warning Canright that unless he conformed to her testimonies, the time for his salvation would pass.

> God has been pleased to open to me the secrets of the inner life and the hidden sins of His people. The unpleasant duty has been laid upon me to reprove wrongs and to reveal hidden sins. When I have been compelled by the Spirit of God to reprove sins that others did not know existed, it has stirred up the natural feelings in the hearts of the unsanctified. While some have humbled their hearts before God, and with repentance and confession have forsaken their sins, others have felt a spirit of hatred rise in their hearts. Their pride has been hurt when their course has been re-

proved. They entertain the thought that it is Sister White who is hurting them, instead of feeling grateful to God that He has in mercy spoken to them through His humble instrument, to show them their dangers and their sins, that they may put them away before it shall be too late for wrongs to be righted.[22]

Notice that Ellen calls herself God's "humble instrument" while she claims for herself the work of the Holy Spirit: it is her job to "reprove wrongs and reveal hidden sins." This is called blasphemy. And this was certainly not the only time Ellen threatened that Canright would lose his eternal life. She accused him of needing to be thoroughly converted, adding that if he wasn't, "he would be in danger of losing his soul."[23] In addition to this, God had "shown her that Canright was "self-righteous" and "self-sufficient," and that he was marked not only by "great spiritual lack" and "human depravity" but also by cowardice. Furthermore, he was "more inclined to fight against the faithful soldiers of Christ than against Satan and his host."[24] Ellen makes all these accusations without providing any examples or a shred of evidence that any of it was true. And if this were not enough, she accuses both Canright and his wife of having "exalted opinions" of their accomplishments, "a hatred for reproof," a "wicked spirit," "vanity and pride," "sanctimonious infidelity," and a "pharisaical" disposition—again with no specific evidence to make her case![25]

And to top it all off, Ellen writes in a spirit of legalism and works-righteousness, which is an insult to the gospel, the perfect finished work of Christ. The prophetess insists that "it costs us an effort to secure eternal life. It is only by long and persevering efforts, sore discipline, and stern conflict, that we shall be overcomers. But if we patiently and determinedly, in the name of the Conqueror who overcame in our behalf in the wilderness of temptation, overcome as he overcame, we shall have the eternal reward. Our efforts, our self-denial, our perseverance, must be proportionate to the infinite value of the object we are in pursuit of."[26] So it is human effort, she contends, that secures eternal life—in complete contradiction to the gospel of the kingdom that Jesus and the New Testament writers preached.

She goes on, "Sanctification is not a work of a day, nor a year, but of a lifetime. Without continual efforts and constant activity, there cannot be advancement in the divine life and the attainment of the victor's crown."[27] This is the same kind of gross legalism I heard in SDA schools growing up, and it was all based on Ellen G. White. She shows much greater ignorance of the gospel than Canright, and yet she doesn't hesitate to aim her legalistic darts at both him and his wife: "If she [Lucretia] does not watch closely and overcome these defects in her character she will surely fail of sitting with Christ in His throne."[28] So Lucretia's eternal life was not dependent on accepting the shed blood and the atoning work of Christ?

This seemingly unending "testimony" is all the more troubling because it all seems to be projection on Ellen's part. There is overwhelming historical evidence and source documentation that specifically shows she was guilty of the very things she was falsely accusing the Canrights of doing and being.[29] Even so, in that very same letter, Ellen makes many self-righteous claims, even comparing herself and her husband to Paul, the author of Hebrews, and Moses. "Our lives are interwoven with the cause of God," she writes. "We have no separate interest aside from this work."[30] Yet it has been proven that the Whites financially manipulated and exploited church members repeatedly through "visions" and that James embezzled the equivalent of half a million dollars from church institutions with the support of his wife's "visions."[31] I would say it is obvious that they did have a separate interest, and it was a very lucrative one.

The idea that God gave Ellen visions of all these accusations, when it is obvious that she was using her claimed visitations from God to humiliate, intimidate, and control the Canrights, who were concerned about the Whites' authoritative leadership style, is beyond credulity. Is this how God operates with His prophets? Is there any other example from history or in the Bible of God using a prophet this way? Common sense and overwhelming evidence tell us that Ellen and James were threatened by Canright and Lucretia because as insiders, they knew as few others did the "prophet's" dishonest and hypocritical ways and her husband's instability, temper, unpredictability, and greed. The Canrights had to be controlled if James and Ellen were to continue their dominance over the Adventist movement, which was very much dependent on Ellen's prophetic charade. Ellen believed that her rebukes of Canright had ensured her control, so she later pushed for him to be reelected as a conference president, despite his objections, and when he quit the church shortly after that, she pronounced her final prophetic condemnation on the man: "If you have decided to cut all connection with us as a people, I have one request to make, for your own sake as well as for Christ's sake: keep away from our people, do not visit them and talk your doubts and darkness among them. Satan is full of exultant joy that you have stepped from beneath the banner of Jesus Christ and stand under his banner."[32]

Once again, in Ellen White's warped mind, to leave Adventism is to leave Christ. And she attributed Canright's move to ambition and a desire for higher position and recognition. But, again, the facts totally contradict this claim. In his 1888 edition of *Seventh-day Adventism Renounced*, we find the following quote in chapter 1, under the title, "How I sought position and popularity after leaving them":

> They said I must have left them for popularity, position, and pay. Did they know my heart? Had they any evidence of this? No, they made it up and said it because they could say nothing else. It was utterly false; for the truth is, I really feared I should be ruined financially by the change. But as soon as I had left them, I received warm invitations from ten different denominations to unite with them, promising me good positions. But in Otsego, where I had lived for six years and was well-known, there was a small Baptist Church, in debt and unable to hire a pastor. They invited me to preach for them but said they could offer me next to nothing as a salary. Here was a church needing help, just such as I felt I could give. I rejected all the other offers and

accepted this and have been their pastor ever since. I leave honest men to judge my motives.

(Chapter 11 elaborates on this.)

Psychologically, we can see why Ellen was so angry at Canright. She had stuck her prophetic neck out to get him reelected as conference president, and then he almost immediately left the church afterward. That is what you call having prophetic egg all over your face, and the cure for that problem was to lash out at Canright with the most condemning testimonies imaginable. Canright was right: God had supposedly shown Ellen that he was to be conference president despite his protests, and when he followed through with his plans to resign, God supposedly showed her that he was every form of evil, even though his faith in God remained strong. This is just another glaring example of how self-serving Ellen's "visions" really were. There is an incredible pattern in Adventism that equates leaving the SDA Church with leaving Christ, leaving God, or leaving the kingdom of God. This kind of thinking is evident in Ellen's false testimonies of Canright and is plastered throughout the history of Adventism over the names of all who dared to challenge the dishonesty, fraud, cover-ups, and blasphemous claims of the "prophet" and the movement. Those of us who have been the recipients of such charges and condemnations can only shake our heads and thank the Lord that He has delivered us from this cultic thinking and abuse!

3

THE DISHONEST OPPORTUNIST

On May 12, 1919, D. M. Canright passed to his rest. During his lifetime, by far, his two most influential books were *Seventh-day Adventism Renounced* (1888) and *Life of Mrs. E. G. White* (1919). For the reasons we have already explored, these books contained the strongest and most powerful arguments exposing Adventism and its prophet that were available to those churches being constantly attacked by SDAs at that time. And though the best and most gifted apologists in the SDA Church had done all they could to counter Canright, the influence of his works remained strong in the 1950s, when Adventists were largely being dismissed as a cult. So it was at this time that two opportunists from very different backgrounds decided to team together to fabricate a book that would be highly promoted by SDAs to discredit Canright and destroy his influence. This book was still being promoted, even in SDA academic circles, decades after it was published. And it is still being strongly promoted by the SDA Church even today if you bring up its title online.

I was trained as a minister and historian in the Adventist system and heard the name of D. M. Canright mentioned with some regularity. The words associated with his name were always negative. He was a heretic, a traitor, a Judas Iscariot, and a Benedict Arnold. He was dishonest; spiteful;

filled with hatred for the Adventist Church and their prophet, Ellen White; and even possessed of the devil. The ultimate evidence for his evil and villainy was that his own alleged secretary blew the whistle on him and exposed him for the miserable man he was. Carrie Johnson's tell-all book, *I Was Canright's Secretary,* was considered all the evidence necessary to condemn this rebellious betrayer to perdition. This was before the age of the internet, so there was no opportunity to google the book and find it linked to Norman Douty's work, *The Case of D. M. Canright.* It was the responsibility of professors to inform their students of such connections. But no SDA professor I had ever mentioned Douty's book or seemed to have the slightest suspicion that the material in Johnson's book was anything but hard, cold facts.

Of course, I read Carrie Johnson's book, but even during the years I taught SDA history, I had no reason to believe that she was a fraud and a deliberate deceiver. Two things dramatically changed that situation. First, while doing the research for my psychobiography of Ellen White, I read Norman Douty's excellent book *The Case of D. M. Canright.* This work demonstrated that Canright was a good and decent man and a much more credible witness and critic of Ellen White and Adventism than the SDA Church and Carrie Johnson had acknowledged. In fact, Douty's book raised several questions about the credibility of much that was contained in Johnson's book. But secondly, it wasn't until my psychobiography was published and I became acquainted with Nancy Paige on my Facebook thread, which discussed my book, that I truly realized the kind of person Carrie Johnson was. Nancy and her brother were raised by Carrie, their grandmother. They lived under the same roof and witnessed firsthand how she behaved. And their observations about their grandmother were alarming to say the least.

I conducted an extensive interview with Nancy,[1] who has also done a great deal of research into her grandma in the years since the *Review & Herald* published Carrie's book. We will be benefiting from her insightful contributions throughout the rest of the book, for she, more than anyone else, truly knew what kind of woman her grandmother was. Nancy has

developed into a remarkable Christian woman, despite her abusive upbringing in Adventism. She told her story in a magazine article, which provides
some important background before we move into the interview and her
other contributions. As you will see, she and her younger brother were
raised by parents and a grandmother who placed a premium on putting
forth a perfect, pharisaical appearance to the public while they engaged in
the most abusive kind of practices in their own home:

> When I was about twelve, my parents gathered my two
> brothers and me for a family conference. We were told that
> we had a roof over our heads, clothes on our backs, and food
> to eat. We did not need anything. From that point on, they
> informed us, we did not need them. They were now going to
> spend their efforts on truly needy people.

> Publicly they were generous and caring, going over-
> board to show non-Adventists the face of Jesus by their
> righteous acts. The reality? They beat my younger brother
> often. I was never physically beaten but was emotionally and
> spiritually beaten down. They helped me believe that their
> anger, sadness, unhappiness, and shame were my fault. They
> believed my older brother could do no wrong, my younger
> brother was possessed, and I was stupid and vain.

> In spite of the way they treated us, though, we wanted
> to believe that Ellen White was sent by God to straighten
> us out. After all, we had the truth! We were the remnant
> church! I used to wonder why my non-Adventist neighbors
> could not see this obvious reality! My dad's parents lived
> close by and were very involved in our upbringing. Grandpa
> was a farmer, somewhat quiet, and probably the only family
> member who showed a bit of love. Grandma used us as her
> personal slaves; we did her yard work, painted her house,

cleaned the apartment upstairs—and she fed us for our efforts. My parents believed that more than two meals a day was gluttony, so, for several years we were sent to school with no lunch. Grandma, on the other hand, was not able to be affectionate, but she fed us.[2]

The more you hear about Carrie Shasky-Johnson, author of the Canright book, the more you will see that this woman had a real penchant for using people in very sociopathic ways. In my interview with Nancy, she was very straightforward about her grandmother's pathology, and this information will become very important as we proceed into the chapters ahead. But before elaborating on this, let me say that my good friend Desmond Ford often used the following quote from James Truslow Adams in his teaching and his preaching: "There is so much that is bad in the best of us and so much that is good in the worst of us, that it hardly behooves any of us to talk about the rest of us." Generally, I strongly agree with this quote. I think it is very important for all of us as sinful human beings to make every effort to extend grace to one another. Jesus was known for extending grace to sinners, even though he was the only sinless human being who ever lived. But the one group he lambasted and condemned were the Pharisees, who were so hard on others while living as total hypocrites themselves (see Matthew 23).

And while I do not compare myself to Jesus in any way, I believe that His Spirit is still about exposing evil, especially the kind of judgmental and hypocritical evil that we find in the lives of Ellen White, Carrie Johnson, and Arthur White. All three of these individuals made every effort to present themselves in the most positive light (like the Pharisees) while they engaged in the most despicable judgment, condemnation, and hypocrisy imaginable. This book, and my psychobiography of Ellen White, are simply exposing the source documentation and historical evidence behind their false claims.

Following is the back cover copy of Carrie Johnson's *I Was Canright's Secretary*:

Carrie Johnson, the daughter of immigrant parents, became an Adventist in her teens and attended a shorthand school in Battle Creek, Michigan. While still a student she became the secretary of Dudley Marvin Canright, a for-mer-Adventist-minister-turned-bitter-opponent.

Sworn to secrecy, for forty years she kept her promise to say nothing. Feeling this pledge is no longer meaningful, she now reveals, from the background of her unique experience with him, the kind of person the real Canright was.[3]

Mrs. Carrie Johnson standing by Rev. and Mrs. D. M. Canright's tombstone. (p. 167)

The publishers wrote of the book:

It is logical that some may question, Who is this Mrs. Johnson who now tells the story of D. M. Canright, fifty years after his death? Mrs. Carrie Johnson, who authored this work, resides at Dowagiac, Michigan, with her husband, and not far from their son, a dentist, who practices in Berrien Springs. The Johnsons are members of the Decatur-Glenwood, Michigan, Seventh-day Adventist Church, in which both currently hold office. A resident of Michigan for a large part of her life, Mrs. Johnson has been in close touch with the development of the Seventh-day Adventist church, both as an eyewitness and as an earnest student of its history.

The reader will learn that she and her husband, now retired, served in the work of the denomination in various capacities in several States, Mrs. Johnson filling positions of secretary, schoolteacher, and literature evangelist. For the past four decades Frank Johnson, her husband, has managed business interests in Niles and Berrien Springs.

The Johnsons are known in their community as being a solid, *Review-and-Herald*-reading Seventh-day Adventist family, with whom many ministers of the church through the years were acquainted as they were graciously entertained at their home. Both husband and wife have filled many church offices, and Mrs. Johnson for eight years was the Dorcas Federation chairman for western Michigan. She served twelve years as the Niles WCTU president and eight years as the Berrien County president in Berrien Springs. During World War II she was cited by Michigan's governor for meritorious service as the Berrien County Neighborhood War Club chairman.

Sworn to secrecy when employed to assist D. M. Canright, Mrs. Johnson, now fifty years after his death, feels that she is no longer bound to this pledge to keep in strict confidence what she heard and saw during the period of time she served as his secretary. Her story, plus the result of her years of painstaking research, combines and forms a new and fascinating portrait of Dudley Marvin Canright.[4]

SDAs continue to market this book even today as a great "faith-building" read, when really it is nothing but a totally false and fabricated attempt to assassinate the character of a humble servant of God who had already become the target of an entire denomination, that is, a big cult. Following is more of their false PR:

A fascinating, faith-building autobiography of Carrie Johnson and biography of Dudley Marvin Canright is presented in the book 'I Was Canright's Secretary.'"

Ironically, the foreword to Johnson's book, claims that "neither Mrs. Carrie Johnson, the author of this book, nor the Seventh-day Adventist Church, of which she is a member, holds any ill will or bitterness toward D. M. Canright, the subject of the volume."[5] Yet, the book is filled with the most damning falsehoods and condemnations one could make against a minister of Jesus Christ, who only wanted to serve Him. In an interview conducted with the author in 1971, the year her book was published, Carrie presents Canright as the most pitiable person imaginable. According to her, Canright looked unkept and homeless, was dependent on Adventists for his food and clothing, and was unable to even support his wife.[6] And that is not the half of it, as you will see later in this chapter. I encourage you to listen to this interview and judge for yourself whether Carrie held no ill will toward Canright.[7]

Most of all, both the book and the interview sought to establish that Canright "died in obscurity," to prove that his end was the fulfillment of Ellen White's prophecy about him. Ironically, Canright may have been the best-known Adventist minister while he was alive, and after his death. The SDA claim that no one attended his funeral is also a lie. Canright's son testified that the church was full of admirers, including many ministers.[8] So, we have seen the pharisaical front that SDAs have put up to present Carrie Johnson to the public as a credible author. Now let's look at the other side of the coin, based on those who knew her best and the most accurate historical documentation available.

As I've mentioned, Norman Douty's excellent, highly documented book *The Case of D. M. Canright* refutes much of what Carrie Johnson claims. But even Douty did not know her the way her own grandkids did.

In my twenty-page interview with Nancy Paige, she said that the earliest memories she and her brother had of their grandmother was that she was abusive, cold, and unloving, and that she forced them to do her work, for which she was receiving rent money from students she rented to. This included fully painting the house, cleaning the house, including terrible messes the renters left, and other physical labor for which they were not paid but were given meager meals (usually two a day). Furthermore, from their earliest years they remembered their grandmother repeatedly lying to them and knew that she could not be trusted. To support this, they both testify to the fact that their grandmother was a thief and was disfellowshipped from her employed position at the Niles Seventh-day Adventist Church for embezzling church funds. For years she and her husband did not apply for membership in any other SDA Church because they did not want their dirty little secret to be known.[9]

Nancy describes her grandmother as a shrewd narcissist and sociopath who was very good at manipulating others socially and great at presenting a false front outside the home but who didn't care about others, including her own grandkids, except to use them. She was always just looking for opportunities to benefit herself–in the most dishonest ways, if necessary.[10] These characteristics will come into full focus as we unpack the way Carrie colluded with Arthur White, and with him, duped the entire Adventist Church, which continues to publish and promote her book to this very day. Let's briefly outline how this process unfolded before we go into greater detail in the chapters to come.

Step 1. The idea. Nancy says that her grandma was an opportunist without morals or ethics. There is no evidence or reason to believe that Carrie Johnson was ever sworn to secrecy about Canright, nor is there any evidence that she ever met Canright, much less worked for him (as we shall see). There is no reason to think that even if it were true, she would have kept this secret from everyone, including her own family, for more than thirty years after Canright's death. In fact, the notion that she would never mention any of this, even confidentially, to someone who could verify her claim is literally unthinkable given the extreme narcissistic patterns that we will uncover in her life. Her claim that she discovered she had leukemia in 1950 and had to get this terrible secret off her chest is also extremely suspicious to any thinking person. First, after the "diagnosis," her doctor told her she would die of old age before she ever died of cancer. And second, why would she have felt any obligation to Canright, much less an obligation that would last more than thirty years after his death? After all, he was full of the devil, if she is to be believed (more on that momentarily). Nancy's explanation—which most reasonable people would embrace—was that Carrie saw an opportunity to become famous and make needed money related to her illness (more on this later) at the same time, so she took it, finding a willing accomplice in Arthur White.

Step 2. Contacting Arthur White. Carrie's scheme by itself would have gone nowhere had she not found an "important person" in the SDA Church who was just as desperate to perpetrate a fraud concerning Canright, as she was. Carrie lived close to Andrews University and the Ellen White vault there, so who better to tell her little "secret" to than Arthur White himself, the head of White Estate for the entire SDA denomination (who often visited the Andrews vault). Canright was the biggest threat to his mother's legacy, so I can imagine that Arthur's eyes got big when he heard this supposed confession from Canright's "former secretary." People who crave power and recognition are typically attracted to others like themselves who can help them accomplish this goal. It had to be love at first sight for these two: Arthur had the position and power to make Carrie wealthy and famous, and Carrie had the ability to make Arthur's dreams come true concerning his "evil" nemesis, D. M. Canright. It was a marriage made in hell, as we shall see.

Step 3. Creating a believable story—at least for SDAs. According to my interview with Nancy Paige, both she and her brother witnessed Arthur White driving up to their grandma's house in his fancy Lincoln Continental on a regular basis for years to help her construct the perfect book that would discredit and destroy D. M. Canright—a book that can now be proven to be completely fabricated.[11] Arthur's heavy involvement was not something he advertised but kept totally secret and even denied when he was questioned about it later.[12] Arthur didn't want fame connected to this book; that was Carrie's role. Nor did he want any money; he had his fancy Lincoln. The cash was all for Carrie and the Adventist Book Centers. Arthur wanted the ammunition to destroy his enemy, and now he had the perfect opportunity to create it himself. Never mind that his claim to be a historian had to be totally compromised in the process.

Step 4. Stealing Canright's diary. We will go into detail about this in the next chapter. But for now, just know that Carrie Johnson deliberately deceived the Canright family about who she was, to get her hands on the diary, and convinced them that she was simply borrowing it to do sympathetic and legitimate research rather than to make up lies about Canright. If that wasn't bad enough, Arthur and the White Estate colluded with Johnson in this theft by taking the stolen property, securing it in the White Estate, and refusing to return it to its rightful owner to this day.

Step 5. A meticulous attempt to make the book look legitimate. As I read Carrie Johnson's book again, with the benefit of now knowing what I do about the author and her secret meetings with Arthur White, many patterns emerged. First, Arthur White did everything he could to provide Carrie with all manner of historical information to make it appear that she was a student of Adventist history. Second, Carrie attempted to compensate for her tragic lack of experiential data by using the material Arthur connected her to and meeting with the Canright family, repeatedly and under false pretenses, to give the appearance that she actually had a genuine relationship with Canright and his family. She also paid a surprise visit to Norman Douty, again under false pretenses, and spent seven hours peppering him with questions and assertions and taking meticulous notes, because Douty knew way more about Canright than she did.

Third, Carrie tragically misused the information in Canright's stolen diary to make multifarious false claims and accusations about Canright, which now could not be refuted because the diary was being held captive.

Finally, because Johnson had already gotten away with the big lie, that she was Canright's secretary, although she had no evidence to support the claim, she tried to appeal to the diary, innuendo, and the above-mentioned resources, rather than personal experience or anecdotes that could be disproven, in the book. This was wise on the part of Arthur and the author because the very few claims based on personal experience that Carrie did make have basically been shown, by convincing evidence, to be false, as we shall see in the chapters ahead. But what Carrie's book lacked in real-life experience and proof of an actual relationship with D. M. Canright, it made up for by doing everything possible to convince readers that the story was true, without evidence.

Step 6. Colluding with Arthur White and the Church to avoid being vetted. When an employee of the Seventh-day Adventist denomination has been caught embezzling from a church institution or congregation, his or her career in Adventism is typically over. The Church will forgive a lot of things, even allowing known pedophiles to stay employed by moving them around to different places (SDAs have way more in common with the Catholic Church than they admit), but they take their money very seriously. Because Carrie Johnson had been disfellowshipped from her SDA church for embezzling church funds,[13] normally, the church would have never trusted her in any significant way again. And Carrie would have known this herself. So, what better way to make amends with the church than to hand them the head of their most hated enemy, on a platter? Carrie started with Arthur White, and once he lost all objectivity regarding her credentials, he became her ticket to convince the rest of the church that she was the greatest God-given gift they could imagine. This explains why there was no attempt to vet her false claims or to hold her accountable for her past actions. Carrie Johnson would die as a hero in Adventism for colluding with Arthur White, the White Estate, and the Adventist Church to commit the worst kind of defamation.

Step 7. An aggressive marketing campaign featuring damaging and deliberate lies about Canright. When you watch the camp meeting interview with Carrie Johnson that has been heavily marketed by the church and continues to be promoted online to this day, it is obvious that SDA leadership considered Carrie to be their fair-haired favorite on the camp meeting circuit and the poster child in their campaign to destroy D. M. Canright. While recently rewatching it, I was both amazed and disgusted to see how Canright was literally demonized by Johnson and the interviewer and presented in the most pitiful terms imaginable, while Ellen White was presented as the most gracious, loving, kind, patient, gentle, saintly human being in her dealings with Canright. Both descriptions were so inaccurate and completely at odds with the historical facts that it is inexcusable.

As I noted earlier, Carrie had claimed that Canright was an indigent who depended entirely on SDA charity for his survival. But far worse, she also claimed that when Canright dictated to her, he was demon-possessed and that it wasn't his voice but a demon's that spoke to her. He "cried constantly," she alleged, and repeatedly declared that he was a lost man and that Ellen was a great woman. I encourage you, again, to listen to this interview and decide his guilt or innocence for yourself as you see the continuing story—and facts—unfold in this volume.

4

THE DIARY THEFT

A diary is a very personal item. It often contains the deepest thoughts and secrets of a person's life and from an ethical perspective should not even be read, much less shared, without the author's permission. As an author myself, I started keeping a personal journal and prayer diary on October 22, 1985, and have continued writing in it every day since, so I have great respect for the privacy of a person's diary. In this day and age, it is not only unethical to violate the privacy of someone's diary, but it is illegal to publish it or to misuse it to hurt the person who wrote the diary. "When it comes to publication of your private facts and thoughts, you have legal privacy protections. Generally, if embarrassing private facts are disclosed publicly, you may be able to take legal action against the person who disclosed your private writings, facts or thoughts."

What Carrie Johnson did to the reputation of D. M. Canright, and to his family, by pretending to be a sympathetic researcher so she could gain access to Canright's diary with the intention of keeping it and misusing it to substantiate false accusations against Canright was unethical, immoral, and illegal.

When my psychobiography of Ellen White was published in 2020, there were some who challenged or objected to my use of the terms *con artist* and *fraud* to refer to the professed prophetess. *Con artist* is defined as "a manipulator who cheats, or tricks, others through persuading them to believe something that is not true."[1] Someone who does so to exploit or take advantage of people is certainly an evil con artist. My daily thread on Facebook, as well as the highly documented evidence in my book, testify that Ellen White deceived and exploited a lot of people. But even she did not have the consistent kind of malicious, sociopathic behavior demonstrated by Carrie Johnson over her lifetime. Ellen was not overtly abusive to her children and grandchildren. She did not embezzle church funds (although she covered for her husband doing so through professed visions from God). She simply attained the status of a prophet at a very young age, at least by seventeen, based on her alleged "visions." She was much more sophisticated in her claims than Carrie Johnson. Still, the bottom line is that both women used religion to support their evil deeds and deceptions.

Jesus Christ could have rightly condemned anyone, given his status as the only sinless human being who ever lived on this earth. But instead, He was known as a "friend of . . . sinners" (Matthew 11:19), one who attracted those whom society condemned. The only exception to this benevolence was the way he dealt with the Pharisees and other hypocritical religious leaders of His day. His words of warning to them took no prisoners and demonstrated His hatred for their fakery, deceptions, and gross exploitations of the people they claimed to serve (see Matthew 23:1–35). The self-righteousness of Ellen White, Arthur White, and Carrie Johnson is remarkably similar to that of the Pharisees. And Carrie's theft of Canright's diary, in collusion with Arthur White, is just one of many actions we will explore that reveal the kind of character, or lack thereof, modeled by this sick woman. For those who don't believe Jesus was God, or believe in God at all, can we still agree that controlling, manipulating, and exploiting people based on their belief in God is one of the worst kinds of evil?

There are so many questions that need to be addressed relating to the theft of Canright's diary that the subject deserves a chapter of its own, and we will spend the remainder of it focusing on three general questions and then seven specific questions related to these general ones.

First, why was Carrie Johnson so desperate to steal Canright's diary? If Carrie really worked for Canright and knew him personally, one would expect this would be the focus of any book she would write about him. But this is not at all the case. The few firsthand details she tries to offer about Canright are filled with holes and contradictions, which naturally raise questions about her credibility. Carrie claimed to work for Canright for seven months at the beginning of 1913,[2] after first being sworn to secrecy concerning the work she would do for him. But the cloak-and-dagger bit just doesn't work. If Canright and the friend fronting for him to hire Carrie were so concerned about secrecy and confidentiality, it makes no sense at all that they would be completely careless and incompetent when it came to vetting the person who would be Canright's secretary. Canright knew a lot of people. There is no reason to believe he would have hired an inexperienced eighteen-year-old of questionable reputation. Beyond this, Carrie's claims about Canright were nearly all proven to be false, as we shall see.[3]

But it was because Carrie's claims were so questionable and could not be verified that it became necessary to find something more to serve as the foundation for the false accusations that would be leveled at Canright. Arthur White was no idiot. He was aware of Norman Douty and his coming book, he was aware of Canright's diary, and he would have been fully aware that Carrie Johnson's shaky story wasn't going to be enough to cut it for the character assassination they were planning. So, he likely encouraged Carrie to pursue Canright's living relatives to try to get ahold of the diary, and Norman Douty as well, to get as much information as she could. According to Nancy Paige, Carrie became quite obsessed with obtaining the diary,[4] and once she had acquired it, "she was like the cat that swallowed the canary."[5] Carrie had every reason to want to steal that diary out of her own desperation to find some credibility.

Second, whose idea was it to try to obtain D. M. Canright's diary? Arthur White and Carrie Johnson had been secretly meeting for many years before Carrie suddenly became obsessed with befriending Canright's remaining family members and winning their trust so she could get her hands on his diary. We have already noted that Arthur White was the brains behind this operation to discredit Canright, and that he kept his visits with his star author completely secret to everyone except Carrie's grandkids, who were usually there when Arthur arrived. Arthur knew what would sell and what would not, and he was the one with the education, position, and influence to get the book published. So, Carrie was 100 percent dependent on him while he called the shots.[6] She was just Arthur's convenient puppet, but he was clearly pulling all the strings. However, the question remained, How could she maintain possession of the diary once it was borrowed?

This is where the evil genius of Arthur White comes into play. He had a lot of his grandmother's shrewdness and deceitfulness in him. White assured Carrie that if she could get the diary in her possession, even for a short time, she could bring it to the White Estate and donate it as the supposed owner, and Arthur would take it from there. What is the proof for this? It is exactly what happened. And once this occurred, no Canright family member and not even Norman Douty could get the diary back. The White Estate still illicitly claims ownership of the personal and private document today. When Canright's family insisted that Carrie return the diary, she lied, stating that she no longer possessed it and was unable to get it back from the White Estate. When Norman Douty contacted the White Estate and met with their officials (including the associate secretary) on July 13, 1962, explaining that the diary had been underhandedly obtained and that it belonged to the Canright family, the officials agreed with him and assured him things would be made right,[7] but that he should put it all in writing and send it to their boss, Arthur White, as he would have to make the final decision. Douty complied with their request and sent the requested material on July 23, 1962. After a long delay, and only after requesting that another SDA official prod him, White wrote Douty the following brief reply on September 20, 1962: "I am not sure that my interpretation of certain matters accords entirely with yours."[8]

On September 24, Douty wrote another letter, sent by airmail to Arthur White, asking him to "elucidate" on his vague reply. After waiting for weeks, White finally replied again, claiming he could only give the diary to the one who had donated it to the estate, despite all the documented evidence that said donor had lied and misleadingly stolen the diary.

> It is our understanding that the D. M. Canright diary for the year 1867 is the property of Mrs. Carrie Johnson, a member of the Seventh-day Adventist Church, it having been given to her by Mr. Clifton Dey. Mrs. Johnson is a layman and her contacts were made on her own volition and without the knowledge of any official of the Seventh-day Adventist Church. Inasmuch as this diary is not our property, we are not at liberty to dispose of it in harmony with your suggestion."[9]

So, the Arthur White–Carrie Johnson plan worked to perfection. Both parties lied about how the diary was obtained, in the face of overwhelming evidence to the contrary; each denied ownership, claiming it belonged to the other; and Arthur White explicitly denied knowing anything about what Carrie had supposedly done on her own, when in reality he had been in league with her for twelve years, masterminding everything she was doing. On top of this, he went back on what his representatives had promised Douty—that things would be made right— and claimed that the SDA Church was in no way responsible for the actions of its acknowledged member Carrie Johnson. Douty was only allowed to view the diary in the White vault itself; he was not allowed to take any notes on what he was reading. Even so, Douty was able to assure his readers that based on what he had read, there was nothing in the diary to support Johnson's claims or that was at all damaging to Canright.[10]

This explains why Arthur denied Douty the right, as a researcher, to make copies or even take notes on a research document. That is unethical for a research institute. But it was the only way that Arthur and Carrie could continue to make false claims, allegedly based on the diary, that were distorted and misrepresentative of what Canright had actually written. Neither Douty nor the Canright family had the necessary wealth to engage in a long, protracted legal fight with an institutional church that had lawyers on retainer, so Arthur and Carrie committed premeditated evil, confident that they would not be held accountable for their actions.

Third, is it clear that Carrie Johnson and the White Estate acted unethically, immorally, and illegally concerning Canright's diary? If you are still uncertain about how to answer this question, let us briefly enumerate what occurred, in chronological order.

- Carrie Johnson and Arthur White met clandestinely for more than a decade planning the book against Canright before they aggressively decided to pursue Canright's diary. The long delay was largely due to Johnson's lack of evidence or any substantial content to justify her claims, which were needed to write the book.[11]
- Carrie Johnson and her husband met with Norman Douty and his wife in April 1962, when she made numerous documented assertions that Douty could prove untrue and that exposed the fact that her claim to be Canright's secretary, or even to have ever met him in person, was manufactured.[12]
- Many of the claims that Carrie made to Douty, documented in their meeting, and which she had made to Canright's family in writing, were clearly false, and forced her and Arthur White to look for more information to use against Canright.[13]
- This is what motivated Carrie to contact the Canright family in the guise of a sympathetic supporter of Canright and his family. She hid her true identity as a hostile SDA to unethically obtain access to Canright's diary.[14]
- In the letters Carrie wrote to the Canright family, she spoke of how she so admired D. M. Canright that she had visited his former churches. She also wrote of how the main street in Grand Rapids, Canright Street, had been named after him, and how she had honored him at his burial place. In other words she gave the family the false notion that she was a real fan of Canright.[15]

- After lavishly praising Canright to his relatives and assuring them that her efforts were purely in the best interest of the Canright family, Carrie arranged to meet Mr. Clifton Dey and his wife, who was in possession of the diary, which was given to him by his uncle Jess Canright (D. M. Canright's son) on Saturday (the SDA Sabbath), August 6, 1960, in the Dey home.[16]
- After a very pleasant visit, where Carrie once again praised Canright, Dey allowed Carrie to borrow—not have—the diary, as can be seen from the overwhelming documentation that follows, to help her with her "positive" research on Canright and his family.[17]
- Having obtained the diary, Carrie celebrated her ill-gotten victory and immediately surrendered the diary to Arthur White as planned, for his safe keeping in the White Estate vault at Andrews University.[18]
- When Canright's family discovered from Douty that Carrie Johnson was a Seventh-day Adventist, who had deceived them about both her identity and her motives, the family immediately fired off letters, made phone calls, and actually visited Carrie's home, demanding their property back.[19]
- Carrie avoided the Canrights for as long as she could, but they finally got ahold of her. She claimed that the diary was no longer in her possession or under her control. This was a prearranged lie, concocted by Arthur White under the strictest secrecy, based on all the evidence available.[20]
- Norman Douty, on behalf of the Canright family, met with officials representing the Adventist Church and the White Estate, their associate secretary, and showed them documentation of all of Carrie Johnson's deception and their responses demanding the return of their personal property. The officials agreed that the diary should be returned but requested that Douty send these documents to Arthur White himself.[21] After stonewalling Douty as long as he could, Arthur sent a letter to Douty, betraying the officials who had met with Douty, and keeping his half of the deal

with Carrie, claiming that only she could request that the diary be removed from the vault.[22] Douty and the Canright family could not afford attorneys to fight this injustice, so Douty requested that he be allowed to see the diary to check out claims he had heard Carrie Johnson make based on the diary.[23]

- Arthur White allowed Douty to read the diary but not to make any copies of its pages or to even take any notes.[24]
- Douty read the diary thoroughly and discovered that it contained nothing whatsoever on which Carrie Johnson could have based her many false claims and nothing that was damaging to Canright.[25]
- But this did not prevent Carrie from grossly misleading readers of her book and listeners to her public presentations that the diary had given her insights on which to base her accusations against Canright.

You can't get much lower as a "researcher" than to steal a dead person's personal diary from his family and then grossly misuse it and misrepresent it to tarnish the good name of its author. I am fully convinced, based on the overwhelming evidence, that the actions of Carrie Johnson and Arthur White were tragically unethical, immoral, and illegal!

So, with that in mind, let's consider seven more specific questions related to the diary theft.

1. **Why did Carrie Johnson wait for a decade before aggressively going after Canright's diary?** As Arthur White held his regular secret meetings with Carrie in her home to help her formulate her book against Canright, it became increasingly obvious to him that Carrie's story was not adding up, and that she had to obtain more convincing and documented information about Canright if their attack on him was to be successful. Arthur had already provided her with the historical filler that took up much of the book, but personal information about Canright, especially the kind of juicy gossip they were looking for, from his personal

secretary was sadly lacking. (In the next chapter we will see the evidence that Carrie Johnson never even met D. M. Canright, much less worked for him for seven months as his personal secretary, a fact well-known to Arthur White.)

So, in all likelihood, it was Arthur who encouraged Carrie to meet with as many members of the Canright family as she could. And it was certainly Arthur who would have been aware that respected author Norman Douty was writing a book about Canright. He probably thought it would be good for Carrie to pick Douty's brain and find out what he knew and didn't know concerning her knowledge of Canright. This was actually a huge mistake on the part of Arthur and Carrie, for although it worked out perfectly where the diary theft was concerned, it backfired tremendously where Douty was concerned, as we shall see in the next chapter.

2. **Why did Carrie Johnson lie about her identity and motives?** The answer to this question is fairly obvious. Carrie's whole idea for the book had absolutely no basis in reality (as we will document in the next chapter). This being the case, Carrie was used to telling the Big Lie, and she was a very convincing liar. After all, she had convinced Arthur White himself, so how hard would it be to convince Canright's family and some man named Douty? But it was her very success in lying, misrepresenting both her identity and her motives to the Canright family, that led her to be way too self-confident when she boldly showed up at Norman Douty's door on a Saturday morning and spent the next seven hours with him, making questionable assertions about Canright and asking a legion of questions.

Douty was a gifted and thorough researcher who was able to see through Carrie's bizarre claims and lies quite easily. It was this that led to Carrie and Arthur's downfall. Had Douty and the Canright family had the money to hire competent attorneys and been inclined to do so, they could have brought Carrie

Johnson, Arthur White, the White Estate, the Review and Herald Publishing Association, and the Seventh-day Adventist Church to their knees. Neither Carrie nor Arthur lived to see their clever fraud exposed, but the White Estate and the Adventist Church are still around and fully deserve to be held accountable for the fraud they perpetrated on their own people and the world at large.

3. **What role did Arthur White and the White Estate play in the theft?** There is very good reason why Arthur White tried to hide and deny his intimate involvement in the construction of the book *I Was Canright's Secretary*. But there can be no doubt that his role was an extremely extensive one. It is here that we owe a great debt of gratitude to Nancy Paige and her brother Ted, who witnessed Arthur's secret visits to their grandmother, week after week, and month after month, for some twenty years, which would have gone totally unknown were it not for their witness. It never occurred to Arthur that two young kids would be his downfall but he certainly did have a number of great reasons for trying to keep his collusion completely covered up. First, it gave him deniability if there was any problem with the book, and as we will see in the next chapter, there were damning problems with Carrie's story. Second, it allowed him to appear objective about the book when he was actually behind it. Third, it gave him the opportunity to help and protect Carrie concerning the diary theft and even allowed him to use the power and prestige of the White Estate to harbor the stolen document. Fourth, it allowed him to insert anything he wanted into the book without having any accountability for what he contributed to the destruction of his enemy, D. M. Canright. And finally, it allowed Arthur White to use his position and power to actively endorse and promote the book in a manner that appeared to be unbiased, and truly objective, which certainly contributed to its popularity in Adventism.

In the case of Arthur White, you can truly say that the apple didn't fall too far from the proverbial tree. Just as his grandmother, the "prophetess" Ellen G. White had engaged in a lifetime of dishonesty, false accusations, and downright fraud (not to mention plagiarism, blasphemy, and gross misrepresentation of God), so did Arthur. He spent two decades helping Carrie Johnson produce a book full of made-up stories intended to smear the reputation of D. M. Canright. Not only did he mastermind this despicable book; he explicitly lied about being involved with it. He spent his whole life trying to present himself as an impartial and objective scholar. Like his pretentious grandmother, he became an expert in claiming to be something he was not!

4. **On what grounds did the White Estate claim ownership of the diary, even to this day?** It should not be overlooked that any reasonable person, including the SDA officials who met with Douty, mentioned above, would be able to see from the documented material presented by Douty that neither Carrie Johnson nor the White Estate ever had a legitimate claim to the diary of D. M. Canright. It was a deliberate theft, orchestrated by Carrie Johnson and Arthur White, and skillfully executed by them both, while at the same time, they both self-righteously claimed to be innocent of any wrongdoing. To this day, the diary is in the possession of the White Estate, and neither the SDA Church nor the White Estate have ever had to be held accountable for the illicit acts that resulted in the theft of this diary.

It is my hope that the publication of this book will so expose the heinous plotting and behaviors of both Carrie Johnson and Arthur White, that one result will be the return of Canright's diary to his family, its rightful owners. In fairness, the vast majority of Adventists have absolutely no clue about what was done to Canright and his diary, and like the SDA officials who agreed with Douty, should find it easy to rise up and insist that the SDA Church take the moral, ethical, and legal action necessary to remove this ugly blight from their history by both returning Canright's diary and ceasing promotion of Carrie Johnson's falsified book. To summarize, there were no legitimate grounds for the White Estate to claim ownership over Canright's diary back in 1962, and there are no legitimate grounds for the White Estate to continue to possess this document today!

5. **How did Carrie Johnson and Adventism misuse the diary to misrepresent Canright?** One of the most important developments that occurred from Carrie Johnson's making a host of rash and false claims, supposedly based on Canright's diary, when she met for seven hours in a documented meeting with Norman Douty, was that it gave Douty both motivation and cause to see the diary for himself. And although he was wrongly denied the ability as a researcher to make copies or take notes, he was able to see for himself that Johnson's claims were false, and to put the White Estate, Arthur White, and Carrie Johnson on notice that they would be held accountable for further misrepresentations where the diary was concerned. This certainly put a cramp in the plans of Arthur and Carrie, who were seeking to attribute the most damaging things possible to Canright based on the diary they possessed, the contents of which no one else knew.

Many of the false claims that Carrie made to Douty in their meeting did not appear in the book for these very reasons. But this did not stop her from smearing Canright with innumerable false claims and innuendo, which she attributed to the diary, in her camp meeting presentations that promoted the book. Adventists were mesmerized by these presentations, which were sponsored and promoted by the Church, and were purported to be fact when they were really just the engineered spewings of the town gossip. Again, I encourage you to view the example I referenced early, which presented Canright as a poverty-stricken, weeping and despairing man, who desperately wanted to return to Adventism but knew it was "too late" because he was sold out to the devil. All of this with generous references to Canright's diary. So, their evil plot was largely realized!

6. **Why did the White Estate deny normal research access to Canright's diary?** One of the stated purposes for the existence of the White Estate is to "provide resources for helping to better understand her [Ellen White's] life and ministry." The estate claims to be a nonprofit entity that facilitates research on the life and work of the SDA prophetess. But when Norman Douty requested to see the diary of D. M. Canright, as stated previously, he was told he could neither take notes on the diary's contents nor make copies of it. This breach of protocol and violation of acceptable research ethics was insisted upon by Arthur White himself, who, quite simply, did not want the truth about Canright to get out. That truth was, his diary would have exposed Carrie Johnson as the liar she was—and Arthur couldn't have that.

As a researcher, I too was denied access to important research materials while an Adventist that would have been extremely important to my academic research on Ellen White, so what the White Estate did to Douty was not at odds with what they have done to many researchers, even those who were Adventists in good standing. At some point the White Estate needs to be accountable for their deceitfulness and cover-ups.

7. **Did the diary contain the kind of harmful information about Canright that SDAs claimed?** If Canright was the emotional wreck that SDAs have attempted to portray, one would expect that his personal diary would be a gold mine of ammunition to expose his pathology. Here we owe a great debt of gratitude to Norman Douty, who went to the trouble of tracking down the diary in the White Estate, reading it thoroughly, and making it clear to all concerned that the diary contained nothing that was harmful or damaging to Canright. In fact, according to Douty, the diary presented Canright for the sincere Christian that he was. The very purpose for which Arthur

White and Carrie Johnson stole the diary was thwarted by the information contained in the diary, based on Douty's testimony. And if you have a hard time knowing who to believe between Douty and the deceitful duo of White and Johnson, know that one is supported by an impressive record of honesty and impeccable integrity, while the other two have been shown to be just the opposite. And that distinction will become even more pronounced in the next chapter.

5

THE NORMAN DOUTY CONNECTION

Had it not been for Norman Douty and the critical role he played in the story we are unfolding and exploring in these chapters, this book would never have been written. That is how important this humble author and researcher was in foiling the worst plans of Arthur White and Carrie Johnson. As it was, they still succeeded in publishing their book of slander against D. M. Canright and doing a great deal of damage to him. But because of Douty, along with Nancy Paige and her brother Ted, the full extent of the fraud that deceived and exploited Adventist church members for decades can now be fully exposed.

It is nearly impossible to find a Seventh-day Adventist who has ever heard of Norman Douty, and even among SDA historians and theologians, his name is seldom if ever mentioned. Despite earning a four-year under-graduate degree in theology from an Adventist university; a three-year master's of divinity at Andrews University, the Adventist seminary in Michigan; and a master's degree in history, specializing in Adventist Church history, from Loma Linda University, I never heard the name Norman Douty men-tioned in any of my classes. It was not mentioned in either of my two doc-toral programs either, but that would be expected, because they were from non-Adventist universities, and Douty's significance is largely related to his book on D. M. Canright and Seventh-day Adventists.

Canright was often attacked in my Adventist courses and training, and the typical reference given was Carrie Johnson's *I Was Canright's Secretary.* As we shall see, even leading SDA "scholars" referred to Johnson's testimony as reliable. Douty's book, *The Case of D. M. Canright,* was published in 1964, whereas Johnson's book was not published until 1971. But it was what transpired between Douty and Johnson before either book was published that is so crucial in understanding the fiction created by Johnson and Arthur White and the fraud they perpetrated on their readers.

UNCOVERING A FABRICATION

How did this strange saga unfold? According to Douty, it all began on June 18, 1960, when he wrote a letter to a well-known SDA scholar (one of the authors of *Questions on Doctrine)* concerning a book that Douty was writing on Seventh-day Adventism. It was a more general book on Adventism, not focusing on Canright. In fact, Douty did not mention Canright in his correspondence. Four days later, he received a reply from this Adventist leader. It contained the following paragraph"

> I am wondering whether you have a real acquaintance with the teachings of Adventists. It would make it possible for you to evaluate them. Walter Martin based quite a few of his strictures upon the statements of D. M. Canright, an apostate Adventist minister who three times left us, was ordained by the Baptists, [and] cast out by them . . . Each time he came back to us he repudiated his former attacks, but finally went out for good, I think, to all concerned. The man considered himself a lost soul who had turned from God and right. I have affidavits from his secretary, and from others that he often said, "I'm a lost man, I'm a lost man!" He was like the desperado who wanted to bring down all he could

before his own life was taken. That is pretty poor caliber of testimony on which to base an antagonism.[2]

Here we see that even in 1960 the SDA leadership was still concerned about the negative influence of D. M. Canright and his books on Adventism. Hardly the obscurity that Ellen White prophesied about Canright and that Carrie Johnson would dishonestly try to prove in her book. Furthermore, notice that this leading SDA scholar refers to "affidavits" from Carrie Johnson—only identified as Canright's secretary. These unproven affidavits were used to support Carrie's false claims that the old deserter Canright had recanted his previous criticisms of Adventists, had been rejected by the Baptists, and had ultimately turned away from God.

Douty knew from his own research that these accusations against Canright were false and resolved that in addition to finishing his book on Adventism, he would research further into the case of D. M. Canright, focusing specifically on these pathological accusations. When Carrie Johnson contacted members of the Canright family, seeking to defraud them of Canright's precious diary, the family contacted Douty. That is when he was able to discover the identity of "Canright's secretary." On April 6, 1962, Douty wrote to Carrie Johnson to see if they could meet and exchange notes about Canright. He received no reply, but without an appointment and unannounced, both Carrie and her husband showed up at Douty's door on the Sabbath, as pointed out in chapter 4, and spent all day discussing her claims and their materials about Canright.[3]

Douty's wife took careful notes on what was said that day, and Douty observed that Carrie Johnson made numerous statements about Canright, trying to convince them that she had been his secretary. This served to accomplish the opposite goal. Some of her most provably wrong claims had also been made in writing to the Canright family members whom she sought to swindle. This visit to Douty was by far the biggest mistake she made, and it ended up exposing her to Douty as the scammer she was. After their seven-hour meeting was over, the minutes from the meeting were drawn up and sent to Carrie for any corrections or additions she deemed appropriate. On May 19, Douty received a reply that "sternly protested making any public record of what she had said." Carrie insisted that Douty not use her name in the book he would be publishing on Canright.[4]

CANRIGHT'S SECRETARY? AND A PEG LEG?

Douty complied with Carrie's demand to omit her name from his book, but thankfully, he did reveal the contents of her claims in his chapter titled "Canright's Secretary." It is critical to examine her claims and to see how they were confirmed in writing to the Canright family to expose the fraud that she and Arthur White successfully put over on the Adventist Church and its members. We will look at these claims in detail, focusing first on the item that revealed more than any other that Carrie Johnson fabricated her whole account and that Arthur colluded with her in this fabrication. Be warned that Carrie claimed to have worked for Canright during three different periods. Her earliest claim was that she was Canright's secretary "for the years 1912 and 1913.[5] When Douty asked her specifically what years she had worked for Canright, she replied, "1912–14."[6] Once the external evidence clearly showed that such claims were impossible to support, Carrie changed her tenure to "seven months" in the year 1913, as seen in her book.[7] With this in mind, let's look at the most convincing evidence showing that Carrie Johnson not only never worked for D. M. Canright but never even met him or saw him in person.

The most strikingly inaccurate claim Carrie made, both in her letters to the Canright family and in her documented conversation with Norman Douty, was that Canright had a peg leg when she was his secretary. She first made this assertion in writing to Canright's son Jess on October 25, 1960, stating that "in 1913, his father had a peg leg."[8] She made the same claim in Douty's home on May 5, 1962, "explaining that he [Canright] had lost a leg in an accident in his father's hay field."[9] To make a claim that she did not know for a fact—and to a man's own son, who would know she was wrong—how dumb is that?

When Carrie Johnson hatched her plan to fabricate her story about D. M. Canright, she first tried to find out as much about the man as she could before presenting her claims to Arthur White in 1950. One of the pieces of information she ran across was an old story that had circulated about Canright, which said precisely what she would end up telling Douty in May 1862: that Canright had lost a leg in a farming accident. Of course Carrie didn't quote this source; she simply claimed to have observed for herself that Canright had a peg leg when she worked for him. Jess Canright confirmed to Douty in a letter dated January 3, 1963, that this rumor had indeed circulated about his father, but went on to say, "As to his losing a leg in his father's hay field, that is pure fiction."[10] And Jess's assertion is supported by testimony from others, as well.

D. M. Canright's nephew wrote Douty on February 4, 1963, disputing Carrie's "peg leg" claim and stating that he had several pictures of Canright during the years in question, 1912–14, showing that he had two perfectly good legs. He even gave one of the pictures to Douty as evidence. Canright's good friend and next-door neighbor, Fred A. Rudy, who worked on projects with Canright during those same years, and who actually did do some secretarial work for Canright when needed, testified in a letter dated February 25, 1963, "Mr. D. M. Canright had two good legs when I knew him, and he was very active from daylight to dark."[11] Another neighbor who knew Canright well during these years, Roxanna North (the former Roxanna Bailey), added her witness to the others, writing on May 27, 1963, "I am sure Mr. Canright did not have a peg leg."[12]

So how had Carrie Johnson become convinced that the false rumor about Canright's leg was true? Perhaps she had read about a relative of his who did have a peg leg and confused him with Canright himself. Or maybe she had read something about Canright having a leg amputated after an accident that occurred later in his life, shortly before he died, and confused this with the rumor about Canright losing a leg in his father's hay field. In any case, had Carrie not made this strong assertion about Canright, it would have been difficult to show for sure that she'd never met the man, despite all her other contradictory claims.

So, we can be thankful, for truth's sake, that she made this foolish error and documented it the way she did. It would be one thing to claim that Mr. Canright definitely had two good legs when he was actually hiding a peg leg under his pants, but to claim that she knew—and saw with her own eyes while employed by—that he had one artificial leg when he actually had two good legs is clear evidence that Carrie Johnson never even saw D. M. Canright, much less worked for him.

Not Even a Smart Fraud

All of Carrie's ruthless claims against D. M Canright are so at odds with historical documentation and evidence that even had she not made the ludicrous claim about his leg, other accusations would have exposed her as a fraud. But the peg leg is the real clincher that reveals not only that she was a fraud, but that she was not a very smart one at that. Beyond what we've already pointed out, there is not a shred of evidence to show that she ever met or worked for Canright, period. Unsurprisingly, she claimed that whatever evidence she had possessed was destroyed in a fire,[13] and (conveniently), that all the people who could have authenticated her story were dead by the time she felt it was safe to bring it before the public. So, there is zero evidence in her favor, but tons of overwhelming evidence against virtually all her claims.

For example, her claim that she was hired as Canright's secretary makes no sense. She lived in a differnt town than Canright's at the time. Canright's own son Jess said he never heard Carrie's name mentioned by his father in any context, much less as his secretary. Jess stated that whatever secretarial work his dad had needed help with was performed by Fred Rudy, whom we mentioned earlier and whom he could fully trust. Canright had been so betrayed by Adventists that the notion that he would hire an SDA without vetting her was unthinkable. The man Carrie claimed hired her, W. E. Cornell, was, like Canright himself, a former SDA. Surely, he would have been protective of his friend Canright, rather than exposing him to potential risk. Of course, Mr. Cornell was long dead by the time Carrie fabricated her story about him.[14]

Furthermore, the date that Carrie claimed to have started working for Canright just happened to be the very day that Canright's wife died and he was mourning with his family in Grand Rapids, where he lived. If that is the case, he was certainly not meeting with Carrie Johnson in Battle Creek.

All the attacks Carrie made on Canright do not comport with the facts, and even the details she tried to give to substantiate her employment under Canright were almost without exception in conflict with documented historical evidence. As Norman Douty put it after his hours-long session with her, "Wherein we [my wife and I] have been able to check her statements with official records, we have found them almost entirely inaccurate."[15] Furthermore, he stated, "She seems adept at misstating things, even when there is nothing to gain by doing so. Her habitual errors regarding the simplest facts reveal the necessity of examining carefully everything she says."[16] From Douty's description and what I have researched on my own, it seems fair to state that Carrie Johnson was a pathological liar, or what we as psychologists refer to as a *mythomaniac*.

So, it is not surprising that after their documented meeting, Carrie wanted nothing to do with Douty again and insisted that her name not be attached to the assertions she had made about Canright in his home, in the letters she wrote to Canright family members. Clearly Arthur White was upset that Douty had been able to poke major holes in Carrie's story, and he was no doubt responsible for telling Johnson to have nothing to do with Douty in the future. Remember that Arthur White had been meeting regularly with Carrie in her home for a full decade before deciding that Carrie was too unreliable to be the only source for their hit book on Canright and that they needed Canright's diary to give the book credibility.

If Arthur White had been a true historian and researcher, he would have vetted Carrie's story himself and come to realize, based on her bogus peg leg claim, that she had never seen Canright. But for whatever reason, White failed to attend to this crucial matter himself, and therefore put Carrie Johnson and the whole book project at risk by having her meet with a legitimate researcher like Douty who was able to easily detect and expose Carrie's deception. Maybe this is why Ted Johnson remembers Arthur White sweating profusely when he would come and sit for hours with Carrie in her home.[17] White knew what was at stake if his visits were uncovered, and this became even more true as he denied all connection to Johnson and Canright's diary in writing. In the next chapter we will explore and evaluate the strange relationship that existed between Arthur White and Carrie Johnson and the important role it played in the ongoing saga that we are unraveling in this volume.

6

DESPERATE COLLUDERS

You are no doubt familiar with the old proverb "Politics makes strange bed-fellows." If you have ever wondered as to the origin of that famous phrase, it can be traced to William Shakespeare and his play *The Tempest*, in which he wrote, "Misery acquaints a man with strange bedfellows."[1] Since his time, Shakespeare's words have been reshaped into the modern "Politics makes strange bedfellows." The meaning of this quote seems to be that people with little to nothing in common sometimes come together simply because of shared political interests. In recent years we have seen classic examples of this, as the Republican Bush family has embraced the Democratic Clintons and Obamas in their common hatred for Donald Trump. Even more striking is the way the extreme political Left has worked hand in hand with radical Islam. Is the Left ignorant of radical Islam's hatred and intolerance for homosexuals, women's rights, left-wing teachings about gender diversity, and so on? No, but leftists and radical Muslims are bound at the hip in their common hatred for traditional Western values, traditional American values, and traditional Judeo-Christian values. If they can ever eliminate their common enemy, then and only then will they turn on each other.

This brings to mind the relationship of Carrie Johnson with Arthur L. White. As we have already seen in the previous chapters, and will see even more clearly in the chapters ahead, Carrie Johnson was a sloppy, careless, and expedient sociopath who made some fatal errors in her attempt to falsely portray herself as someone she was not. Arthur White by contrast was a snobbish wannabe academic who was a high-functioning sociopath like his grandmother, Ellen. Carrie and Arthur at one level had very little in common except their resolve to deceive as many Adventists as they possibly could for their own respective self-interests. And even these self-interests differed markedly. Carrie didn't really care about D. M. Canright or about Adventism. She had already betrayed the Adventist Church through her uncovered embezzlement, and she admitted that she didn't even know who Canright was at the time she was supposedly called on to work for him. All the evidence points to her fabricating her story about him for money and whatever fame she could acquire from getting it published.[2]

By contrast, Arthur White did not seem to be the least interested in fame, book royalties, or even getting recognition for his part in creating Carrie's book. In fact, the opposite was true. Arthur went out of his way to meet in secret with Mrs. Johnson in her home to help her shape the book while he denied any acquaintance or involvement with her until the book was written and she sought his help to get it published shortly before it went to press. Arthur didn't even sign his name in the foreword to the book, which he wrote, instead simply signing, "Publishers." The only reason Arthur was so dedicated to laboriously and patiently working with Carrie so frequently and for so long was that he desperately wanted to take advantage of her and the opportunity she brought to him to disparage and destroy the reputation of by far the most effective critic, Dudley M. Canright, who had ever exposed the tragic truth about his "prophet" grandmother, Ellen G. White, to that time. Canright was public enemy number one to the White Estate, and he had to be stopped through any means necessary, no matter how dishonest and evil they happened to be.

One definition of *psychopathology* is "the scientific study of mental disorders."[3] More specifically, it is the study of abnormal cognition, behavior, and experience that focuses on the individual. In the chapters to come we will analyze the psychopathology of both Carrie Johnson and Arthur

White. But in this chapter, we want to zero in on their shared sociopathy. In contrast to psychopathology, *sociopathy* is defined specifically in reference to sociopathic behavior: sociopathic means "of, relating to, or characterized by asocial or antisocial behavior or exhibiting antisocial personality disorder."[4] But in general, *sociopathy* can describe social pathology on a scale that ranges from major social problems to the relational dysfunction and pathology that occurs with couples, partners, workmates, and so on. In the case of Arthur White and Carrie Johnson, they partnered together to engage in gross deception and defamation of character under the guise of religious self-righteousness. In the remainder of this chapter, we will look at five specific sociopathic similarities that Carrie and Arthur shared, and then we will briefly explore five specific areas where these two people were very different.

SIMILARITIES

An extreme desire to be thought well of by others. Most people want to be thought well of by others. But when this desire becomes so excessive and pronounced that it produces myriad sociopathic behaviors, it is not only abnormal; it is dangerous and harmful to its victims. Carrie Johnson did her best to convince Arthur White and the Adventist Church in general that she was a candidate for sainthood. When one reads what was written in her book about her, and the various promotional materials about her that SDAs used to market and sell her book, she comes off as a wonderful, humble, dedicated Adventist who is only interested in revealing the truth after years of secrecy. But when one digs a little deeper, one learns that her own grandchildren expose her as a manipulative, controlling wife; an uncaring, unloving, and abusive grandmother who exploited her own grandkids; a dishonest church member who was fired and disfellowshipped from her church for embezzlement; and a sociopathic liar willing to engage in libel and antisocial behavior purely for her own self-benefit. And the reality is she went to her grave believing she had pulled off her amazing fraud.

Arthur White was very much like Carrie Johnson in his desperate need to be thought well of. He did everything he could to convince SDAs that he fit the part of the saintly, scholarly grandson of Adventism's famous "prophet." He repeatedly went out of his way to persuade SDA leaders and church members that he was an objective historian who was interested only in seeking and protecting the truth upon which the church was supposedly founded. Yet he was willing to sneak around to visit Carrie Johnson for years to ensure that her book would do the unfair damage to Canright that he envisioned. White knew good and well that Carrie was a fraud, at least from the time that Douty exposed her ridiculous claim about Canright's peg leg. But he did all he could to cover for her lies, to lie about his relationship with her, and to push the book to publication knowing that its author was a pretender and a pathological liar. To me, this makes Arthur White every bit as bad as Carrie Johnson, and in some ways worse because of his heritage, status, and position. The thing that Jesus hated most was people-pleasing pretense and hypocrisy (see Matthew 23), and in Arthur and Carrie, we find a tragic collusion that contains plenty of them both.

Moral expediency. The term *moral expediency* refers to thinking and behavior that chooses convenience and selfish benefit over moral principles or values.[5] Sociopaths are classic examples of expediency in the way they manipulate and exploit for their own benefit, with no regard for the people they hurt in the process. Both Carrie Johnson and Arthur White demonstrated a remarkable pattern of expediency in their dealings both with each other and with everyone affected by the fraud they collaborated to produce. Carrie seemed to take no thought about the potential damage she could do to Arthur and his reputation when she exposed him, so she drew him into their risky collusion by her fabricated story. And Arthur went out of his way to keep his relationship with Carrie totally secret, so he would be better able to discard her or to deny having anything to do with her (which he did anyway) if her hoax was exposed by outside sources.

But far worse than their willingness to damage each other was their premeditated assault on the integrity and reputation of D. M. Canright, a committed minister of Jesus Christ. What they did to Canright deliberately was nothing less than total character assassination. This demonstrates clearly the level of evil that both individuals were willing to embrace for their own respective selfish gain as strange bedfellows and desperate colluders. And the fact that the *Review and Herald* publishers made no serious effort at vetting this book or its author, and that the SDA Church launched a major campaign to promote and market the book, featuring Carrie on their camp-meeting speaking circuit, demonstrates that the sins committed against Dudley Canright after his death were not just the responsibility of two but of many, a point we will further unpack in the next chapter.

During my years working as a psychologist at Riverside Juvenile Hall, I encountered numerous clients who functioned with a default tendency to engage in expediency. In most cases these kids came from dysfunctional families, where expediency was modeled to such a great degree that it became almost automatic behavior for everyone in the family. These kids generally used expediency as a form of self-protection and survival. They were just trying to keep from getting crushed by a very pathological family system. And while that doesn't make their behavior healthy, it at least makes it understandable. And there is a huge difference between juveniles who have been conditioned to act in expedient and immoral ways to survive, and adults who model the most malignant expediency to destroy others for their own benefit. This is what we see in the lives of Carrie Johnson and Arthur White even as they tried to present their behavior as a righteous pursuit of the truth! True, we are all flawed human beings, and it is important to be as gracious and forgiving as possible, but the line has to be drawn at gross, deliberate evil!

Extreme dishonesty. Like expediency, dishonesty tends to be a learned behavior. When it is modeled in a home, the likelihood that children or grandchildren will adopt it is great. Both Nancy Paige, and her brother Ted spoke of lying/dishonesty being an overwhelming force with both their parents and their grandmother, to the point that they felt it was difficult to survive without it.[6] Clearly, lying and expediency go together. Lies are typically told for the convenience or protection of the person telling them, to avoid being embarrassed or getting into trouble in some way.

But pathological liars take dishonesty to a whole new level. They conjure up an alternative reality with a certain grandiosity and delusion, which gives them a sense of meaning, importance, or even greatness. In Carrie Johnson's case, her true reality was far from glamorous. So as her lifetime patterns of lying and deceiving escalated, they culminated in her last great deception, that she was D. M. Canright's secretary, and that she alone was in a position to save the Adventist Church from the terrible criticisms that Canright had leveled and documented.

As we've established, this along, with a whole host of terrible accusations that she hung on Elder Canright, were a Big Lie. And the more she lied about him, the more new lies she invented, to the delight of her captive audiences and avid readers. After all, it is only human nature to want to hear the worst about your most despised enemy, and Carrie Johnson had a very receptive group of Adventists eager to hear her tales wherever she went and wherever her book was sold. But the SDA who was most eager to baptize her horrendous stories into documented truth for the ages and to help her generate new ones, was Arthur White.

How does a grandson who serves so proudly in the lineage of the great last-day messenger to the world/prophet of Adventism become a deliberate liar and deceiver? Clearly, Arthur was way more familiar with his grandmother's lifetime patterns of lying, deception, and fraud than he ever let on. Arthur claims to have known his grandmother well during the eight years their lives overlapped. In my own experience, given the time I spent with my grandparents (which was less than Arthur's), I came to have a very strong insight into each of their characters and personalities. If Arthur had any kind of normal insight, he would have recognized the real Ellen White, the one behind the façade. Furthermore, Arthur's father, Willie, was closer to Ellen than anyone else, and he made it very clear to Ellen's assistant, Fannie Bolton, during her orientation, that the way the church and its members had generally understood how Ellen received and communicated her "visions" had nothing to do with reality as he knew it. He refuted the notion that she got those detailed downloads from God.[7] Arthur would have had this same understanding from his father, but he had a vested interest in misrepresenting his grandmother, just as he completely distorted the truth about Canright.

Unrestrained immorality. It is possible to be a people pleaser and a habitual liar and still not be an evil person. This does not apply to either Carrie Johnson or Arthur White. The evidence is overwhelming that they not only engaged in prolonged, premeditated evil, but that they both delighted in it. Two of the books in my library that address the topic of sin and evil from a psychological perspective are Karl Meninger's bestseller, *Whatever Became of Sin,* and M. Scott Peck's *People of the Lie* (the follow-up bestseller to his record-setting blockbuster, *The Road Less Traveled*).[8] What makes the latter work particularly interesting to me is that Peck shows from his clinical encounters with certain clients how an external force of evil literally possessed them, convincing him of its vivid reality. Meninger's book was more concerned with addressing why the concept of sin and evil was disappearing from a culture that was becoming increasingly secular in the West, and especially in the formerly Christian America.

Clearly, a person can be evil without believing in demons or a devil, much less being possessed by such powers. But not only did Carrie Johnson believe in demons; she and her husband had personal encounters with demonic forces that shook them both to their very cores, according to their granddaughter.[9] This becomes important in the case of D. M. Canright, because Carrie chose to present Reverend Canright not only as a miserable wretch of a man, but as a demon-possessed one who spoke with a heinous demonic voice that was nothing like his own when he dictated to her. This of course made for very dramatic presentations to the Adventist camp-meeting crowds she addressed, who were thrilled to hear that their longtime antagonist was actually a pawn of the devil and functioned under his control. Never mind that all of this was fabricated by a woman who had never met Canright. So, what was really occurring here, it seems obvious, was that Carrie Johnson was projecting her own demons onto Canright, to discredit him in the most punishing way possible.

Arthur White, by contrast, demonstrated a level of evil that was equal to Carrie's, but in keeping with the academic reputation he desperately tried to project, he wanted nothing to do with her demonic narrative, much to her frustration and annoyance.[10] So, Arthur left the demonic characterizations of Canright out of the book, while he left Carrie free to mesmerize the crowds she spoke to with such stories. What made Arthur's behavior particularly immoral was his secrecy, denials, and premeditated plotting with Carrie to produce what he knew to be both fraudulent and purposely designed to destroy a good man's reputation for his own self-interest—*and* to do so while claiming to be an objective historian of the highest integrity! Had it not been for Carrie's grandkids, he would probably have gotten away with it in this world. But time tells the tale on us all.

Willingness to use and exploit others for self-benefit. Sociopaths are users; they use and exploit people to their own ends, whether they are high-functioning or not. Carrie Johnson cleverly used and manipulated Arthur White for her own benefit at the very same time that he was using and exploiting her to accomplish his malevolent goals. These two deserved each other, and maybe the SDA Church deserved them both, based on the total lack of vetting of which the publishers and Church were guilty in reference to this book. The denomination was fortunate that it was not held accountable for this fraud with a multimillion-dollar lawsuit from the Canright family. The best we can do now is to present the truth to all who are interested. And the truth in this case is very ugly.

Johnson and White not only exploited each other; they exploited the White Estate, the Review and Herald Publishing Association, and the entire Seventh-day Adventist Church. And in chapter 8 we will see how each of these entities was eagerly and willingly duped. But for now, the question will be, Who in positions of responsibility in Adventism will admit to this fraud and call sin by its right name? Will Andrews University post-humously revoke the honorary doctorate they awarded to Arthur White? Will the White Estate acknowledge what Arthur did and sever their name and association from his actions? Will the Review and Herald Publishing Association (or Teach Services) take Carrie's book off the market and apologize for ever printing it? Will the General Conference of SDAs admit that they have wrongly promoted a fallacious hit piece on D. M. Canright and apologize to all concerned? I'm waiting, and the world will be watching.

Differences

Education: Even though Arthur White was not overly educated, and certainly was not educated as a historian to the degree that he projected, he was a lot more educated than Carrie Johnson. In fact, there is legitimate evidence that Carrie Johnson never received the meager education she claimed to receive at the Cornell Business College. She wrote, "I was 18 and an advanced student of Cornell Business College, in Battle Creek, Michigan."[11] She goes on to claim that W. E. Cornell, owner and director of the college (which was never called a college) and a former SDA, singled her out to become Canright's secretary. Of course, she waited until after he was dead to produce this story. There is no record of her ever attending the school, much less being an advanced student there. There is no reason in the world to believe that Cornell or Canright would have ever trusted her to be Canright's secretary. We have already proven that Carrie Johnson never met D. M. Canright and that she was a pathological liar, and finally, Carrie's own granddaughter, Nancy Paige, was able to obtain her original manuscripts for her book and from her testimony found that they were so messy, error-laden, and unprofessional that they revealed no secretarial training at all.[12]

Arthur White, on the other hand, was certainly literate, and not in the habit of fabricating his education, but he was not educated in the area in which he would spend the greatest part of his career. He earned a certificate of business administration at Pacific Union College in 1928, and a year later was called to work at the White Estate as an accountant and general assistant to his seventy-four-year-old father, Willie White. When his father passed away in 1937, Arthur replaced him as the secretary of the White Estate, a position he would hold until 1978, when he asked to leave to work on the multivolume biography the church had commissioned him to write about his grandmother Ellen White. After his promotion, Arthur oversaw the transfer of the White Estate from Elmshaven (California), the two-story Victorian home where Ellen had lived until her death, to Washington, DC, where the church headquarters and seminary were at time. He taught courses about Ellen White at the seminary and was awarded an honorary doctorate of divinity from Andrews University in 1973. All of this transpired without anyone having knowledge of his collusion with Carrie Johnson, or the trumped-up story they constructed together to destroy Canright.

Status: The head of the White Estate is a big deal in Adventism because Ellen White herself has been made into such a larger-than-life figure. SDAs love to boast about how the Smithsonian named Ellen one of the 100 most significant Americans of all time, along with Joseph Smith, Mary Baker Eddy, and L. Ron Hubbard, three other religious figures of dubious background. The list also includes eleven criminals or outlaws, so it is hardly a list of honorable people. "Significant" does not mean great or positive. Hitler was significant; Bernie Madoff was significant, but is the world a better place because of them? We have already noted the absolute claims Ellen White made for herself,[13] and because Adventists have at least given lip service to believing these claims, the White Estate is seen as the bastion of the prophetic truth of Adventism—they house the very words of God that were given directly to His last-day messenger to the world.

There is only one reason that Arthur White was put in charge of the White Estate: his status as the grandson of Ellen White. It was not his education, training, talent, or ability, and as is clear from this book, it was certainly not his character. For its first sixty-plus years of existence, the White Estate was simply an exercise in nepotism, dominated completely by Willie and Arthur White. By contrast, Carrie Johnson had no status to speak of, despite her attempts to present herself as something she was not. For years she couldn't even apply for membership in an SDA church lest her thievery be uncovered and exposed.[14] Carrie was a very insecure woman, for good reasons, who was always searching for significance through any dishonest means she could muster. She hit the gold mine when she first conned

Arthur White, then the SDA Church, through her fabricated book. But her posthumous fortunes will not be so fortunate.

Position. Arthur White lived in the shadow of his famous grandmother all his life. It was this relationship that gave him his status and position as head of the White Estate for more than forty years. This relationship was also the reason he was commissioned to write the six-volume biography, or hagiography, of his grandmother that the church considers to be the last word about her life.[15] If his integrity in that work is the same that he demonstrated in the construction of Carrie Johnson's book, it clearly wasn't worth the paper it was written on. But Arthur did hold an important position in the church, and it was why Andrews University issued him an honorary doctorate. The evidence presented in this book demonstrates that both the position and the doctorate were undeserved and are now an embarrassment to those who granted them.

Carrie Johnson, in contrast to Arthur, held no prestigious position in her life, and based on her proven lies, it is difficult to know if she held any of the positions she did claim to hold. Certainly, her position as Canright's secretary is the one she tried to capitalize on, but now we know she never held such a position at all. The one position that we can confirm that of a denominational employee, from which she was fired for misusing church funds. And yet, the woman goes down in Adventist history and SDA lore as the heroine who slayed the evil villain D. M. Canright. How long, O Adventism, will you celebrate the deliberate character assassination of a humble, honest minister of Jesus Christ?[16] That is a question for the SDA denomination to seriously consider and address.

Motives: It is easy, given her track record, to assume that Carrie Johnson was purely driven by self-serving motives in everything she did. And this certainly fits with her lifetime sociopathic patterns. By contrast, some may believe that Arthur White was motivated to do what he did for the sake of the church he loved, a seemingly more altruistic motive. But let's break this down. Was it love for the church that led Arthur to deliberately deceive the whole church about his grandma, Carrie and Dudley Canright? This can hardly be called love. More realistically, his motives were to protect his grandmother's disintegrating reputation, on which his position, and the White Estate itself, were dependent, and to destroy the man who had threatened that reputation more than any other. These motives were very different than Carrie Johnson's, but at their core were just as self-serving.

Clearly, no one can know with certainty the motives of another, but as in a court of law, we must look at all of the evidence and make the most informed decision that we can. It is difficult to look at the evidence presented thus far in this book and at the same time believe that either Carrie Johnson or Arthur White had any healthy or moral motives for the evil acts they committed. The common denominator in their motivations seemed to be a willingness to mock and ridicule the truth to pursue their own selfish desires and goals, which we will turn to next.

Goals: Even though Arthur White and Carrie Johnson had goals that were very different in their desperate collusion, they were not mutually exclusive. Arthur was glad for Carrie to become an Adventist celebrity by selling a successful book, making good money from it, and being featured as a prominent speaker on the Adventist camp-meeting circuit.[17] These were all goals that Carrie was more than happy to realize by her fabricated book, which found such acceptance in Adventism. A woman who was more of a criminal than a Christian fulfilled all her fantasies at the last stage in her life with the help of a very dishonest Adventist icon who was willing to say and do anything to realize his own goals.

And Arthur White's singular goal was to discredit his grandmother's greatest critic, D. M. Canright, in the most effective way possible. As by now it must be clear, that included machinating with a pathological liar, becoming a blatant liar himself, being an accessory in the theft of a diary, harboring it for all eternity, and helping draft and publish a tall tale allegedly based on it. Clearly, this man had learned a lot from his very dishonest grandmother.

7

PUBLISHING A TOTAL FABRICATION

When a publisher releases a nonfiction book, they are of course concerned with making a profit from the publication. But there are two much more basic and foundational concerns that are prerequisites for any publisher who is going to survive or function with any credibility. First, how will the publisher's reputation be affected by the release of the book? But even more critical, what liability issues must be resolved before a publisher puts their name on a book? Because the liability issue can be fatal for a publisher, they typically go out of their way to ensure that what they publish is properly vetted. So, the question that jumps out from the evidence presented thus far in this book is, How did the Review and Herald Publishing Association ever agree to publish Carrie Johnson's *I Was Canright's Secretary*?

The research I have done as an author is more than enough to convince me that this book was a total fabrication written for the purpose of character assassination of a sincere and honest minister of the gospel. If this can be so clear to me, as a researcher and an author, how could a publisher, with so much to lose, have failed to find the same material that was available to me? I think the simple answer to this question goes back again to Arthur White. It was he who oversaw and facilitated this project from inception to fruition, and because of his elevated position and status in the

Church, there can be little doubt that the scrutiny that would normally be required for such a publication to be processed was simply bypassed.

This raises two more very important questions about Arthur White's behavior that have never before been addressed. That Arthur White was willing to risk his entire reputation and position as head of the White Estate to ensure that Carrie Johnson's totally fabricated book was published to destroy his enemy is hard enough to believe. But, one, why was he also willing to risk not only the reputation but the potential bankruptcy of the Review and Herald Publishing Association to fulfill his fantasy of destroying Canright? And two, why was he willing to subject the White Estate itself, his own baby, to potential humiliation, shame, and even possible dissolution by his risky engagement with Carrie Johnson? We will consider these questions individually.

The Review and Herald: The Review and Herald Publishing Association (R&H) always seemed to operate on small margins. All it takes is one lost lawsuit to send an operation like this into huge financial straits. An example of this is the lawsuit that the Pacific Press lost to Merikay McCloud Silver over sex discrimination back in 1983, described in her book *Betrayal,* which cost $600,000 to settle (approximately $1.8 million today), a lot of money back then. And of course, Richard Utt, the publisher who hired Merikay, blamed her for the whole embarrassing mess, claiming that she was too impatient and should have been more willing for the church to make things right.[1] I have yet to see Adventism ever make anything right when they were not forced to do so.

What the Review and Herald Publishing Association did to D. M. Canright and his family's reputation by publishing Carrie Johnson's fabricated book went way beyond discrimination, to total, deliberate character assassination. Of course, some of the worst accusations, such as Canright being demon possessed when he dictated to Carrie were omitted from the book by Arthur White. But these accusations were fully documented in the promotion and marketing of the book at Adventist camp meetings and are still available on the internet today. So, the liability connected to the R&H and the Adventist Church would have remained. There is really no other word to use than evil for what the R&H publishers did to Canright. And being misled by Arthur White was no excuse.

Certainly, all the church entities that were liable in this horrendous fraud, including the Review and Herald Publishing Association, dodged a bullet when Douty and the Canright family were intimidated into not pursuing a lawsuit based on the vain threats of counter-lawsuits that Arthur White generated. After all, who generally has the money to take on a huge corporation with lawyers on retainer, who can drag legal action out for years until the wronged parties are finally forced to go bankrupt because of their own attorney fees? This kind of intimidation happens all the time but is even more despicable when conducted by church organizations and entities. It is also significant that E. S. Ballenger played an important role in discouraging the Canright family from suing the church.[2]

In any case, it seems that Review and Herald Publishers should at least do the moral and ethical thing today, now that the evidence exposing what was done under their name has been made available to the public. Further, they should repudiate the publication of Carrie Johnson's book, rebuke Arthur White posthumously for the sinister role he played in its production, cease publishing the book in any form, and insist that all recordings of the false marketing and promotion of this book that remain on the internet today either be removed or issued with a disclaimer and an apology to the Canright family for the grave injustice that was done to them in the name of Seventh-day Adventism and their god. And *god* is deliberately not capitalized in this context!

The White Estate: The White Estate has a long history of dishonesty and cover-up where Ellen White's writings and reputation are concerned. This is not terribly surprising because their whole mission revolves around the protection and promotion of Ellen White and her writings, and when one is familiar with the extensive dishonesty practiced by Ellen White herself,[3] it would be expected that protecting her legacy would involve similar dishonesty. And that is certainly the case. Well before the White Estate was established, Willie White made it clear that how the church had been taught to understand his mother's "visions" had virtually nothing to do with the truth about those alleged visions.[4]

Adventists, in general, were educated to believe that Ellen received detailed downloads from the Almighty, from which she wrote her many books and "testimonies." Willie and his associate, Doris Robinson, by contrast, informed Fannie Bolton, when she was being oriented as Ellen's assistant, that "matters revealed to Mrs. White in vision, were not a word for word narration of events with their lessons, but that they were generally flash-light, or panoramic views of various scenes in the experiences of men, sometimes in the past, and sometimes in the future."[5] In other words, these supposed visions were of a general nature, and not in any way similar to the detailed messages that SDAs and Ellen herself had claimed for her writings and that church members had been taught to believe.

Of course, today we know that it is extremely unlikely that God gave Ellen White visions of any kind and that those she claimed can be traced to other sources.[6] More likely, based on the overwhelming evidence, is that she fabricated most of the so-called visions for her own purposes. But the White Estate has been built on the myth that Ellen did receive thousands of "visions" from God, and that they were responsible for her voluminous writings. So, let's return to the White Estate's dishonesty. In addition to Willie White hiding the nature of Ellen's "visions" from the general church membership, he was also part of the SDA leadership that intentionally buried the very revealing minutes of the 1919 Bible Conference. Even though Willie didn't attend the meetings himself due to time-sensitive work commitments, he was fully aware of what transpired, and the White Estate, more than any other entity, should have ensured that these minutes were preserved and made available in their vault (more on this later).

But Willie was part of the very SDA leadership that colluded to deprive the SDA people of this crucial information and who were responsible for the minutes being buried and lost for more than fifty-five years. The damage done to Adventism and its members by this tragic cover-up is impossible to estimate, but the church was sadly and certainly left in the dark for decades concerning the one attempt on the part of SDA leadership to come clean about Ellen White and her writings. Arthur White replaced his father, Willie, as head of the White Estate in 1937, during the dark ages of Adventism, and worked with his mentor Francis Nichol to promote the most dishonest apologetics and hagiographic materials about the "prophetess" that have ever been printed.[7] And of course, as we have already documented, Arthur started working with Carrie Johnson, as head of the White Estate, in 1950 to carry out the culminating and most despicable deception of his career.

Since 1978, when Arthur left the White Estate to work on his six-volume hagiography of his grandmother, the White Estate has made some attempts to improve their reputation. They hired men such as Robert Olson and Ron Graybill to give the appearance of objectivity, and these leaders did make some very candid admissions about Ellen and her writings. But the bottom line has been that the White Estate is in the business of trying to make Ellen White look good, despite the overwhelming evidence to the contrary. As a researcher writing academic dissertations on Ellen White, I was assured that I had access to all relevant documents. But like other researchers, I was deliberately lied to, based on the reality that very important materials were withheld.

In 2012, the White Estate was hacked with the help of an anonymous insider, and by 2014, many of these hidden documents were exposed on the internet. It was these exposed writings that rekindled my interest in Adventism, after having left the church four years before, with no plans to look back. Examples of these materials were excerpts from Ellen's diary about her alcohol/vinegar addiction, which almost killed her; her prolific role in making homemade alcohol when she explicitly condemned the use of a single drop of it as a strict prohibitionist; and her insistence that God hated children of various kinds, particularly unruly ones. But even after the hacking, the White Estate could not resist the temptation to be dishonest.

Instead of admitting that they had withheld documents from researchers and that they had been hacked, exposing their secrets, they came out with a claim that in the spirit of their new openness, they would be releasing all of Ellen White's materials in honor of the 100th anniversary of her death in 1915. So, rather than acknowledge that the information was already available online, they falsely portrayed themselves as candid in a self-congratulatory way. Most recently, when I finished my psychobiography of Ellen White, Albert Timm, present director of the White Estate, wrote a highly critical review of the book that included numerous false claims. Not only did he ascribe motives to me that were completely inaccurate as well as untrue accusations about both me and the book, but he concluded with the following sanctimonious statement about himself and the White Estate: "Since we cannot read the heart of another, let us beware of ascribing wrong motives to any man, lest we find ourselves involved in guilt similar to that of Miriam—condemning those whom the Lord is teaching and guiding—and thus bring upon ourselves the rebuke of God."[8]

As we close this section, I would challenge Dr. Timm and his current White Estate staff to acknowledge and admit that the White Estate, under the direction of Arthur White, not only judged Rev. D. M. Canright's motives but ascribed to him the most horrendous and demonic characteristics to purposely assassinate his character while falsely defending Ellen White's documented evil deeds. I am tired of the White Estate's lies and moralistic tripe. They need to apologize to the Canright family and renounce the actions of Arthur L. White. He should be expelled from the White Estate legacy for what he did. It is time for the White Estate to put up or shut up, and while he is at it, Timm can apologize for his false attributions concerning me and my book.

The Importance of Secrecy: We all have things in our lives that we are not proud of and that we would prefer to keep secret. Growing up in Adventism, and before I had any clue about the true gospel of Jesus Christ, certain texts troubled me in this regard:

> "For nothing is secret, that shall not be made manifest; neither any thing hid, that shall not be made known and shouted abroad." (Luke 8:17)

> "But there is nothing covered up that will not be re-
> vealed, and hidden that will not be known. Accordingly,
> whatever you have said in the dark will be heard in the light,
> and what you have whispered in the inner rooms will be pro-
> claimed upon the housetops." (Luke 12:2–3)

As to most people, the notion of having my secret sins broadcast for all to see was not particularly appealing to me. And it was not until I came to understand the perfect finished work of Christ and His substitutionary work in my behalf that I was able to move beyond such passages with assurance. But embracing the gospel never empowers us to engage in immorality or evil. The continual secrecy with which Arthur White practiced evil over decades clearly demonstrates that he not only failed to grasp the gospel but made no effort to take seriously the many moral mandates of Adventism as well.

The fact that this well-known SDA leader sneaked around like a thief to plot with Carrie Johnson in her home year after year to fabricate a book designed to destroy an innocent man cannot be emphasized enough. No wonder he was always sweating profusely![9]

Arthur White's greatest fears are now being realized. The words of Jesus are coming true for him, well before the final judgment. His secrets and his lies are now being exposed after his death in a way that would surely be the source of great shame were he still alive. Mr. White (I will not call him Dr. White because I believe his honorary doctorate was illegitimate) was willing to pursue every dishonest means to take down the man he despised. But now the truth is finally coming out—truth that vindicates the falsely accused Reverend Canright and condemns the hypocritical and underhanded behavior of Arthur White.

The Importance of Johnson's Grandkids: It is noteworthy that Arthur White treated Carrie Johnson's grandkids as if they did not exist when he was in their home.[10] He showed no interest in them and saw them as a bother and a distraction from the task he was pursuing. Ironically, they were the only witnesses who were able to place him in their grandmother's home for all the years that he colluded with her. Were it not for Nancy and Ted, Arthur would have gotten away with his sinister plan, and none of us would have ever known the difference.

But as the old saying goes, "Be sure your sins will find you out" (Numbers 32:23). And in the case of Arthur White, we are not talking about some personal, secret sin that may have been embarrassing. We are talking about a premeditated plan to portray a man who had done nothing wrong in the worst possible light as a matter of history. Again, it is not easy to take on a religious icon who had built a false reputation through years of dishonesty, and I want to personally affirm the courage and commitment to truth that has led both Nancy Paige and Ted Johnson to persistently tell their stories through the years, even when no one seemed to listen.

The story of Arthur White and Carrie Johnson's fabricated book is just one more nail in the coffin of a false prophet; a dishonest legacy of that prophet, called the White Estate; and a dishonest denomination that has covered all the lies with false claims based on bogus "visions." In this age of the internet, the abilities of entities like the Seventh-day Adventist Church to cover their sins and the evil deeds of their false prophet are rapidly diminishing, and thanks to people like Nancy Paige, and Ted Johnson the words of Jesus ring true today, more than they ever have before: "Nothing is concealed that will not be revealed!" (Luke 8:17, paraphrased).

Will There Be Accountability? When I wrote my psychobiography of Ellen White, I knew it would be greeted with great opposition and resistance from SDA leaders who dared to speak about it. After all, these are people who have invested their whole careers and make their living from the dishonest doings of their "prophet" and the cult she created. Yet, none of them were able to effectively dispute or refute the overwhelming source documentation that the book contained. Now, in this book, we move to a much simpler case where Arthur White and Carrie Johnson are shown to be guilty of penning a fraudulent book that was intended to destroy the reputation of one of Ellen White's most effective critics. Here again, SDA leaders have a lot invested in keeping Canright as a villain in their history and protecting their self-proclaimed "prophetess" from the serious charges that she mustered. But there is much less concern and loyalty to Arthur White and the White Estate itself in Adventism.

So, it seems that any SDA with any integrity at all who views the evidence presented in this book should be willing to acknowledge that Arthur White and Carrie Johnson were wrong in what they did and that the Adventist Church as a whole needs to condemn their evil actions and make every effort to reverse the tragic results. This means that the church must renounce their connection to this false book and all the interviews they conducted with Carrie Johnson that leveled even more ridiculous charges against Canright than were contained in her book. Carrie Johnson herself should posthumously be condemned, as a fraud and Arthur White should be formally condemned by the SDA Church for his secret collusion and manipulation of Johnson to commit fraud himself. He should be formally disowned by the White Estate for his unthinkable behavior, and Andrews University should withdraw White's honorary doctorate and release Canright's diary, which is housed in their White Estate vault. And along with all of this, the Canright family should receive a formal, official apology from the Adventist Church for the terrible deeds done against them, with appropriate financial compensation.

8

THE WILLINGLY DECEIVED

Any Adventist church member who wants to know the truth about Ellen White—and now her grandson, Arthur White—can easily access this information. For most of its history, this has not been true in Adventism. The dishonesty, secrecy and cover-ups that have characterized SDA leadership from its inception made it very difficult for honest Adventists to find the truth, especially given the way whistle blowers in the church have been treated. And in fairness, it is important to point out that many more people have left the Adventist Church than have ever remained in it.[1] So, despite their difficulty with getting good information, many have still turned their backs on Adventism. But access to information has changed with the dawning of the internet and the flow of information that is available through it.

This does not mean that the church has become open to this flow of information or that they welcome criticism, for this is certainly not the case. Every day I hear from people on my Facebook thread about how they came to access new information about Adventism on the internet that had been hidden from them for years in the church. They have also expressed how grateful they are to have a person of my education and background providing the historical documentation that helps them weigh this information. On the other hand, we also hear from many SDA apologists who are in denial about what has been exposed and do their best each day to defend Ellen White and the SDA Church, against all evidence and reason.

But the good news is, now that Adventists have a clear choice, they don't have to live with being kept in the dark anymore. There are many who will remain, for a whole host of reasons that are very powerful and that briefly deserve to be identified. One is fear. Two is the desire to be special, Three is employment, Four is the sociological pull of Adventism—social isolation. Let me briefly expand on each of these.

Fear: I can't count the number of times I've heard SDAs say, "If I leave the church, I feel like I will be lost." Where does this feeling come from? In most cases, it is the direct brainwashing of the church itself. In her very first "vision" as part of what would develop into the Seventh-day Adventist Church, Ellen White warned her followers that if they fell off the narrow path that God had provided for them, they would be lost for eternity, with all the "wicked world" that He had already rejected.[2] If this sounds cultic, it is because it is. And throughout Adventism's history, Adventists have been more condemning of other churches than almost any denomination you can find and have either given the impression or outright taught that leaving the SDA Church was the equivalent of being lost for eternity.[3]

Special status: Many Adventists are quick to claim that fear has nothing to do with why they stay in the church, but these same individuals will often boast that they stay in the church because it is the true church, it is the Remnant Church, or it is the most Bible-based church you can find. All these claims are, of course, nonsense, to anyone who has a true, Christ-centered, Spirit-filled understanding of what Jesus said and modeled. But fear and the desire to be special or elevated above others are the two traits that false and unhealthy religion use the most to keep their followers. If you can't scare them into the fold, delude them into the fold. SDAs have been experts with both strategies.

Employment: In 2021 there were approximately 330,000 full-time employees of the SDA Church worldwide. When you include retirees, the number is closer to half a million, and when you add the family members of these individuals, the number goes way beyond one million. So, a good number of people who remain Seventh-day Adventist have a financial motive or incentive to do so. After I wrote my last book, exposing Ellen White's lifetime patterns of plagiarism and dishonesty and how the SDA Church is directly connected to this dishonesty, I was surprised by the number of church employees who have confidentially shared with me that they know the documentation in the book is true and accurate, but they feel trapped in the system and can't get out because they don't feel they have any other viable options.

Social pull: Finally, there is a huge and growing number of "social Adventists," many of whom are in the United States, especially in Southern California. These are people who do not fit in the previous three categories but have friends or family in Adventism or have placed their kids in the Adventist school system, which ties them to the insular social subculture of Adventism. They may know the church's theology and teachings are questionable, and in many cases are not inclined to take the SDA lifestyle or demands too seriously. But for the most part they find Adventism to be a safe subculture and a convenient group to identify with, if for no other reason than that Adventists are the most upwardly mobile church in the world.[4] They place a premium on education, health, status, and wealth and produce a much higher percentage of doctors and health workers than any other church in the world.

The SDA Church is fully aware of these factors and therefore attempts to appeal to them as reasons for staying in the church by aggressively attacking any person or research that threatens their control over the people they have cleverly manipulated into "needing" the Church. In 1974, the lost and buried transcripts from the now-famous 1919 Bible Conference, which revealed major doubts about Ellen White from top church leaders, were rediscovered, and this would set the stage for numerous other discoveries that were very embarrassing to SDAs. Hence, during my lifetime I have seen one honest seeker after the next unfairly attacked by the Church. Let me just give a few of the most prominent examples.

Ronald Numbers: In 1976, historian Ronald Numbers had his ground-breaking book, *Prophetess of Health,* published by Harper & Row.

I was a newly hired minister at the time, and I bought and read the book as soon as it came out. At my first worker's meeting in the conference, President Charles Cook got up and told us that we were forbidden to read the book (which I had right there in my briefcase) but that we were all required to read the rebuttal, which they handed out to each of us. This is the SDA way: suppress every voice that threatens to expose the dishonest history of the church and its prophet. Distort, deny, and attack. Numbers himself described the way he was treated once the church discovered that he wasn't writing the typical apologetic hagiography of EGW: "But after I had written several chapters, somebody leaked them. The White Estate saw that what I was writing was going to be a contextual study, not an apologetic one, and that scared Arthur White and some others. After that he went out of his way to make sure I didn't get crucial material."[5]

Once again, we see Arthur White suppressing truth so he could continue to spread his lies about his grandma. And he was not alone, at the White Estate, in this regard. Ron Graybill, who was being groomed to become a director there, took advantage of Numbers as a friend, only to betray him when his book was published. As Numbers continues in his interview.

> One interesting note: I was in Baltimore at Johns Hopkins when Graybill was studying for his PhD. He used to come up every week and stay with me. He spent the rest of the week working at the White Estate. When my book came out, the White Estate sent him to camp-meetings and college campuses to denounce me.
>
> The most memorable phrase he used about me was: "A wildly irresponsible historian."[6]

Here was Graybill, pretending to be Ron Numbers's friend, then trying to publicly discredit him. This is quite laughable when you compare Numbers's credibility and reputation to Graybill's. Fritz Guy, who also claimed to be Numbers's friend was equally unethical, attacking Numbers's book in a review in *Spectrum* and playing amateur psychologist in the process, hurting both Numbers and his father by his irresponsible and inaccurate speculations. Again, Numbers describes this for himself: "Fritz Guy, who ventured into psychobiography, suggested I had ventured into this as a reaction to the rigid religion of my father. That hurt my father. And it wasn't true. We disagreed a lot, but we always had totally open communication. My father was getting it from both the conservatives and the liberals."[7]

The interesting thing is that today, Numbers is an award-winning historian who gets high marks from Adventist academics, as can be seen in a piece by Loren Seibold, editor of *Adventist Today* (*AT*), talking about Numbers at the fiftieth anniversary of the Adventist Forum: "I was thankful that Dr. Butler also gave homage to Dr. Ron Numbers. He described *Prophetess of Health* as 'the most significant book ever written regarding Adventism' and 'a transformer of the history in Adventism.' I can't help but agree, and only wish Dr. Numbers had been there to hear it."[8]

Now Numbers is a hero, even though he was treated like dirt by the church and even its academics when he wrote his book on Ellen White. And it is not surprising that Arthur White (if you can call him an academic) was at the top of the list.

Desmond Ford: If ever there was a man who could have brought the SDA Church to its knees and forced them to face up to their flawed and dishonest history, it was Desmond Ford. There were so many ministers of my generation (including me) who were ready to leave Adventism and follow Ford if he started a gospel version of Adventism. But when he failed to do so, the disappointment was difficult to bear, and many left on their own without him. I preached for Des at his Good News Church once he was rejected by the SDA Church and talked with him privately on various occasions. He was a remarkable Christian and someone who treated the church so much better than it treated him and than it deserved.

In 1975 Gillian Ford, Des's wife, wrote a treatise on the nature of Christ, which asserted that Jesus had a sinless human nature, in contrast to the SDA party line at the time.[9] She drew on the theology of *Questions on Doctrine* (1957), Edward Heppenstall, and Robert Brinsmead to make her case, and Des wrote an appendix to this document, which attracted the attention of SDA leadership because he was a professor at Avondale College, where the Adventist ministers were trained in Australia. The Brinsmead connection in particular worried SDA leaders, for he more than any other Adventist theologian had taken a stand against the SDA position on law and gospel that was adamant![10] The Palmdale Conference was called in 1976 to resolve these conflicts, and the results were ambiguous enough that all parties left claiming their positions had been vindicated.[11]

But this attempt to sweep the problem under the rug was not sufficient as far as Ford was concerned. He continued to strongly oppose SDA perfectionism as taught by its traditional Sanctuary and Investigative Judgment doctrines, and in 1979, publicly announced that he did not believe in these doctrines. This set the stage for the Glacier View Conference, which was called in 1980 to punish Ford for his audacious announcement, and where, despite the fact that more than a quarter of the theologians and church administrators present also rejected these doctrines, Ford was singled out and relieved of his church employment and ministerial credentials. To fire a man of Ford's integrity simply because he stood for the New Testament gospel and opposed the gross and indefensible perfectionism of Adventism, speaks for itself!

Walter Rea: The rate of official SDA apostasy increased by more than 10 percent in the early 1980s in reaction to Glacier View, Walter Rea's publication of *The White Lie*, and the Davenport scandal, which also rocked the church. Rea, more than any other critic of Ellen White, documented a great deal of her plagiarism and claimed that it was responsible for 80–90 percent of her writings. In reaction to his book, pastor John Robertson was commissioned to write an apologetic work entitled *The White Truth*. The Adventist Church hired a Catholic attorney, Vincent Ramik, who wrongly concluded that plagiarism was not illegal in the nineteenth century. And the Church commissioned Fred Veltman, a well-respected academic, to conduct an eight-year-study on several chapters of Ellen White's *The Desire of Ages* to determine its actual amount of plagiarism.

Veltman's conclusion was certainly more conservative than Rea's, showing that at least 31 percent was found to be copied from other authors, but he also stated that his findings showed all her writings to be largely derived from others, if not directly copied. "The content of Ellen White's commentary on the life and ministry of Christ, the *Desire of Ages*, is for the most part derived rather than original."[12] So, while SDAs did everything they possibly could to try to discredit Rea, their own, paid-for study did not vindicate the professed prophetess at all but did the opposite. Like other SDA critics, Walter Rea was attacked and punished in every way the church could muster, including having his pension revoked. But Rea sued the church and forced a settlement, in which church leadership agreed to restore his pension as long as he didn't publish his book, *Pirates of Privilege,* which exposed details of the Davenport financial scandal that were extremely embarrassing to the SDA hierarchy.[13]

Rea, like Numbers and Ford, was just another honest person amazed to find that he had been duped by the church, until he was able to study the issues at stake, in depth, for himself. When you read his story, of how he was repeatedly lied to, misled, and betrayed by the church he loved and tried to work with to discover the truth, it is just another testimony that the SDA Church does not value truth or the pursuit of truth where their sacred cow, Ellen White, is concerned. Nor do they value independent thought or honest inquiry on the part of their members. The quickest way to become marginalized and viewed with suspicion in Adventism is to ask honest questions that leadership cannot answer. This is the subject to which we will now turn.

CONFORMITY VERSUS INDEPENDENT THOUGHT

Adventists place a premium on conformity and generally have a disdain for independent thinking. Many years ago, when I was still an SDA, I wrote an article entitled "'Milgram's Pilgrims,'" which was expanded into a chapter in a book that documented this strong pattern in Adventism.[14] Two of the classic and best-known studies in conformity were those of Solomon Asch and Stanley Milgram. Asch was the first researcher to scientifically document the powerful influence that groups had to change the decisions of individuals, even when those decisions blatantly contradicted the individual's own senses. His key studies found that 75 percent of people were willing to conform to inaccurate group decisions even though their own senses clearly told them these decisions were wrong.

The surprising results of this research were replicated by many other studies that followed and led to Milgram's astounding findings at Yale University that 65 percent of its students were willing to obey commands from an authority figure that were thought to do significant harm, even to the point of death, to actors who were functioning as subjects. Unfortunately, Milgram's experiments were replicated in many other settings, and the results proved to be alarmingly general in scope.[15] How does this apply to Adventism? In many ways! Adventists have been brainwashed into believing that their movement was supernaturally established by God's last-day messenger/prophet, Ellen White, who was supposedly given downloads from the Almighty on almost every conceivable topic. This means that when you resist the party line, or church traditions (and there are a lot of them), you are really rejecting the direct revelation of God. This kind of group pressure produces an even more powerful conformity than what you find in the population in general. So, church leadership, who are the interpreters of their prophet's words, are given a much greater power than what leaders have under typical circumstances. And to quote Lord Acton, "Power tends to corrupt and absolute power corrupts absolutely."[16] Where this becomes ugly is in Adventism's historic patterns and practices of supporting or failing to oppose totalitarian governments for the sake of their own institutional self-preservation.

The most glaring example of this occurred in Nazi Germany, where Seventh-day Adventists and their health institutions managed to remain in favor with Hitler, while all the other churches in Germany gradually opposed the Fuhrer and were then persecuted by the Nazis. Hitler was initially attracted to Adventists because, like him, they practiced vegetarianism, did not drink or smoke, and generally seemed to emphasize health principles with which the Fuhrer strongly agreed. He was reciprocal in his praise for SDAs, giving the church a favored status and their health institutions special commendations while relying on them for his own personal medical treatment. For their own self-protection Adventists never did officially oppose or condemn Hitler, even when he engaged in atrocities.[17]

This conformity at the expense of principle by the official SDA Church has been repeatedly demonstrated under other totalitarian regimes as well. It became a frightening pattern in the former Soviet Union and in various other Communist countries where dissident Adventists who opposed the church policies were persecuted by these governments, but the official SDA Church remained unharmed. It was the case in South Africa, where the SDA Church refused to take a stand against apartheid.[18] On my daily Facebook thread, I hear from former SDAs consistently who speak of how they were ostracized, marginalized, or mistreated for trying to think for themselves, and as a researcher I have certainly been lied to and lied about by the denomination and its leaders simply because I have tried to do honest research about Ellen White and SDA history. The bottom line is that Adventists have marketed themselves as nonconformists, who will be persecuted by the whole world, as they stand for truth as God's Remnant Church, when in really they are some of the most conforming thinkers on the planet. And conformity plus dishonesty is a very bad combination.

9

WHO WAS CARRIE JOHNSON?

As previously stated, this book would never have been written without the powerful insights and contributions of Nancy Paige, the granddaughter of Carrie Johnson. I knew relatively little about Carrie except for what I learned from Norman Douty's book, *The Case of D. M. Canright*, before meeting Nancy on my thread. Since that time, I have not only learned a great deal about Carrie from Nancy but have explored as much as possible about her from other sources. As a licensed psychologist, I am fully aware that it is unethical to diagnose a person who has not been one's client and without consent from the person. This is informally called the "Goldwater rule," after a major lawsuit, and is found in section 7 of the American Psychiatric Association's (APA) Principles of Medical Ethics. So, in this chapter we will not be diagnosing Carrie Johnson but simply viewing the overwhelming historical evidence connected to her life and comparing her traits to the characteristics that describe sociopathy or antisocial personality disorder in the *Diagnostic and Statistical Manual* (DSM) used by psychologists.

In my psychobiography of Ellen White, we compared how the historical evidence from Ellen's life fit with the characteristics of a high-functioning sociopath. When you look at her lifetime patterns, there is strong source documentation to suggest that Ellen White was one of the most shrewd, political, manipulative, dishonest, controlling religious leaders who ever lived, and that she was so successful in this regard because she hid under the guise of a weak, humble uneducated vessel of God who could do nothing on her own. When one compares Ellen White to Carrie Johnson, one can see they shared a good number of sociopathic qualities, but the level of sophistication in their deceptions makes for a major contrast. Ellen was able to fool and mislead an entire religious denomination into believing that she was God's final last day messenger to the world and that she had received thousands of detailed visions from the Almighty on every conceivable subject.

Carrie Johnson, by contrast, was not a high-functioning sociopath but exhibited very common sociopathic characteristics typical of someone with an antisocial personality disorder. *Antisocial personality* and *sociopathy* are often used synonymously, but a high-functioning sociopath demonstrates other unique qualities. We will unpack what a high-functioning sociopath is in the next chapter. But in the remainder of this chapter, we will conduct a mini-psychobiography of Carrie Johnson, looking at the prominent historical evidence that has been documented in this book, with some additions, and its relationship to the traits of APD.

Antisocial personality disorder signs and symptoms may include the following:

> **Disregard for right and wrong:** Based on the host of immoral behaviors we have discussed in the previous chapters, it is obvious that Carrie Johnson had lifetime patterns of evil, unprincipled, and unscrupulous tendencies and actions that fit this characteristic. Of particular interest, in this regard, is the following claim from her granddaughter:
>
> "Grandma saw demons frequently. I have a story from her manuscript which she had hoped to be in her book. In it she claimed that there was a woman in the apartment below

her who was demonic. She said she could look down from her apartment into the apartment below and could hear the devil speaking. This story did not make it to publication. I am certain Arthur White nixed it. That would have angered Grandma greatly."[1] Not only did she claim to see demons but had visitations and attacks from them as well, according to Nancy.

"In the mid-1970s, after Grandma's book had been published in 1971, Grandma and Grandpa called Dad and told him they had just been beaten up by a demon. It tried to strangle them; lifted up their bed, with them in it; and slammed it into the wall. The devil threatened them (I can't remember what he said).

"I never saw Grandma or Grandpa read the Bible. They never had a Bible anywhere in the house."[2]

Carrie's evil behaviors, coupled with her preoccupation and obsession with evil itself, certainly seems to help explain her disregard for right and wrong. Those who see the devil everywhere in others are often projecting their own demons.

Persistent lying or deceit to exploit others: Lying and deceit seem to have been Carrie Johnson's specialty. Nancy testifies that from her earliest years she remembers her grandmother being a pathological liar. Norman Douty, in his book, also identified Carrie to be a pathological liar,[3] and we can see from the evidence presented concerning her claims about Canright that this pattern is firmly in place. Not only does she lie about an untold number of little things that don't even seem to matter, but she excels at the Big Lie as well, claiming to have been the secretary of someone she never even met, writing a book based on that claim, and establishing her whole reputation in the Adventist Church on the foundation of that lie.

Callousnous, cynicism, and disrespect of others: From the evidence we have, Carrie Johnson exhibited all of these. She was neither loving nor caring, even to her own family, and was in fact abusive to all of them, including the children and grandchildren.[4] She was a user of others, and only seemed to enter into relationships with them for whatever personal benefit she could derive from the relationship. She even lied to, manipulated, and exploited Arthur White to achieve notoriety. But, of course, he was equally exploitative in this relationship, although, as Nancy points out, these two did not even like each other.[5]

Use of charm or wit to manipulate others for personal gain or pleasure: It seems clear from available evidence that Carrie sought positions of influence that would make it appear that she was a caring person. But then she would in turn use these positions to lie, cheat, and steal for her own benefit. An example of this was the use of her Temperance Leader position to cheat so her granddaughter would win the temperance oration contest. Another would be her use of her church treasurer position to embezzle funds, which, as you have read, got her fired and disfellowshipped from her church. And the most notable was her position as a celebrated author in Adventism, based on a fabricated book that committed character assassination.[6]

Arrogance, a sense of superiority, and extreme opinionatedness: What kind of arrogance does it take to fabricate an entire book to damage the reputation of a dead person, and then to falsely accuse the person—a humble minister of the gospel—of being devil possessed, in public interviews and presentations viewed all over the world? Carrie Johnson rose to stardom in the Adventist Church with this perverted tale and played the part of a celebrity, speaking at one camp-meeting to the next, with large audiences enthusiastically inhaling her rancid, deliberate falsehoods. She became the expert on Canright even though she never met him. What information wasn't overtly fabricated, she stole from his family under false pretenses.

Recurring problems with the law, including criminal behavior: The two most notable examples of Carrie's engaging in behavior that was criminal in nature were embezzlement and libel. For her embezzlement, obviously, the church could have pressed charges against her, but SDAs typically like to handle such problems in-house to avoid bad publicity. And D. M. Canright's family could have sued for libel and defamation of character had they had the money to hire attorneys. But instead, Carrie and her cohort, Arthur White, threatened to sue Douty, who also lacked the money to hire lawyers, so he took his book off the market.[7] This is the SDA way: when caught in wrongdoing, go on the offensive and accuse your accusers of your wrongs.

Repeated violation of the rights of others through intimidation and dishonesty: When Norman Douty caught Carrie Johnson red-handed telling ridiculous lies about Canright to his family members, and to Douty himself, both Arthur White and Johnson knew that their whole book fabrication was in big trouble. So, their solution to this problem was intimidation. Arthur White had the whole

White Estate behind him, as well as the SDA denomination, with its lawyers on retainer. Carrie Johnson had no such backing, but she was backed by Arthur White, who had such resources and had colluded in the book creation for more than a decade with Carrie, when Douty exposed Carrie's lies. It is easy to act the bully when you are backed by bullies, so that is precisely what Carrie did!

Impulsiveness or failure to plan ahead: Carrie Johnson may have been impulsive when she decided to help herself to the church till and the tithe payers' money, but evidently she learned from this greedy mistake and became much more deliberate, methodical, and premeditated when it came to her plan to concoct an entire book. The plotting, secrecy, dishonesty, and outright evil generated from the twenty-plus-year collusion with Arthur White were anything but impulsive. So at least with respect to these traits, Carrie seemed to have learned some hard, but productive lessons from her failures.

Hostility, irritability, agitation, aggression, or violence: According to Nancy Paige, her grandmother's relationships with their biological and extended family were not fun or positive at all. In fact, the opposite was largely true. Carrie was hostile, easily agitated, and exceptionally gifted at manipulating and exploiting those around here. This applied even to her own grandchildren, who felt no affection from grandma but were required to do free labor for her, even though she herself was getting paid by renters. And when things did not go Carrie's way, there was hell to pay. She was irritated by very small things and was willing to hurt others for her own benefit.[8]

Lack of empathy for others and lack of remorse about harming others: Again, the Johnson home was not a safe place in terms of finding emotional comfort, or even the kind of love and care one would expect from a grandma. Carrie Johnson had little ability to empathize or apologize. She was not one to ever admit she was wrong, although there is some evidence that she secretly made a deathbed confession regarding the evils she had committed, shortly before her death. This seems to be more out of a fear for what judgment might await her than any genuine remorse or repentance, for it is clear she never made any apology to the Canright family for the terrible wrong she had done to them by destroying D. M. Canright's reputation. Neither is there any record that she ever publicly, or even privately, confessed to or apologized to the SDA Church and its members whom she had deliberately deceived.

Unnecessary risk-taking or dangerous behavior with no regard for the safety of self or others: As mentioned above, the most notable example of Carrie Johnson taking a huge risk that could easily have landed her in prison was her willingness to embezzle church funds as a church employee. Though she was fired and disfellowshipped from the SDA Church, fortunately for her, the church never pressed charges. As stated. it prefers to handle such sensitive and embarrassing problems in-house to maintain control, avoid negative publicity, and prevent members from losing faith in the institution. It was also a huge risk to pen her false biography of Canright, but in that case she had the protection of Arthur White, the White Estate, and the SDA Church.

Poor or abusive relationships: Carrie Johnson was abusive in the way she helped raise and treated her grandkids. And according to Nancy, she was controlling and abusive in her other family relationships as well.

Failure to consider the negative consequences of behavior or learn from them: For most people—who are not sociopaths—the experience of getting fired and disfellowshipped from your church for stealing church funds would be a real life-changer, particularly if the act was kept relatively quiet and no charges were filed, which would have given one a criminal record. But when one demonstrates the attributes of an antisocial personality disorder, the degree to which one gets away with negative or harmful behavior only produces an incentive to attempt something even more evil or despicable. This was certainly the case with Carrie. Because she showed strong sociopathic tendencies throughout her lifetime but was never truly held responsible for her behaviors, she had the chutzpah to fabricate a book that resulted in character assassination.

Consistent irresponsibility and repeated failure to fulfill work or financial obligations: This may be the characteristic, among those listed, that is the least notable in Carrie Johnson's life. She generally did a pretty good job of trying to appear responsible, with a few glaring exceptions, such as theft and defamation of character. But she generally held down jobs and positions of responsibility in a manner that did not make it immediately obvious that she had the traits of an antisocial personality disorder. This goes back to her acute need to look good, and to hide the negative and destructive characteristics that actively loomed beneath the surface.

Most individuals who have strong sociopathic tendencies are also much likelier to have narcissistic personality disorders than others. Nancy concluded that her grandma had a strong case of narcissism, which seems very likely from the evidence, so without listing all that evidence (most of which overlaps with what we have already presented) let me invite you to apply what we have already documented to the traits of narcissistic personality disorder.

NARCISSISTIC PERSONALITY DISORDER

In 1980, the APA designated narcissistic personality disorder as a formal classification, in the following words:

> A pervasive pattern of grandiosity (in fantasy or behavior), need for admiration, and lack of empathy, beginning in early adulthood and present in a variety of contexts, as indicated by five (or more) of the following:[8]

1. Has a grandiose sense of self-importance (e.g., exaggerates achievements and talents).
2. Is preoccupied with fantasies of unlimited success and power.
3. Believes that he or she is "special" and "unique."
4. Requires excessive admiration and attention.
5. Has a sense of entitlement, i.e., unreasonable expectations of especially favorable treatment or automatic compliance with his or her expectations.
6. Is interpersonally exploitive, i.e., takes advantage of others to achieve his or her own ends.
7. Lacks empathy: is unwilling to recognize or identify with the feelings and needs of others.

8. Is often envious of others or believes that others are envious of him or her.
9. Shows arrogant, haughty behavior or attitudes.[9]

There is a great deal of overlap between these disorders that all seem to be strongly represented in the life patterns of the author of *I Was Canright's Secretary*. I don't think a person has to be a licensed psychologist, or even professionally trained in counseling, to see the similarities between these two disorders and their lifelong presence in Carrie Johnson.

10

ARTHUR L. WHITE: A PSYCHOBIOGRAPHY

One of the criticisms I was repeatedly bombarded with from Adventists who objected to my psychobiography of Ellen White was that it was biased, one-sided, or too focused on the negatives about Ellen White, without balancing that out with all the positives. And I'm sure the same criticism will be leveled concerning Arthur White in this volume. But it is very important to put these criticisms in perspective. Both Ellen White and her grandson Arthur were given a tremendous amount of positive publicity and media coverage by the Adventist Church throughout their lifetimes. And in the case of Ellen White, she made claims for her writings and ministry that were absolute and in many cases blasphemous but which the Adventists embraced and supported as evidence that they are God's true Remnant Church.[1] Arthur White based his reputation and writings entirely on his grandmother's claims, which he spent his entire life defending and perpetuating.

Let me shift gears. Had Bernie Madoff died in his early seventies, before his fraud was exposed, he would have been celebrated as a great man. Not only was he a world-famous investor who had made unprecedented amounts of money for his clients, but he was also president of the Nasdaq, an extremely prestigious position in financial circles. But once his scam, or pyramid scheme, was exposed, how many authors or reporters spent their time writing articles or books about what a great man Madoff was or what positive things he accomplished in his life? Such writings would have been an insult to those who were fooled, deceived, and exploited by Madoff. And the same is true of Ellen White, Arthur White, and the Adventist Church, who honor these individuals as great people.

As humans, we are all subject to confirmation bias, which is defined as "the tendency to interpret new evidence as confirmation of one's existing beliefs or theories."[2] But when a person is convinced by new evidence to take a position that is the opposite of what he or she has previously held and how he or she was raised, this defies confirmation bias. As a Seventh-day Adventist minister, I was trained to believe that Ellen White was a true prophet of God, and I held this view for many years, despite having to deal with more and more evidence that she was a plagiarist and a person with many other faults. My doubts about her continued to build through a master's program in history, where my thesis focused on the 1919 Bible Conference and its examination of EGW, as well as two doctoral dissertations that also focused directly on EGW and Adventism.

By the time I left Adventism in 2010, I was fully convinced that Ellen White was not a true prophet of God, but it wasn't until I explicitly researched the question, Will the extensive accusations of pathology and immorality leveled against Ellen White, both during and after her lifetime, stand up to historical and psychological scrutiny? that I became totally convinced that EGW was an absolute fraud as well as a deluded human being. And it wasn't until after I wrote my psychobiography that I became aware, through my acquaintance with Nancy Paige, that Arthur White had so many of the characteristics of his grandmother. When it was revealed to me that Arthur White had secretly colluded with Carrie Johnson for more than twenty years to fabricate a fraud against Canright, I dug into his background a great deal more than I had before.

So, let's consider Arthur's background and childhood a bit. Arthur White was "one of seven grandchildren of James Springer White and Ellen G. White, Arthur White was born to William C. White and Ethel May

White on October 7, 1907. He grew up in Pratt Valley, just below the St. Helena Sanitarium in northern California."[3] Arthur's life overlapped with that of his famous grandmother, Ellen, for seven years, nine months, and nine days. And he lived quite close to her Elmshaven Estate, where she spent her final years with her extensive staff of some twenty-one people. Not only was Arthur the grandson of the matriarch whom Adventists considered God's final last-day prophet to the world and the prophetic voice from the Almighty, who made them God's exclusive Remnant Church. But his father, William, was the favored son of Ellen White who was designated by Ellen to head the White Estate in the aftermath of her death.

Given the elevated status of both his grandmother and his father in Adventism, a relatively isolated subculture, it would not be unreasonable to assume that Arthur was raised with the notion that he was special. To what degree he was privately taught this, we don't know, for the Whites were intensely secretive and private about what transpired in their close-knit inner family circle. But we can be quite certain that Arthur was at least aware, growing up, of the things his father had disclosed about Ellen on the record and even under oath, to say nothing of the discussions he would have heard from his father in their own home. The bottom line is, William (or Willie, Arthur's dad) was very candid with Fannie Bolton when she was hired to work for Ellen that what she and other SDAs had been taught about Ellen's "visions" being detailed downloads from the Almighty was completely inaccurate and that at best, her "visions" were more general "flashlight or panoramic views" that did not involve dictation from God.[4]

Even more significant was William White's admission under oath in the H. R. Henry libel case that his mother's professed visions concerning the case were not "visions in the night" as she had claimed, but rather that they were not. He stated plainly, "I cannot lie."[5] In this high-profile case, all it took was the threat of perjury to get the Whites to tell the truth! Arthur would have been well aware of these facts, and many others growing up, which would have made it clear to him that what the church generally believed about his grandmother and the reality were miles apart. But the family name and reputation were at stake. Arthur would have known he was privileged growing up and that the family had a lot to hide to keep it that way.

The monumental work that Arthur White was most known for, during and after his lifetime, was the six-volume biography of his grandmother Ellen, *Ellen G. White: A Biography*, which took six years to complete. It is considered the definitive biography of Ellen White by the SDA Church, and the writing of it was started in 1979 and finished in 1985. The six volumes are divided into the following sections of her life:

> The Early Years: 1827–1862 (vol. 1)
> The Progressive Years: 1862–1876 (vol. 2)
> The Lonely Years: 1876–1891 (vol. 3)
> The Australian Years: 1891–1900 (vol. 4)
> The Early Elmshaven Years: 1900–1905 (vol. 5)
> The Later Elmshaven Years: 1905–1915 (vol. 6)

The project was first initiated in 1966, when the White Estate board of trustees, in consultation with the General Conference of Seventh-day Adventists officers, asked White to author these volumes on the life of Ellen White. Arthur was at first hesitant to agree because of his personal relationship to the subject of the biography, but based on his stance taken early in his ministry, that he would relate to Ellen White as would any other loyal Seventh-day Adventist, viewing her as "Sister White" and not as "my grandmother," White accepted the assignment. In 1978, he resigned as secretary of the White Estate to focus on the biography commitment, working at his home but accessing the nearby White Estate vault.

It is interesting to note that when the notorious 1919 Bible Conference Minutes were rediscovered in the General Conference archives in 1974, after being lost for more than fifty years, Arthur White managed to obtain custody over these critical documents and kept them from church members. He was well aware that this information did not make his grandmother or the church look good, so he took it upon himself to deprive SDAs of this crucial material. When Arthur left the White Estate in 1979, the minutes were leaked to *Spectrum* magazine, which provided a summary of them to church members. And according to Ron Graybill, who also worked in a leadership role at the White Estate, Arthur took every opportunity to suppress or distort the truth where his grandmother was concerned.

For example, in his book *Visions and Revisions,* Graybill reveals how Arthur supervised the editing process that suppressed the mention of Ellen's love for oysters. He also attempted to discredit Prescott's landmark letter to Willie White lamenting his grandmother's deceptions, and he did everything in his power to present Prescott's many changes to Ellen's *Great Controversy* as "few and minor in nature," when this was hardly the case. Jonathan Butler also documents Arthur White's dishonesty in denying that his grandmother took her kids to a phrenologist to have their heads examined, when Ronald Numbers was doing his research in this area, only to have Graybill sneak the info to Numbers behind White's back. Arthur was not about presenting his grandmother as an objective historian, as he claimed. The fact is, Arthur White was all about control, suppression, and distortion, and not about the truth![6]

In light of the revelations contained about Arthur White in this book, it is fascinating to see what efforts he made to present himself as an objective scholar where his work as a historian was concerned, and particularly with regard to his grandmother, when in reality, the exact opposite was true. Arthur was willing to go to any strides to protect the reputation of his grandma, and to any extremes, including deliberate lying, theft of a diary, and twenty years of secret meetings fabricating the most dishonest book he could help Carrie Johnson produce, to destroy his grandma's most threatening critic. And up until the present, it seemed that Arthur had successfully accomplished his deception. At the General Conference session in New Orleans in 1985, White was presented with the church's Distinguished Achievement Award. The following year he received the Charles E. Weniger Award of Merit from Pacific Union College. And, as we've already mentioned, he received an honorary doctorate from Andrews University during the previous decade. All this recognition was intended to present A. L. White to the church as a great scholar and researcher who was worthy of being the biographer of Adventism's great last-day prophet and most famous personage. But the reality was that just like his grandmother, Arthur had lived a double life. Whereas, on the one hand, he presented himself to church members and his colleagues as a very virtuous person of great scholarship and integrity, on the other hand, he was living out lifelong patterns of gross dishonesty and general immorality.

Compulsive dishonesty is a trait that often exists in dysfunctional families and is common with antisocial personalities, and especially with high-functioning sociopaths. Sociopaths typically engage in behaviors that harm others in some way for their own benefit. High-functioning sociopaths may seem to be very successful in their work or careers and manage to maintain marriages and families as well. But their actions and attitudes, which are meant to come across as warm and charming, are intended to deceive, manipulate, exploit, and control others to benefit themselves.

High-functioning sociopaths differ in a number of significant ways from their low-functioning counterparts and from antisocial personalities who have psychopathic traits. Unlike psychopathic personalities, they do not have a strong genetic or biological link to anger and rage, do not usually have abusive backgrounds, and do not generally engage in behavior that is overtly cruel or violent. Unlike low-functioning sociopaths, they do not generally lack education or have average or below-average intelligence. In this case, Arthur and Ellen White were remarkably similar. You could almost say, based on the historical evidence, "Like grandmother, like grandson" in terms of them both meeting the qualities of a high-functioning sociopath!

In fact, they both seemed to have high levels of emotional intelligence. Neither of them had poor interpersonal skills or generally made overt attempts to intimidate, coerce, or threaten others to get their way. They were much more subtle and sophisticated in their methods of manipulating, exploiting, controlling, and deceiving others to ultimately benefit themselves. There are many symptoms and components of the high-functioning sociopathic personality that overlap with, or mirror, the narcissistic personality disorder, as we noted before. Based on the historical evidence,

Ellen White fit with both disorders, and in this regard she differed from her grandson, who only seemed to share her characteristics as a high-functioning sociopath.

THE HIGH FUNCTIONING SOCIOPATH

1. *Above-average intelligence.* The high-functioning sociopath is capable of manipulating others without making their attempts to exploit and control obvious. Where Ellen White was concerned, even though she did not seem to have a lot of creative intelligence, she did have the intelligence to overcome her very meager formal education and to con or manipulate an entire religion into believing she was the anointed last-day prophet of God. Arthur was also able to con the same denomination into believing he was an objective scholar who saw his grandmother as any objective scholar would and who had no animosity toward D. M. Canright, when the opposite was true.

2. *Lack of empathy.* Like the narcissist, the high-functioning sociopath is concerned with accomplishing his or her ends, not with understanding or caring for other people. But this kind of sociopath is generally tremendously effective at deceiving people and making them think they are cared about, to use them for self-centered reasons. In Ellen's case, she secretly stole from other authors and, again, basically used and manipulated an entire denomination of church members to become a revered "prophet" and religious icon. Arthur White gave the impression that he was a humble, serious scholar, content to live in the background, even though he devoted much of his life to destroying the reputation of D. M. Canright and was ruthless in the way he treated Norman Douty and the Canright family.

3. *Calculating behaviors.* High-functioning sociopaths are generally strongly driven and determined individuals. They typically

possess a high level of self-love (narcissism) and a sense of grandiosity, which justifies their plans to control and manipulate others through means that are often unethical or immoral. As in the case where Ellen premeditates a faked vision to dupe Joseph Bates into embracing her "prophetic gift" and giving her and her husband financial and emotional support, behaviors are often predetermined and highly calculated. Arthur White was not grandiose or attention-seeking in the way his grandmother was, but he was very controlling and conniving, working secretly behind the scenes for more than twenty years to destroy a good man's reputation. He was very accomplished at calculating and premeditated evil.

4. *Secretive tendencies.* High-functioning sociopaths tend to hide their real selves and their real motives with great success. They don't really like people, but they are great at pretending to like others. They seldom confide in others or reveal private information about themselves unless it is to manipulate people. Where others are concerned, they generally live a lie. This certainly exemplifies the life of Ellen White, who hid her plagiarisms, denied them, covered up and refused to acknowledge her false prophecies, and engaged in repeated activities that were in direct conflict with the "testimonies" she imposed on others. The same patterns can be seen in her grandson, who was extremely secretive, managing to cover and deny his working relationship with Carrie Johnson and the major role he played in the construction of her evil fabricated book throughout most of his career.

5. *Charisma and charm.* Again, the high-functioning sociopath is not generally an extrovert, who enjoys socializing with people, but generally displays excellent social skills and has very high emotional intelligence. It is striking to see what a high percentage of politicians, elected church administrators, and even pastors in general have sociopathic tendencies or personality traits. Ellen was extremely gifted at appearing to be a very

humble, loving, and caring person. As she got older, she became the sweet little grandmother—except to those who dared to cross her, in which case she became the master of passive-aggressive behavior. Arthur White also seemed to be a very nice, meek, unthreatening person outwardly but was grossly dishonest, vicious, and malicious behind the scenes when his agenda was threatened. He was a vindictive and evil person , as evidenced in how he treated Canright.

6. *Hypersensitivity.* High-functioning sociopaths are typically very defensive. They are generally easily threatened because they have a lot to hide related to their secrecy and deception. Therefore, they tend to be quick to anger when they perceive that they don't have someone's approval or may be potentially exposed. This is because, like the narcissist, they crave admiration from others. Ellen was extremely sensitive to criticisms and reacted to them with "visions" and "testimonies" that released the wrath of God on her critics. Arthur didn't have the threat of "visions," which made his grandmother so effective, but he was very successful at hiding behind a virtuous reputation. He put Carrie Johnson up to the dirty work while he claimed no association with her or knowledge of what she was doing and acted self-righteously offended at any suggestion that he was ever guilty of wrongdoing.

7. *Addictive behaviors.* It is common for a person who is a high-functioning sociopath to struggle with an <u>addiction, or multiple addictions</u>. Compulsive, controlling behaviors and reactions can lead to issues with eating disorders, shopping addictions, gambling, sex, alcohol, and drugs. Where the "prophetess" was concerned, she hid an addiction to home-made alcohol for years, until it became life-threatening, and then only admitted it in her private diary. But rather than admitting that she was addicted to alcohol, which she vigorously condemned as an avid prohibitionist, she claimed to have an addiction to

vinegar, which is not addicting. Clearly, it was the vinegar wine she made that could have had a high alcohol content. Arthur did not seem to have the classic addictions of his grandmother, but he was certainly addicted to compulsive controlling behavior, including lying and other forms of dishonesty. And he seemed to be addicted to living a double life, one as the pristine head of the White Estate, and the other secretly plotting the destruction of D. M. Canright.

8. ***An incapacity to experience guilt.*** Sociopaths in general, including high-functioning sociopaths, rationalize and justify their behaviors so that they believe they are almost never wrong and almost never truly need to apologize. They basically function without a conscience, no matter who they hurt or how many they hurt to get their way. In Ellen's case, she was able to rationalize plagiarism and literary theft to destroy people's lives with "testimonies" she attributed to the Lord, exploit church members for money, and commit other forms of hypocrisy, deception, and fraud, all in the name of God. Arthur White was also guilty of plotting and committing evil against those he considered to be a threat, while denying bold-faced that he had any involvement in such activities. Again, he never seemed to confess any of these actions, repent of them, or even show any evidence of ever feeling guilty about his dishonesty and cover-ups. In his mind, no one knew what he had done, and he wasn't about to tell them.[7]

Again, it is not my intention to diagnose either Arthur White or his "prophetess," grandmother, but to provide you with the historical evidence and the components of certain pathologies and let you draw your own conclusions. To me, what makes Arthur's and Ellen's pathologies so dangerous and damaging was not just their willingness to hurt others, steal from others, and deceive multitudes for her own self-promotion and benefit, but in Ellen's case, her willingness to project her own tragic and damaging errors, condemnations, and character flaws onto God, and in Arthur's case to strongly perpetuate those lies. From my perspective, based on thirty-five years of experience in the Adventist ministry, there is an interesting parallel between the pathological tendencies of the "prophet," her grandson, and what I have found with Adventist Church leadership throughout its history and during my lifetime. Why did I stay so long, in an effort to try to help the church move in a healthier direction, until I was pushed out?

In closing this chapter, it seems fair to say that Arthur White closely mirrored most of the traits in his grandmother that fit with a high-functioning sociopath. But he did not seem to take on the characteristics that closely fit with a narcissistic personality disorder, as his grandmother did. Arthur did not have an attention-seeking personality or the need to be in the limelight. He was content to work in the shadows and in secrecy for the twenty-odd years he collaborated with Carrie Johnson on her book. Again, this was what he perceived to be in his own self-interest, but clearly Arthur did not have the same level of grandiosity and delusion that his grandmother had. He was content to work behind the scenes to do all he could to further the Big Lie that she generated about herself.

11

WHO WAS D. M. CANRIGHT?

In the Adventist mindset D. M. Canright was the equivalent of a Benedict Arnold in American history. He was seen as a successful young minister who showed great potential, largely because of the influence and support of Ellen White, only to ultimately betray her, turn his back on her, and become her greatest and most effective critic. SDAs who know anything about Canright, tend to look on him with great disdain and condemnation. And the book that cemented this image in their minds was the fabrication that Carrie Johnson and Arthur White colluded to produce, *I Was Canright's Secretary.*

But long before this book was published, even while Canright, himself was alive, the SDA Church leadership did everything possible to try to discredit Canright in whatever ways they could. Much was made of Ellen White's prophecy that Canright would fail outside of Adventism and "die in obscurity" because he had opposed her and supposedly wanted to make a name for himself in the "world." When one studies the life of Ellen White carefully and objectively, one of the lifelong patterns that emerges is that she did not care about people except as they impacted her own position, power, and control. She became very invested in the lives of individuals like Fannie Bolton and D. M. Canright, who were in the strongest positions to expose her, particularly when they were struggling with doubts, and did everything she could, even manipulating "visions," to keep them under SDA employ and her control. But the moment they expressed doubts, even those that were based on very good evidence, Ellen released the "visionary" hounds of hell and condemnation on them, until they either confessed and repented or became so discouraged and depressed that they could no longer function in their positions.

It is obvious that Ellen never really cared about Fannie or Dudley, even though they both deeply cared about her. She was only concerned with how their doubts and very powerful testimonies could hurt her. She would go to any extreme to condemn them and shut them up so their influence would not be heard by others. We see this in her warnings and testimonies trying to silence their tongues. In Canright's case, she expected him to "keep away" from all Adventist people when he was not under her direct control. It was a case of either stay and do as I say, or go and stay away from all of the Adventist people (including friends and family) if you are to leave.

"Satan is full of exaltant joy that you have stepped from beneath the banner of Jesus Christ, and stand under his banner. . . . Keep away from our people, do not visit them and talk your doubts and darkness among them. . . . You have ever had a desire for power, for popularity, and this is one of the reasons for your present position. You have wanted to be too much, and make a show and noise in the world, and as the result your sun will surely set in obscurity."[1]

Here we see the SDA prophet claiming to speak for God *and* Satan. She has been shown that the enemy of Christ is "full of exaltant joy" over Canright. She equates Elder Canright leaving the Adventist Church with no longer serving God and instead actively serving the devil. This of course has been typical Adventist thinking over the years: anyone who leaves the one true Remnant Church (cult), cannot possibly be saved, no matter how devoted to Jesus Christ he or she happens to be. And Canright was a humble minister and servant of Christ who just wanted to quietly move into a healthier expression of Christianity than what he had found in Adventism.

Both Douty's heavily documented research[2] and Canright's own testimony make it clear that Canright wanted to leave the SDA Church without any controversy or animosity and that it was the Adventists who broke the truce and publicly attacked Canright in their church paper before he could ever give reasons for why he left. I agree with Douty's assertion that this was "the greatest tactical blunder in its [Adventism's] entire history."[3] In Canright's own words:

> Though I went out quietly and peaceably and let them entirely alone and even spoke favorably of them, they immediately attributed to me all sorts of evil motives, base sins, and ambitious designs. They seemed to feel it a sacred duty to blast my reputation and destroy my influence. . . . "Apostate" was the epithet all applied to me. I was compared to Balaam, to Korah, Dathan and Abiram, to Judas, Demas and a whole list of evil characters. Not one honest or worthy motive was granted me. The meanest and wickedest reports were circulated as to what I had done or said—things that I would despise even to think of. Yet all were eagerly received and accepted as undoubted truth. But I expected it, for it is the way all are treated who dare to leave them and give a reason for it.[4]

SDA leaders told every lie they could to ensure that Ellen White's false prophecy about Canright was fulfilled, but instead, their efforts to attack and oppose Canright ended up making him famous, along with the powerful reasons he had for leaving. Ironically, despite Canright's humble attempt to leave Adventism quietly, with no controversy, and his choice to pastor a poor, small Baptist church that needed his help instead of several larger churches that made him offers, Canright may well be the best-known pastor who ever served in the Adventist Church. And his legacy has only increased over the years. His life and well-documented books have been quoted more and translated more as evidence that Ellen White was a false prophet and that Seventh-day Adventism is a cult than any other. Hardly what you would call dying in obscurity.

And while every form of evil, weakness, and selfish motivation were attributed to him by SDA leaders, both during and after his lifetime—including apostasy, desire for fame, greed, anger, bitterness, envy, hatred, mental instability, immorality, ungratefulness, pride, character weakness, and demon possession[5]–the truth is that it took tremendous courage and self-sacrifice for Canright to make the decision that he did, and the personal pain and loss he experienced from it had everything to do with why he vacillated over several years before leaving for the last time. Canright was a caring person, with very close friends in the movement, family ties, and his whole identity tied to Adventism. Leaving a cult is no easy thing under such circumstances, and it took incredible integrity on Canright's part to finally pull the rip cord.

Canright exposed the irony of the SDA accusations against him in chapter 8 of his excellent book, *Seventh-day Adventism Renounced*, under the sarcastic heading, "How I Sought Position and Popularity After Leaving Them."

> They said I must have left them for popularity, position and pay. Did they know my heart? Had they any evidence of this? No, they made it up and said it because they could say nothing else. It was utterly false; for the truth is, I really feared I should be ruined financially by the change. But as soon as I had left them I received warm invitations from ten different denominations to unite with them, promising me good positions. . . . At the time I left I was getting higher pay than ever before, and was on friendly terms with all. All the leading men, as Butler, Haskell, Smith, etc., were my warm personal friends, ready to do all in their power to assist me. Had I desired office, or better position, all I had to do was to go right along without wavering, and positions would come to me faster than I could fill them. But if I left them, where

could I go? What could I do? How even make a living? I took this all in, and it required all the courage and faith in God I could master [muster] to take the risk. It cost me a terrible struggle and a great sacrifice, for in doing it, I had to leave all my life-long friends, the cherished hopes of my youth, the whole work of my life, all the means of my support, every honorable position I held, and bring upon myself reproach, hatred and persecution. I had to begin life anew, among strangers, with untried methods, uncertain where to go, or what to do. No one who has not tried it can ever begin to realize the fearful struggle it requires . . . fairness can see readily that self-interest and personal ambition would have held me with them.[6]

When you compare the integrity of Canright (overwhelmingly demonstrated by an abundance of testimonies in his behalf from others) to the tragic lack of integrity displayed by those who produced the book *I Was Canright's Secretary*, you can see that the contrast is so stark and undeniable that Adventism desperately needs to own up to its slander of this noble man.[7] So, with this brief background, let's circle back and try to understand Canright's life from a psychological perspective, as best we can.

In addition to all their other attacks on him, SDAs continually come back to the argument that Canright had to be a weak, indecisive, and unstable person because of his many years of vacillation and his decision to take leave of the movement and then return. Because he couldn't seem to make up his mind about EGW and SDAs, he is presented in the worst light. But is this fair? Was it because Canright was a very healthy, caring man who was highly conflicted, for good reasons, that he demonstrated such behavior?

Let's start with his family of origin. Unlike Ellen White, who demonstrated some significant pathology and abnormal fears, even in her childhood, including suicidal ideation, Canright seemed to have a very healthy childhood, and in the words of Norman Douty, after sharing sixteen pages of research into Canright's family background, "He had come from the very best kind of stock."[8] His family history was solid as a rock, and his personal history is impressive as well. Dudley grew up on a farm in Kinderhook, Michigan, and had many pleasant memories of his boyhood, which he shared with his own children and with his SDA Church family.[9] Unlike Ellen White's, his childhood was not filled with fear and trauma. But also unlike Ellen, he was not raised in a religious home.

The three generations of Canrights before his father were all committed Christians, but this was not the case with Dudley's dad or mother. His father was well-known in his community and served in several influential positions, while keeping a farm at the same time. He seemed to be a good father but was not a man given to books or religion. Dudley was quite different from his dad in this regard and had a tremendous intellectual curiosity and desire for an education, even though his father did not encourage this at all. But Dudley was a very determined young man, despite his father's wishes, he walked to town, got a job on his own, and earned enough money to work his way through school.

When the time came for him to leave home for high school, he would walk for miles barefoot, carrying his shoes to preserve them, to catch the train that took him ten more miles to his educational destination. Coldwater High School was the name of this institution, and while attending there, Dudley also received the first formal religious education of his life.[10] This came from Methodists, who worked with him for two years. In his own words, "I was converted among the Methodists under the labors of Rev. Mr. Hazzard, and baptized by him in 1858."[11] It was the next year, 1859, that Canright would come to know SDAs, as he started attending Albion Academy in New York, near where his uncle Joel lived.

It was also during this year that Dudley was introduced to James and Ellen White for the first time. The SDA movement only had a total of five thousand followers during that period, and while the Whites had settled in Battle Creek in 1855, they did a lot of traveling, speaking at churches and schools as they were able. Dudley was a very self-motivated young man with great academic potential, but he was also new to Christianity and easily influenced by religious founders such as James and Ellen. The

Whites were always on the lookout for such young talent and were quick to not only convince him of the seventh-day Sabbath but to make it clear to him that the Methodists were wrong and only Adventists had the truth. As Canright put it:

> As I was anxious to be right, I began keeping Saturday, but did not expect to believe any more of their doctrine. Of course, I attended their meetings on Saturday and worked on Sunday. This separated me entirely from other Christians and threw me wholly with the Adventists. I soon learned from them that all other churches were Babylon, in the dark and under the frown of God. Seventh-day Adventists were the only true people of God. They had "the truth," the whole truth, and nothing but the truth.[12]

When Dudley left Albion Academy, the Whites invited him to live in their home in Michigan and to do secretarial work for them.[13] To the Whites' credit, they were quick to spot talent in young men that they thought had potential as ministers, doctors, or leaders in their movement, such as Canright and Kellogg, and didn't hesitate to nurture and groom them on their own turf, to keep them from outside influences. This also allowed James and Ellen to mix church and personal finances in ways that brought them a great deal of legitimate criticism.[14] Not only did the Whites have Dudley live with them but had his younger brother Jasper move in with them when he was much younger than Dudley, so they were able to convert him to Adventism as well.[15]

This was also during the period (the 1860s and 1870s) when James White exercised the greatest influence and almost absolute power in the Adventist Church. He had just won the battle over church organization in the late 1850s and early 1860s, making sure that Seventh-day Adventism became an official, legal denomination. Then he served three different terms as the General Conference president after that (1865–1867;

1869–1871; and 1874–1880). For most of the years between the time the church was officially organized (1863) and his death (1881), James was the General Conference president, and Ellen, his prophet-wife, made it clear during those years that the General Conference in session was the voice of God on earth. Of course, after her husband died, and there were GC presidents she disagreed with, she contradicted this view from later "visions," claiming God had changed His mind about the GC being His voice on earth.[16]

But the last two decades of his life, James wielded absolute authority and expected unconditional loyalty from those he took under his wing or gave positions of leadership. Again, even the secular newspapers of the day commented on the extreme authority, power, and influence that James White commanded in Adventism.[17] So, it was a great honor and privilege for anyone to be taken into the inner circle of James and Ellen White. And what made Dudley Canright even more a part of this inner circle than most was that he married a young woman, Lucretia Cranson, who had also been taken into the Whites' home and had been treated by Ellen as the daughter she never had. So, on April 11, 1867 ,Canright married into what was for practical purposes, the White family, while he was quickly becoming a rising star in the Adventist ministry and one of their leading debaters.[18]

Canright and Lucretia were so close to the Whites that they actually vacationed together, and it was on one of these vacations, at one of the Whites' vacation homes in Colorado, that the dogmatism and overbearing dominance of James White rubbed Canright the wrong way, and the two of them got into a heated argument that was not resolved. Canright was clearly tired of being treated in a condescending manner by the Whites and was becoming increasingly disturbed by the way James abused those under his authority, to such a degree that they often felt humiliated and shamed but were afraid to speak or defend themselves based on the retribution that had been dished out to any who had dared to do so in the past.[19] From Canright's perspective, James was not only overbearing and mean to his "underlings," but continually exploited them by misusing their education and talents, taking credit for their knowledge and work himself:

Elder White was not a literary man, not a student of books, not scholarly, not a theologian. He understood neither Hebrew, Greek nor Latin, read only the common English version of the Bible, and seldom ever consulted other translations . . . He attended high school only twenty-nine weeks, and learned enough simply to teach a country school. Though he published and edited papers for thirty years, he produced no commentary, no critical work, no book on any doctrinal subject. He published two bound books: *Life Sketches*, a simple story of his and his wife's lives, and *Life of Miller*, taken almost wholly from another author. He drew his knowledge from observation and from conversing with leading men who were students. All doctrinal subjects requiring study he turned over to these men for them to dig out, after which he used them himself.[20]

So, like his wife, James was quick to steal the thoughts and ideas of others, without giving them credit. And by this time, Canright had also witnessed firsthand the Whites financially fleecing and exploiting church members for their own personal gain in a manner that had raised major concerns about the integrity of their leadership.[21] So, they were not really in a mood to be scolded and lectured by the Whites during their Colorado getaway. And yet, that is precisely what happened. James and Ellen did not feel their underlings were showing them the proper reverence and honor they deserved as the founder and co-founding prophet of the movement, and the dispute between James and Dudley seemed to be the trigger that launched a barrage of criticisms that had clearly been escalating in the prophetess for some time. As soon as Canright and Lucretia cut their stay short by leaving, Ellen started writing a massive testimony that judged and condemned them both without mercy.

This letter from Ellen White to the Canrights covered more than twenty-five pages; was sent from Black Hawk, Colorado; and was dated August 25, 1873. It was published in volume 3 of Ellen's *Testimonies for the Church*, under the title "To a Young Minister and His Wife." And the "prophetess" began her "testimony" with these words: "Dear Brother and Sister A: For some months I have felt that it was time to write to you some things which the Lord was pleased to show me in regard to you several years ago. Your cases were shown me in connection with those of others who had a work to do for themselves in order to be fitted for the work of presenting the truth."[22]

Canright had been a leader in Adventist ministry for some time when Ellen wrote these words, yet she claims God gave them to her years before as things that needed to be corrected for him to be fitted for the work of presenting "the truth," as she "humbly" referred to the SDA message. In other words, Ellen had been negligent in failing to deliver this testimony when she "got it"!

She continues, "I was shown that you were both deficient in essential qualifications and that if these are not obtained your usefulness and the salvation of your own souls will be endangered. You have some faults in your characters which it is very important that you should correct."[23] So, this testimony was critical to prepare them for ministry and likely to affect their eternal destinies, but Ellen had waited years to send it yet coincidentally decided to unload the whole thing right after Dudley had had a strong disagreement with her husband.

Some other highlights, or lowlights, from the letter included the following: They both had a "lack of reverence and due respect for others," and they were both guilty of being "very self-confident," having an "independent spirit," being "headstrong," following their "own minds," and "selfishness." She goes on to attack their diet and their parenting and to accuse them of being "sanctimonious," of having an "infidel" spirit, of being "self-righteous," of having a "wicked spirit" with "vanity and pride," of being "unconverted" and of being "in danger of losing" their souls. She goes on to refer to them as Pharisees, guilty of "murmurings" against God's anointed pioneers, and failing to see "grievous sins" in their "true light." Of course, Ellen could see their sins, for as she reminded them, "God has been pleased to open to me the secrets of the inner life and the hidden sins of His people . . . the angel of God has spoken to me."[24]

This letter kind of reminds me of Ellen's testimony directed at the Elders of the Battle Creek Church, who had a disagreement with her, and whom God showed her in "vision" leaving the "most solemn, impressive discourses on the judgment" and going to their rooms to indulge "in their favorite bewitching sin, [of secret vice/masturbation] polluting their own bodies." God had given her pornographic "visions." And their children were presented to her as "corrupt as hell itself."[25] If you want to hold power over people, just convince them that God is giving you "visions" of their secret sins. Ellen had a way of getting church leaders to fall into line when she didn't like the direction they were going. But the problem with Canright and Lucretia is that they had lived in Ellen's home and knew first-hand that she and her husband were far more guilty of the sins of which she had accused them of than they were themselves.

I believe it is fair to say that Canright and Lucretia, who died on March 29, 1879, never fully recovered from this hypocritical "testimony." Dudley lived another forty years after his first wife passed, but during the fourteen years between when he received this letter and when he finally left Adventism, he was psychologically conflicted to such a degree that, as he said, it took all the courage and faith he could muster to sever all ties with a movement that had almost totally given him both his professional and personal identity. Once Canright left, in 1887, SDAs tried to accuse him of leaving them four different times and of being an unstable personality.[26] But these were the typical false charges of Adventism.

The truth was that Canright did take three leaves, two of them very short, from his preaching and ministry during that fourteen-year period to try to honestly deal with the conflicts and questions about Ellen White and SDA theology that continued to surface. But in no case did he leave the movement, or he wouldn't have been given the important assignments and positions he was given when he returned from these leaves. Canright's first voluntary leave from his ministry occurred right after he and his wife left their vacation with the Whites in 1873. He was clearly disturbed by what had occurred at their vacation home, and both he and his wife were even more offended by the hypocritical and condescending "testimony" they received from Ellen White. During this period Canright worked on a farm in California for three months to sort out his thoughts and feelings but was chosen shortly thereafter to represent the whole SDA denomination.[27] Canright was picked over James and Ellen White and Elders Loughborough and Cornell (who were all available) for a week-long series of debates with Miles Grant, the most formidable opponent of Adventism at the time.

Canright's next leave was even more dramatic because it included his resignation from the Ohio Conference presidency and came seven years later, in the fall of 1880. Canright protested that he did not want to be reelected as Conference president but was voted in at the insistence of Ellen White.[28] I've personally known a lot of SDA Conference presidents in my life, and not a one of them seemed the least bit inclined to resign from his position of power for any reason. But, again, Canright gave up his presidency and left. Then, for three months he reflected on his concerns about Adventism and spent the rest of his time lecturing on the subject of elocution, which was a budding interest of his. And once again, Ellen, greatly embarrassed by what had transpired, hit him with a "testimony," which denounced him as a "child of hell."[29]

However, soon thereafter, James White wrote Canright personally, expressing that he had greater interest and confidence in Canright's abilities than those of any other man.[30] And shortly after this letter, Canright was elected to the executive committee for the Michigan Conference. Finally, Canright's third withdrawal occurred two years later, in the fall of 1882, and this time it was a more extended leave, lasting for two years. During this period Canright worked on his farm in Ostego, Michigan, trying to sort out doubts and concerns about the church that continued to plague him. Canright pointed out that such leaves among SDA leaders were not uncommon and were taken by such notable men as J. N. Andrews, Uriah Smith, G. I. Butler, and J. N. Loughborough, but these leaves were never described as "leaving the church," as his were. And even after this two-year leave, Canright occupied a number of very important positions in Adventism before he finally decided that he could no longer be a SDA.

When he did finally sever ties with the denomination in 1887, he never looked back or regretted his decision, contrary to SDA false claims.[31] This decision, as mentioned before, left prophetic egg on the face of Ellen White and provoked her ire in a "testimony": she now insisted that the very man God had shown her was to be Conference president, and one of the great leaders among them, was now a seeker of vain ambition who sought "through disobedience to rise to greater heights, to gain some flattering position."[32] Ellen also claimed to have had a dream concerning Canright in which she saw him leaving the ship of Adventism and becoming a lost soul. The Captain of the SDA ship, who was supposed to be Christ, twice told Canright that He would not permit him to leave the ship, but then gave him a final warning: that only his ship will make the harbor; the other vessel will be smashed on the rocks. Ellen added, "I am deeply concerned for your soul . . . This may be the last trial that God will grant you. Advance not one step in the downward road to perdition. . . . If you yield to impressions, you will lose your soul . . . Satan is taking advantage of everyone who is not fully established in the truth.[33]

Here again, Ellen was equating God's true church with the Adventist "ship" and clearly stating that if Canright left Adventism, even to pastor in another church, he would be on the "road to perdition" and would "lose" his "soul." This kind of thinking alone, especially given that she attributed it to God, should make it obvious why Canright felt it necessary to escape. But the "prophetess" wasn't done. Her last "testimony" to Canright was dated April 20, 1888. In it, Ellen even accused Canright of lying about his first wife's own faith. Lucretia, who was equally offended by Mrs. White's testimony against them as her husband, and who had died nine years earlier, had died disbelieving the "Testimonies," according to Canright. But Ellen insisted she had received a letter from Lucretia before her death stating that she had implicit faith in the Testimonies, so Mrs. White was calling Canright a liar regarding his own wife. However, Ellen never produced this letter, nor was it ever found in any of her documents.

This was a despicable lie, where the "prophet" tried to claim she knew Canright's first wife better than her husband did, based on a nonexistent letter. Nor did she spare Canright's second wife: "Your present wife has had no deep religious experience in self-denial, in self-sacrifice, in communion with God, in belief in the truth." The prophetess once again extended blanket judgments, despite abundant evidence that her claims weren't true. Finally, she did not miss her last chance to condemn Canright himself again: "You now take the side of the first great rebel to make void the law of God. . . . You will stand guilty and condemned . . . You will have no words of excuse for your late defection."[34] The "prophetess" sees everything from her own cultic perspective and describes a deeply dedicated Christian minister who departs from that distorted perspective as joining hands with the devil. In this context, it is not hard to see why Canright rejected the cultic teachings of Adventism and its false prophet.

But psychologically, it is also not difficult to understand why this decision took so long and what tremendous pain and conflict it caused for Canright. The first factor to consider is that Canright did not have the advantage of a Christian upbringing, yet he sincerely sought for spiritual guidance, and it is not surprising that he would be greatly impressed when the cofounders of an up-and-coming religious movement took such interest in him, were willing to mentor him, and even allowed him to live in their home. The point is, Canright did not have the education, training, or discernment at this young age to properly counteract the strong recruitment and opportunities that the Whites offered him. In many ways Canright became a classic example of the power of cognitive dissonance.[35] He bought the sales pitch that the Whites presented concerning Adventism, and then every aspect of his life became so entwined with and indebted to the Whites and to Adventism that it was virtually a miracle that he ever found the later discernment and courage to leave.

As Canright described it in his books, noted already, his connections to the Whites and Adventism were so strong, and these connections provided him with such tremendous opportunities, given his considerable talents, that it was nearly unthinkable to the Whites that Canright would ever leave them. It took an overwhelming amount of evidence to finally convince Canright that he could no longer stay, despite the following strong ties:

Canright was personally recruited into the movement by the Whites themselves.

He lived in the Whites' home for a significant period and became like family to them.

He vaulted into prominence in the Adventist ministry based on the Whites tutelage and his own considerable gifts. He married Lucretia Cranson, who had also lived in the Whites' home and was also like family to them. They were so close to the Whites that they vacationed with them and clearly saw their many faults.

The Whites sought to control Canright, first through very lengthy "Testimonies," which condemned his doubts/questions, and finally, by entrusting him with very high church positions of leadership, which they felt he would not leave.

So, while Canright was experiencing tremendous cognitive dissonance as he struggled with the possibility of losing everything–his family, his ministry positions, his income, his identity, his reputation, and so on– if he left, he was also having to deal with emotional and spiritual abuse, or "emotional blackmail," a term popularized by psychotherapist Susan Forward to describe controlling relationships. Forward also coined the term, or acronym, FOG–fear, obligation, guilt–as the primary methods used in emotional blackmail.[36] The Whites were very good at controlling and manipulating all their subordinates through these three factors, and Canright was no exception. He had a genuine love for the Whites, and a true appreciation for all they had done for him.

But from the Whites' perspective, they owned Canright, and he was obligated to show them absolute loyalty, regardless of their hypocrisy and evil actions. He and his first wife were two of the few people who had been taken into the White's inner circle, so when they failed to show the proper "reverence" to Ellen and James that the prophetess expected from them, she tried to overwhelm them both with guilt–attributing divers criticisms and condemnations to her "visions" from God. And when this ultimately did not work, she attempted to scare Canright back into submission by appealing to fear. If he left her, and the church, he would be lost for eternity and fall into league with the devil himself.

Canright had to struggle and deal with all this spiritual abuse from his spiritual mother. So, it is not surprising that it traumatized him to the core. But the more he saw and heard from the Whites, the more he realized that they were not well. James showed extreme paranoia. And James's own wife, who lived across the country from him for years, questioned his sanity and mental stability in letters to a friend, as noted earlier in this chapter. And after the death of her husband, Ellen became increasingly paranoid herself, lashing out with more fabricated "visions" against all who dared to question her authority or challenge her prophetic claims. In my psychobiography of Ellen White, a great deal of historical evidence was provided that suggested that Ellen suffered from mental illnesses including depression, somatic disorder, narcissistic personality disorder, and high-functioning sociopathy, but there is also plenty of documented material that strongly indicates that Ellen may have had a paranoid personality disorder as well.[37]

Ellen's paranoia is quite understandable given her deliberate attempts to hide her extensive plagiarism from her own assistants and her documented hypocrisy in terms of how she grossly violated the very "testimonies" she had claimed to receive from God and used to condemn others.[38] Canright was privy to much of this information and was therefore more threatening to Ellen White and her stranglehold on power and control than any other person, with the possible exception of Fannie Bolton. Fannie, one of Ellen's top two assistants, was literally driven insane by Ellen's attacks on her.[39] Ellen tried to have the same effect on Canright, but this man showed amazing character, courage and conviction. He ultimately gave up nearly everything that had given his life meaning, except Christ, to cling to Christ alone.

In summary, what can we say about Dudley M. Canright?

- He was born into a good home, with loving parents, but one that lacked spirituality.

- He felt the spiritual deficit and sought out spiritual meaning for himself and found it.
- Ellen and James White saw his great potential and made it their task to nurture and mentor him, even in their home.
- Canright quickly rose to prominence in SDA ministry based on his considerable skills and the Whites' support.
- Canright married Lucretia Cranson, who was also like family to the Whites.
- Canright became one of the best-known ministers in Adventism and their chief debater against other denominations.
- Canrights had a falling-out with the Whites while vacationing with them, followed by a twent-five-page "Testimony" from Ellen.
- This "Testimony," which contained many false accusations attributed to God, greatly increased Canright's doubts.
- In the next fourteen years, Canright would take three leaves of absence from Adventism to sort out his doubts.
- After each of these he returned to Adventism, occupying high positions of influence in the denomination.
- In 1887 Canright left Adventism for good and never regretted or questioned this decision, despite SDA contrarian lies.
- Ellen White thoroughly condemned Canright, again based on "visions," as being lost, and in league with Satan.
- Canright had sought to leave Adventism peacefully and proposed a truce, but the church and its leadership chose to flagrantly break it.
- This choice to irresponsibly violate the truce with Canright probably hurt SDAs more than any decision they ever made.
- Canright had attractive offers from ten different denominations after he left Adventism, but chose to pastor a poor Baptist church.
- Canright proved to be a humble and effective pastor after he left Adventism, receiving great accolades from those who knew him.

- Canright never confessed any desire to return to Adventism, despite SDA's false claims to the contrary, which have all been debunked.
- Canright's two books, renouncing SDAs and EGW, had a great and world-wide impact exposing Adventists, which continues today.
- Canright's book on Ellen White was published the year of his death, proving that he never changed his mind about EGW.

And finally

- Canright's legacy was so great that, as we've already shown, a main street of his hometown was named after him. What a contrast to the "obscurity" Ellen White had "prophesied" and SDAs falsely claimed after he died.

12

WHY IS THIS BOOK IMPORTANT?

In conclusion and summary, I believe this book is a very important one,- for the following reasons, which have all been documented in the previous pages.

1. **Adventism's very beginnings were that of an extreme cult and filled with dishonesty because of Ellen G. White.**[1] Some cults are clearly more extreme than others, and any honest person who is familiar with the documentation relating to the origins of the Seventh-day Adventist movement would have to agree that this movement started as an extreme cult. Not only did the movement consist entirely of individuals who had believed the world would end on October 22, 1844, as William Miller had predicted, but after that date passed these same people doubled down on their madness by embracing the belief that the entire world was lost except for their 150-member group, that the world's probation was closed, and that Christ would indeed return in a very short period (the shut door doctrine, discussed in chapter 1).

   The other Millerites, including Miller himself, at least had the self-awareness to admit they had been wrong about their date-setting.[2] But not the followers of seventeen-year-old "visionary" Ellen White. She claimed in "vision in December of 1844 that God showed her the exact day and hour of His coming, and that the whole wicked world was lost (cementing the Shut Door Theory in her follower's minds). Ellen would go on to claim God showed her He would return before the end of June 1845, and when that failed, that He would return before the end of September that same year. Ellen would claim to have many other "visions" in the seven years between 1844 and 1851 that continued to specifically promote the shut door view. In 1849 she would claim that God gave her a "vision" that believers were to sell their homes and possessions and give the money to "the cause" which she and her husband controlled.

Adventism never admitted this documented cultic thinking but instead tried to delete it or cover it up in their publications. And later, in 1874 and 1883, the prophetess herself issued formal denials of these early "visions," which the church has used ever since to try to discredit them. Which leads us to the next point.

2. **Adventism's dishonesty regarding Ellen White has been a continual pattern throughout its history.** The Adventist Church and its leaders have never been honest about Ellen White's documented dishonesty, deception, plagiarism, fraud, financial exploitation, manipulation, control, false "testimonies" condemning various people, false claims for her writings, and gross misrepresentation of God, including blasphemy. In fact, church leadership in every stage of the movement has done everything in its power to marginalize, misrepresent, and even destroy anyone who attempted to expose these problems.[3]

D. M. Canright was one of the first and possibly the most successful critic of Ellen White and Seventh-day Adventism, so he became a special target of the SDA Church, as I have shown. This book demonstrates, documents, and reveals for the first time the extent to which Arthur White and Carrie Johnson would go, supported by the entire Adventist system, to fabricate an entire book dedicated to misrepresenting Canright and ruining his reputation. It is an outrage that the book was never vetted or ever published, and now that the truth has been revealed, it will be critical to see how the church responds.

3. **D. M. Canright, more than any other person, was responsible for exposing this fraud and dishonesty.** Due to his close personal relationship with Ellen and James White, Canright was treated like family and given great opportunities by the Whites, who recognized his tremendous talents and nurtured them by mentoring him in their own home. Canright felt tremendous loyalty and love for the Whites, but his gradual doubts about them and Adventist theology, which grew over time, caused tremendous conflicts and cognitive dissonance in his thinking. But when Canright finally decided that the fraud and dishonesty he had witnessed was more than his integrity could tolerate, he left the movement in 1887 and never looked back or regretted his decision, though, as stated earlier, SDA said otherwise.

   Part of the purpose of Carrie Johnson's book was to try to document the false claim that Canright did regret leaving Adventism, that he wept bitterly and continually over this decision, but that he felt it was too late to return. And as a result, Johnson claimed she repeatedly heard him lament that he was a "lost man" because of his departure from the "remnant church." This kind of Adventist arrogance was not only meant to try to discredit Canright but to warn any others with doubts that leaving the church would result in the worst agony and eternal loss. But for those who are not bound by Adventist lies, Canright was greatly blessed outside of Adventism and was a tremendous blessing to those to whom he ministered.

4. **Both Ellen White and the SDA leaders of her day treated Canright with extreme dishonesty and disrespect.** Ellen

White clearly made up the "visions" she claimed God had given her to rebuke Canright and his wife to manipulate them into conforming to the Whites' control. The Canrights saw this and were deeply grieved by it. They did their best to try to cope with the situation, but in the meantime Canright's doubts continued to grow, and he lost his wife to disease. Ellen falsely claimed that Canright's wife had written her a letter before her death, claiming she accepted Ellen's "Testimonies," but Canright disputed this, and Ellen never produced the letter, nor was it ever found. The evidence is that such a letter was never sent. Once Canright decided to leave Adventism in 1887, he called a truce with the denomination so they could part on good terms, and the church leaders agreed to this.

But no sooner had Canright officially left, than the church began to publish articles in the *Review & Herald*, their main church paper, calling him an apostate and a Judas Iscariot, as well as defaming him in other ways. Then the SDA General Conference president, G. I. Butler, tried to deny that SDAs had broken the truce, despite irrefutable evidence. Canright was forced to defend himself against the false charges, and from that time forward he was at war with the Adventist Church, which continued to treat him in ways that were totally dishonest, as has been repeatedly documented. But what SDA leaders did to Canright while he was alive was nothing compared to the total fabrication that Carrie Johnson and Arthur White would invent.

5. **Despite this mistreatment, Canright lived a life of great integrity and great productivity.** Not only was Canright offered highly attractive positions by nearly a dozen denominations when he left Adventism; he chose instead to help out a small, poor Baptist congregation in his hometown that couldn't even afford to pay him a decent salary, because they were hurting and needed his help. This shows the kind of man Canright really was, in contrast to the SDA accusations that he had left

them to seek fame and fortune. Ellen White specifically accused him of such prideful motives, supposedly based on "visions," without evidence, and she also prophesied that the Lord had shown her that Canright would die in obscurity.

SDAs tried to make a big deal of this prophecy, and Carrie Johnson, with the help of Arthur White, tried to claim this prophecy had been fulfilled. Ironically, and largely because of the Adventists' refusal to observe the truce they had agreed to with Canright, he probably became the best-known Adventist pastor to ever live. His books had a great influence throughout the twentieth century, continue to have great influence today, and have been translated worldwide into more languages than the books of any others who have exposed the evils of Ellen White and Adventism.

6. **The great contributions of Norman Douty, which SDAs attempted to discredit, need to be recognized.** From all the evidence I could gather, Norman Douty seems to have been a man of impeccable integrity and a careful and thorough researcher. His books are well written and well documented. Douty was a Christian gentleman and was probably kinder and more cordial in his relation to the dishonest and intimidating Arthur White, and to a lesser degree Carrie Johnson, than what was in his own best interest. It is understandable that a man of limited means would be hesitant to enter legal warfare against a whole denomination of attorneys, but right was so clearly on his side that I would have liked to see him try.

In any case, his book about Canright was spot-on, and had he not documented the critical information contained within the book, my own book, documenting the fraud and fabrication of White and Johnson, would have been impossible. So, Douty needs to be remembered and honored as a champion of truth and an author who presented D. M. Canright in a fair and professional manner. He was even quite restrained in his criticisms of Carrie Johnson, Arthur White, and the Seventh-day Adventist Church at large. Douty's should be celebrated, as it is in this book, to the same degree that Carrie and Arthur's dishonesty is appropriately shamed.

7. **The dishonesty, secrecy, and fraud of Carrie Johnson and Arthur White have never been exposed before.** The most significant revelation of this book is its documentation of the role that Arthur White played in the production and publication of Carrie Johnson's book and the fact that this hit piece was a complete fabrication that had no basis in fact. It is truly scandalous that these two individuals, colluding together, with the full enabling of the Review & Herald Publishing Association and the entire SDA Church, could commit such a fraud. Not only have these individuals not been exposed for their shameful acts, but Carrie has been celebrated as an SDA celebrity. Her words and behaviors were so vile that I'm sure the SDA Church will want to make things right now that the facts are out.

    And even though Arthur kept his role in this fiasco hidden, now that he has been exposed, it only seems right that the SDA Church will censure his actions, return the diary, and strip him of the false honors and recognition he received, when the reality was, he was a partner in evil at a level that even Adventism surely cannot ignore! How can this man be held up as the official historian of the SDA Church where EGW is concerned when he was clearly willing to do anything, no matter how unethical and immoral, to destroy an innocent, God-loving man? If Adventism does nothing about this, it truly speaks for itself!

8. **This fraud has been perpetuated by the entire SDA system without acknowledgement or accountability.** I'm sure that the facts presented in this book will cause any Adventist who cares about integrity (and there are many) to blush or at least feel a good deal of embarrassment for those SDAs who played a role in this fraud. Many in my reading group for this book,

on my Facebook thread, speculated that the church and most of its members will try to ignore the material or pretend that it never happened. If this occurs, it will only serve to cement the perception that SDAs are so willing to function as a cult that virtually nothing will wake them from their cultic brainwashing and slumber.

And even though Arthur White and Carrie Johnson are clearly most responsible for this reprehensible behavior, it cannot be ignored that the entire SDA system played a significant role as well. Not only did the R&H fail to vet the book but it was featured and promoted, along with its author, throughout the SDA camp meeting circuit, through all their PR avenues, and the book and its author are still being promoted by Adventism on the internet to this day. This is about as despicable as it gets. And it demonstrates the expediency by which Adventism tends to operate. They will utilize every dishonest means to promote every dishonest end that seems to benefit the false narrative of "God's Remnant Church"!

9. **The important contribution of Nancy Paige needs to be recognized and credited.** We have already noted the critical role that Norman Douty played in preserving the evidence of the fraud described in this book. But it is equally important to recognize the crucial role that Nancy Paige has played in her testimony and interview, which have identified the previously hidden part that Arthur White played in directing what would be written or not be written in Carrie Johnson's book. Had it not been for the input and promotion that he gave to Carrie in his influential position as head of the White Estate, her lies would have never been published. White came very close to pulling off his deception except for the witness of Nancy and her brother Ted, which you will read in appendixes 1 and 2.

Nancy is not only an eyewitness to what Arthur White did, but she has spent many years studying and researching what her grandmother did as well in the process of generating their slanderous fabrication. It is my hope and prayer that the Canright family will receive D. M. Canright's diary back from the White Estate, which wrongfully took it and has unlawfully withheld it from its rightful owners for so many years. I also pray that the White Estate will confess and apologize for the scandalous behavior of Arthur White on their behalf. This seems to be the least they should do. And to the degree that this occurs, we all have Nancy Paige to thank and acknowledge for it.

10. **The question remains, Why can't the Adventist Church do right?** Many years ago, I remember reading an article in *Spectrum* magazine, titled "Why Can't the Church Do Right?" The article rang true then concerning Adventism, and it applies even more today. In fact, now the same question can be asked of *Spectrum* itself, and *Adventist Today* (*AT*), as well. These two publications used to give me hope that the SDA Church might someday act with a modicum of honesty and integrity. But in recent decades both magazines, while claiming to be independent and objective, have badly compromised themselves. When my psychobiography of Ellen White was published at the end of 2020, it didn't take long for *Spectrum* to publish a review of the book, by Jonathan Butler, which was somewhat objective but also unduly harsh and inaccurate in numerous places.

I quickly wrote up a response, answering each point that Butler made in a concise manner, and sent it to *Spectrum*, expecting that they would have the editorial decency and integrity to publish it. But to my surprise the editor refused, claiming some shortage of available space in the journal. So, I requested that it at least be published on their website, which had no shortage of space. Again, *Spectrum* refused, showing that their initial excuse was just that: a feeble excuse! I mentioned to my friend Jonathan, who was part of the reading group that previewed my book, that *Spectrum* had refused to publish my response. He, too, seemed surprised and encouraged me to try the new editor who had just taken his position. So, I did, and got a similar kind of refusal. At this point I realized the problem was not with the editors, for they were simply acting as sycophants of the boards that controlled them.

It just so happens that both AAF (Adventist Forum, formerly the Association of Adventist Forums) and *Spectrum* currently have very influential board members who were former university presidents of mine and who happened to be the two most dishonest SDA administrators I'd ever known. Enough said! In the case of *AT*, I served on their editorial board for more than a decade, starting in the 1990s, but lost my enthusiasm for the publication when on three separate occasions I was asked to write very specific articles, for which I had carefully researched and documented and which had been accepted for publication, only to have them censored at the last minute by one of the university presidents referred to above. It just so happened that *AT* was housed on his campus at the time, and he couldn't handle the truth that was revealed in each of these articles.

More recently, long after leaving *AT*, the new, young CEO of the publication offered to interview me after my psychobiography came out, and the hour-long interview was published on the *AT* website. But the old guard quickly reared its ugly head, the CEO took tremendous flack and was soon gone, and the interview was taken down, with all existing copies of it suddenly disappearing! It will be interesting to see if *Spectrum* and *AT* are equally dishonest and suppressive where these new revelations of Arthur White are concerned. I expect the White Estate to be dishonest, as they certainly have been, regarding my psychobiography, as well as so many other things, but when *Spectrum* and *AT* follow suit, one has to seriously question whether there is any objective voice left in Adventism at all. This is why I have included appendixes 3 and 4 in this book.

To conclude, the White Estate fraud, concocted by Arthur White, with the help of his pawn, Carrie Johnson, represents one of the saddest chapters in all of Adventist history. In contrast to the way the church has trumpeted and promoted this fabricated hit piece, *I Was Canright's Secretary*, the book itself will go down as a testament to the desperate dishonesty Adventism has been willing to engage in, right up to its highest levels, to try to shield themselves from criticism, even if it meant destroying the sterling reputation of the great and courageous D. M. Canright! Will the Church and the White Estate be willing to take responsibility and accountability for their behavior? It remains to be seen, though it seems highly unlikely based on their history. God only knows, but at least He knows that it *will* happen someday, whether they want it to or not!

Appendix I

INTERVIEW WITH NANCY PAIGE

by Steve Daily
Friday, September 24, 2021, 1:56 p.m.

Steve Daily: How well did you know your grandma, Carrie Johnson, who authored *I Was Canright's Secretary*?

Nancy Paige: I was born in 1951. Dad was stationed in the Air Force in Salina, Kansas, in 1952–1954. His parents, Frank and Carrie Johnson, had lived in Niles, Michigan, since the 1930s. Dad attended academy at EMC/Andrews, graduated in 1939 at age twenty. I believe he had been kicked out at one point. He attended college at EMC from 1940 to 1944. Married mom in 1947. When Dad got out of the Air Force in 1954 and moved to Niles, he had his dental practice in Berrien Springs. We attended the Niles SDA church. My grandparents lived about three miles from the church but never attended church. After church we always went to the grandparents' house for lunch every Sabbath. As a five-year-old, I would ask them why they didn't go to church. They just said they were tired or sick.

It wasn't until about five years ago that my brother, who had asked a lot of questions, told me that in the 1950s Grandma and Grandpa had been the treasurers of the church. They were disfellowshipped for financial fraud.

(Side note: [Abraham] Terian had been the pastor of a church of an SDA church about thirty miles from Niles. Grandma and Grandpa attended that church for several years. I asked Terian if they had placed membership. He said they did not. I asked him if Grandma had confessed to him that they had been disfellowshipped. He said she had not. But, he said, he had always wondered why they had not placed membership. My brothers and I were at Grandma's nearly every day when they moved from Niles to Berrien Springs.)

In the summer we helped Grandpa in the garden. They lived in a big house across from the Dairy Queen. And they used the upstairs as a rental to foreign students at Andrews. The renters they had were from countries that did not have indoor water, toilets, bathtubs, and no kitchens. Every time renters moved, it was our job to clean it! There would be an inch of grease above the stove. The bathroom . . . poop on the floor; they used the toilet to wash their feet, peed in the bathtub, and they washed their clothes in it. Grandma had us paint her house, inside and out. We trimmed trees, pulled weeds, harvested the garden, and basically worked our little butts to pieces. Grandma was the president of the Women's Christian Temperance Union in Niles in the 1960s. She forced me and my brothers to memorize temperance stories, and we would compete with other kids. I remember when I was probably eleven or twelve, the day of the competition, I was sick with a temp of 102. I was miserable! She would not allow me to stay home.

I had to compete in front of several hundred people. I know I did not deserve to win! I could barely speak. But at the end of the competition, I had won the top medal! Grandma cheated! After they moved a little farther out, I did not see them as often. In 1969 I was engaged. Grandma invited me to go through her house and tell her what furniture, dishes, and other things that I might need. She wanted her only granddaughter to have what she needed to start her new home. But it was a lie! A classmate of mine, who was also going to get married, took a trailer to Grandma's house, gave her a sob story. Grandma gave her everything she had promised me, except a set of dishes.

Grandma fed us. Our parents had us on a two-meal-a-day program. One day she was feeding us soup. The can said bean and bacon. I had been taught that we should never touch a pig! I asked her why there was bacon in the soup. She said it was vegetarian bacon.

Grandma was not trustworthy. My mom and dad were liars! I figured it out when I was six years old. I remember I decided that from then on, I could not ever trust them. And in order to do anything a normal kid would do, I had to lie to my grandparents and parents.

Steve Daily: What was your opinion of your grandma's character, apart from the book?

Nancy Paige: Grandma was very narcissistic. Grandpa was her slave. He was not allowed to voice his opinion, so, he would go about his work and stay out of her reach. Grandma's brother, Uncle Fred, bought an acre plot of land. Grandma accused him of stealing it from her. I don't know why she would think he stole it from her, but she hated him to the death. When he died, his niece, who was his executor, refused to give anything to Grandma from his estate. The executor can only do what the deceased has stipulated in his will. The niece could not give Grandma what she demanded. Grandma died holding a grudge against the niece.

My mom was a sociopath. Her mother-in-law (Grandma) was her worst enemy. The two hated each other with a vengeance. Dad was caught between them. He followed his dad's footsteps. Dad would work three hours a day and disappear for the rest of the day. He stayed away from his mom and his wife. At the end of every spat, Grandma got her way, which galled Mom to no end. Grandma saw demons frequently. I have a story from her manuscript which she had hoped to be in her book. In it she claimed that there was a woman in the apartment below her who was demonic. She said she'd look down from her apartment into the apartment below and could hear the devil speaking. This story didn't make it to publication. I am sure Arthur White nixed it. That would've angered Grandma greatly. Fast-forward, in the mid-1970s (after Grandma's book had been published in 1971). Grandma and Grandpa called Dad and told him they had just been beaten up by a demon. It tried to strangle them; lifted up their bed, with them in it; and slammed it into the wall. The devil threatened them.

I never saw Grandma or Grandpa read the Bible. They never had a Bible anywhere in the house.

Steve Daily: Did Grandma ever meet Canright?

Nancy Paige: I always figured she was telling the truth, but I really could have cared less. When I first read the book at age twenty, it made me cringe. The preface was full of lies! It made no sense. In my thirties I found Canright's book, *Adventism Renounced*. By that time, I had been out of the church for several years. As I read his book, it just made sense! A few years later I found Douty's book, *The Case of D. M Canright*. The last two chapters are about Grandma, the unnamed secretary. Douty nailed her. The reason her name was not used in Douty's book was because Grandma forbade him not [*sic*] to quote her or use her name. After the book was published, the R&H threatened to sue Douty over the book, claiming that it libeled Carrie Johnson. So, instead of getting sued, he stopped publishing the book. In Douty's book, he outlined the lies Grandma used on the Canright family as she tried to get them to agree with her. And then there is the story about how she stole Canright's diary from his grandson.

I remember how excited she was after a trip to see the grandson. She had been trying to get that diary for a while, with no luck. When she finally got it, she had told the grandson that she wanted to borrow it. But instead, she gave it to Arthur. The reason I believe she gave it to him is because he was the secretary of the White Estate, and he was in charge of the EGW trustees. Who else would have locked up the diary in the White vault? In 2015 I started looking for clues about Grandma's book. It just didn't add up. However, it was quite daunting to find information. Who was Abraham Terian? He claimed he was her pastor. I was unaware that she and Grandpa were attending church. One day, in 2019, I told God that I would like to have Grandma's manuscript if there was one. Within two weeks my mom's sister-in-law (mom's second husband's sister) called me. Mom's husband had died a few weeks before. His sister knew nothing about Grandma, or her book. She urged me to go to her brother's home (shared with Mom but not in her name) and take anything I wanted. And she sent me a key. I hated the thought of even stepping in the house. But I felt God was pushing me.

Well, as I started looking through the books, there were two manuscripts of Grandma's book! But that was not all. There were notes of Mom's correspondence with people who had been trying to prove Grandma was legitimate. They were very upset with Douty. They said he was uneducated and had not done any research, which of course, rendered his book invalid.

Since I have continued my search in the last two years, I started to look for evidence that Grandma knew Canright when she was eighteen. With the help of a friend, we have found documentation that makes it very hard to believe she ever even met him.

For instance, Grandma claimed that she met Canright in W. E. Cornell's office at 9:30 a.m. on January 2, 1913, on the morning Canright's wife died at his home in North Park, just north of Grand Rapids. Grandma said Canright took a trolley from Grand Rapids to Battle Creek and was in Battle Creek by 9:00 a.m. Why would Canright have decided to leave his family that morning and go to Battle Creek in the middle of winter? According to a historic book about Battle Creek, in 1913 trolleys did not run in the winter. It also says that the rails for the trolley between Battle Creek and Grand Rapids had just been started in September of 1912. Battle Creek had a very large snowstorm in October or November in 1912, which shut down the transportation for a few weeks, which most likely stopped the trolley project. Even if the trolleys were running, it was a sixty-seven-mile ride from Grand Rapids to Battle Creek. Back then, on a clear day, the trip would have taken three hours. In the snow, it would have been hours longer. If Canright had been in Battle Creek by 9:00 a.m., he would have to be on the trolley, in the snow, by 5:00 a.m. He would have had to leave his house earlier than that. I don't know what hour his wife died, but I doubt he would have left his adult kids so he could go to Battle Creek. Grandma said Canright had rented a room in Battle Creek during the time he spent there. There is no evidence that he stayed in Battle Creek.

His family said that he never rented a room, nor did he spend time there. If he had gone to Battle Creek between January 2 and July or August 1913, his family said it might have been once or twice, for a single day or possibly for one night.

In March of 1913 there was what they called a snow hurricane. It closed down everything for weeks. Canright would not have been traveling to Battle Creek in March. And he was not living there at the time. Grandma called Canright "Jekyll and Hyde"! She said she was terrified because she believed her life was in danger. Did she have any documents with Canright's name and her name on them? No. Why? She had a very convenient alibi! Supposedly she had walked, in the heat, from the cafeteria to the Battle Creek Tabernacle to pay her tithe for the first time in her life. She had no lunch because she was broke. Her shoes had holes in the soles. She walked into the office at the tabernacle, where two of the staff were working. They began asking her questions about her job. She told them about Canright and how she believed he was dangerous. One man told her to go to the office where she had been working for Canright and gather up everything of his and bring it to them. She brought an armload to them. They said they would put them in a safe place. Two weeks later they called her back and asked her to take all of Canright's things and keep them herself. She hid them in the second story of her dad's house, six miles out of town. Does that make sense? If Canright was such a threat, why wouldn't the church have wanted to keep the evidence? Three months later, her dad's second story of his house was burned, and Canright's things were supposedly burned up. It is true that there was a fire in the second story of her dad's house. It was considered to be arson. Obviously, after her alibi had been destroyed and she could not prove that she had ever known, or worked for, Canright, the fire became her best explanation.

I believe Grandma did not know Canright at all. In her book she described him as dirty, unkempt, poorly dressed, shabby. She portrayed him as a delusional man who was sometimes normal, but he could quickly become angry, afraid, talking to himself, sad, mood swings . . . and on and on. If you read Canright's books and pay attention to the people who knew him, there is no way he was anything like Grandma described. He was educated. Grandma was barely out of high school. My brother believes she did not finish school. Canright was well traveled. He was an orator and debater. In Douty's book he lists the hundreds of trips Canright took all over the U.S. and Canada, helping churches grow, preaching, organizing the General Conference, fixing problems caused by the Whites.

Grandma said that a pastor of a Sunday church gave her Canright's book, *Adventism Renounced*, in 1910 or 1911. She took it home to her mom, who could not read. Her mom asked her to read it to her. After a chapter or two, her mom told her that the book was evil. Her mom had been getting pamphlets from the SDAs. Even though she could not read, she was certain that the Adventists were right. Grandma never read Canright's book! She said she could not understand it. Because of all her false ideas about Canright being so far off who he really was, I think it is safe to say she never met him. Because she lived in Battle Creek during a time when the Adventist leaders were trying to destroy him, it makes sense that Grandma would have heard the lies about him. She only lived there less than a year, just long enough to soak up the false stories.

Steve Daily: What evidence is there for the claims and accusations she made in the book?

Nancy Paige: The short answer is that there is no evidence! Not a photo, a document, letter, signature, or a book, NOTHING but her seventeen-to-eighteen-year-old imagination. No one has ever come forward to validate her story. No one in her family ever said anything that I know of. My parents were not even aware of her story until she contacted Arthur. In fact, Canright's family disagreed with every one of her claims. Douty's research is very well documented, thorough, and scholarly. Grandma's was hearsay, and much of the dialogue which she wrote was her guessing what Canright was thinking.

She would write a few sentences from the R&H, or from a letter, then make a remark about what Canright was thinking, and then continue with another quote with an ibid. She made it look like the whole thing was a quote. Also, I suspect that she copied some of Douty's research. When his book came out, she had access to it. It appears to me that she changed it to suit her narrative. This is another clue that makes me think she did not know Canright. Douty's book was published in 1964. Her's was not published until 1971. She and Grandpa just showed up at the home of Douty and his wife one Sabbath (before his book came out) and stayed with them for seven hours. He thought it was odd that she would drive several hours to see him, without calling, then spent seven hours trying to tap into his research. He sent her a letter outlining their conversation and asked permission to quote her. She refused. Douty did not use her comments, but he had other sources, namely, Canright's family.

Grandma visited all of the Canright family members numerous times. And each time she would tell them how she had been their dad/granddad's secretary. She never told them she was an SDA. She misrepresented herself to them. Grandma was very adept at schmoozing and buttering up people. She played the sweet, little old lady. And (what an idiot) she would tell them things about Canright that were made up by her, as if she knew him better than they did! Remember, even if she had been his secretary, she was only in Battle Creek for about eight months. She claimed she worked for him for seven months. But in her book, she admitted that Cornell (the owner of the "Cornell Business College") had to find other work for her to do because Canright would disappear for weeks at a time. Which is it? Either she worked for him for seven months, or she only saw him a couple of times . . . OR, more than likely, she lied about the whole thing!

There seems to be a thread that is incongruent through her claims. For instance, in the first chapter she said called herself "an advanced student at Cornell Business College." She had only enrolled in November of 1912, if we can believe her. How does one become an advanced student, who did not even finish high school, in two months? Then, in the same page she called herself "better qualified." Later in her book she called Cornell's Business College the "Battle Creek Business College." But just a year ago a friend found Cornell's obituary. His school was called the Cornell School of Shorthand.

My question is, Did Grandma actually attend that school? If so, was she trying to elevate herself to college level in order to make it appear that she was more educated? Or was this little change in the name of the short-hand school a suggestion of Arthur? In the first manuscript of her book, it is completely typed by Grandma. If she had been an advanced student, I would have expected it to be quite neat and tidy. But it looks like a child typed it. You see? Things just do not add up.

Steve Daily: When did she meet Arthur White, and under what circumstances?

Nancy Paige: It took years before I found the answer of this one. After Mom died in 2017, I received a box of documents. There is a page from the *Focus* magazine. It was published by Andrews University. There is a photo of Grandma standing next to Arthur, possibly in the White Estate at Andrews. The caption reads, "Mrs. Carrie Johnson, author of the forthcoming book, *I Was Canright's Secretary*, confers with Elder Arthur White on the manuscript at the Seminary." The article was written by Ray Dabrowski, Seminary Reporter.

This is the article:

> "I am a lost man! I am a lost man! She was a good wom-
> an" were often-repeated words of D. M. Canright concern-
> ing Ellen G. White. Mrs. Carrie Johnson, seventy-seven
> years old, recalled these words of her boss while visiting at
> the Seminary, November 17. Mrs. Johnson, author of the

forthcoming book, *I Was Canright's Secretary*, told the story of how she was instructed to keep secret what she "saw and heard" while working for this former minister of the SDA Church. It was in the year 1950, on finding that she had leukemia, she decided to reveal what she had kept in her heart for almost forty years. Elder Arthur L. White of the Ellen G. White Estate was the one to whom she disclosed her story. [Her secret conveniently made it impossible for anyone to know if it was true or not. Obviously, Arthur had never heard of her until she contacted him at Andrews.] TOGETHER they worked on the manuscript of the two-hundred-page book which will be published by the Review and Herald Publishing Association in the early part of 1971. Mrs. Johnson's association with Mr. Canright and his writings dated back to May 1912, when, after expressing the thought to another Protestant minister that she might join the SDA Church, she was advised to read Canright's book, *Adventism Renounced*, which he lent her. Later in the same year she met Canright (known to her as Mr. X) while working in the cafeteria of the Battle Creek Sanitarium. After attending a course in typing and shorthand with the financial backing of M. E. Cornell in a business school in Battle Creek, she was "offered a job" with Canright. Beginning January 2, 1913, Carrie Johnson (then Carrie Januszewski) worked for some six or seven months as a personal secretary to the "seedy and dejected" Canright. Her work included answering a multitude of letters addressed to him and recording his dictation of two books—one on the Lord's Day and the other against Ellen G. White. In mid-July 1913, after an incidental and providential "confession" about her work with Canright to George Israel and the treasurer of the Battle Creek Tabernacle, she stopped her "mysterious" job by removing all the notebooks. tracts, etc., from his office to the Tabernacle, and then to her home. Shortly afterwards these documents burned together with the house.

On her association with Canright who at one time "led thousands of men and women to baptism," Mrs. Johnson said, "He treated me as if I didn't exist." About Canright himself she said, "Poor man who sold his soul." Mrs. Johnson, who lives near Dowagiac, Michigan (twenty-five miles from Andrews), was leader of the Dorcas Federation in Western Michigan during the Second World War and contributed to sending some twenty thousand pounds of clothing abroad. For this and other social services she was twice honored by the Governor of Michigan.

This is Nancy again:

Paragraph 1: Canright denied that he ever said he was a lost man. Neither did he ever say he wished he could return to the SDA church. There is plenty of documentation to support his statement.

Paragraph 2: She has no documentation at all for her claim.

Paragraph 3: Arthur White had never heard of Carrie Shasky Johnson. She did not go by her Polish surname when she was in Battle Creek.

Paragraph 4: For Carrie to have met Canright on January 2, 1913, she would need to provide proof, which she did not have. The evidence against her is much more believable that her crazy claim that Canright left his wife, who had died that morning, and his family that morning; took a trolley in the snow; made it to Battle Creek in less time than any trolley could run on a good day; and end up in Cornell's office at 9:30 a.m. According to her own words in her book, she said that Canright went back home for three weeks in January. And she also admitted that Canright would be gone for many weeks during the time she claimed to have worked for him. She could not even keep her own story straight!

Paragraph 5: It is feasible that Carrie went to the tabernacle to pay her tithe? Yes. But it is not likely that she told them of her work with Canright. For one thing, she most likely never met Canright. If those men had believed her story, why didn't they keep all Canright's stuff? Isn't that sin? Carrie did not live with her abusive, probably alcoholic dad. She lived with a family in town. Why didn't she keep the evidence? Isn't it odd that the two men did not give Canright's letters, books, and documents to the church leaders? They were always looking for evidence that would condemn Canright.

Paragraph 6: Anyone who knew Canright knew he was a warm-hearted man. He loved God, his family, his church, and the Whites. He wept at Ellen's funeral. I have to laugh at her statement that Canright treated her as if she did not exist. The truth is, he never knew her. So yes, he ignored her! Her portrayal of him simply did not match his character. Arthur obviously had never heard of Carrie. She went after him. Why did she wait until she was sick to reach out to him? I believe it was money. She could not validate her story. Arthur saw an opportunity. If he had been honest, he would have verified her claims, but he didn't. And neither did the R&H. I have personal experiences with SDA editors. The ones I knew lied. They were not concerned about the truth. They just wanted the story that fit their ideology.

Steve Daily: What role did Arthur White play in helping your grandma write the book? And for how long did they work together?

Nancy Paige: Grandma contacted Arthur in 1950. As far as I know, that is when they began working on the book. Because of her leukemia, she would check herself in at the Battle Creek Sanitarium from time to time. Her doctor told her she would die of old age before leukemia would kill her. The first time I remember seeing Arthur, I was about five or six years old. He came to my grandparents' house in Niles, Michigan. He always wore a black suit, white shirt, and black tie. He was not interested in us kids. Kids were to be seen but not heard. He and Grandma would discuss her book for hours. At my age I did not know what they were doing, but it certainly was not a friendship.

When I was about ten, my grandparents moved to Berrien Springs. Arthur had a new, shiny, black Lincoln Continental with suicide doors. He'd arrive up their driveway, walk into the house, and sit at Grandma's kitchen table. He would point out her mistakes and tell her to "fix it." That book was largely his creation. Arthur visited Grandma whenever she was feeling well enough. Her book was supposed to have been published in 1970, but a letter from R&H apologized for taking so long to publish the book. They said they had too many other books ahead of her book. Didn't Arthur have clout? He had been working with Grandma for twenty years. What does that tell you about how important the book was to the church?

In 1971–1972, Arthur helped promote her around the Great Lakes on book tours, where she was interviewed by various church leaders. I have a cassette tape of Arthur interviewing Grandma about her book. He would give her leading questions. Sometimes he would tell her story and then say, "Isn't that right?" Of course, she would agree with him.

Douty and the unknown secretary of the EGW Estate

In chapter 14, page 159, in Douty's book, *The Case for D.M. Canright*, he received a letter from the Adventist leader whom he knew well because he [Douty] had worked with him on *Questions on Doctrines*. Douty's book was not yet finished. He knew that someone was going to write a book about the life of Canright. (In Douty's book he did not identify Arthur or Grandma by their names.) Page 159, paragraph 1:

> In the letter received on June 22, 1960, from the Ad-
> ventist leader who collaborated in the writing of *Questions
> on Doctrine,* he said that Canright's secretary, along with
> others, had taken an oath that he had often said, "I'm a lost
> man, I'm a lost man!" Although the name of the secretary

was withheld, I discovered her identity. When she began to correspond with Jess Canright (Canright's son) 1, and Clifton Dey (grandson), seeking information about D. M. Canright, they shared the letters with me. Then, on April 6, 1962, I wrote her, asking if we could meet to exchange notes on Canright. I had no reply, but on a Saturday (the Adventist Sabbath) she and her husband called at our home and remained about seven hours.

That is when Douty found out that Carrie Johnson was writing the book. Douty proved at least two dozen instances of "misstatements" by Carrie. Page 166, last paragraph:

> Yet this is the party cited by one of the authors of *Questions on Doctrine*, in order to discredit Canright. She [Carrie] told me in my home on May, 5, 1962 that this author had written her repeatedly for data on him [Canright]. When I informed him what I had discovered about her unreliability, he professed to have no need of any information she possessed! Documentation which I had sent him on the charges he had made, apart from her testimony, he ignored. Impartial men can judge the morality of such procedure.

In chapter 15, page 171, there is another mention of a different leading Adventist which Douty asked to help get the secretary of the White Publications to answer his request to restore Canright's diary to the Canright family. Douty had been asking Carrie and different people who worked in the White Estate to return the diary to its rightful owner, with no success.

Arthur White's characteristic lies and roundabouts were all over this thievery. He was the only one who would have hounded Grandma for data. It was up to him to get the book finished.

Steve Daily: Did Arthur White acknowledge his role with your grandma to Douty, the true Canright biographer?

Nancy Paige: I don't know if Arthur ever made any comments about Grandma's role with Douty. He certainly disliked Douty. He and Arthur had known each other for a number of years at Andrews. In his book, *Another Look at Seventh-day Adventism*, he mentioned Arthur White.

Douty had many angry Adventists after his books were published, but the Church threatened to sue him because they said he had "slandered" Carrie Johnson's character! His detail and huge documentation scared them to death! My parents had emails between themselves and a number of leading Adventists, which were full of lies about Douty. They said he was uneducated; had no understanding of Adventism; he had put this book out in just a few weeks; we don't need to worry about him!!

After Grandma visited him unannounced, that is when Douty found out that Carrie Johnson was writing the book, and that she had stolen the diary and given it to Arthur White. In chapter 15, page 171, Douty wrote:

> It was not until I had asked another leading Adventist to prod the memory of the Secretary of the White Publica-tions that I received a vaguely-worded letter from him, writ-ten Sept. 20, wherein he said: "I am not sure that my inter-pretation of certain matters accords entirely with yours."

Arthur White was accustomed to lying and telling half-truths. He was the secretary of the White Publications at that time. There was no other person who would have hounded Grandma for data. He also acknowledged that he gave her access to the EGW vault, which means she did not have to hunt for documentation. But from watching Arthur putting words in her mouth and quotes in her manuscript, and knowing she was a very poor writer and typist, she could not have written that book.

Side note: If you read Arthur's books, he always wrote in the third person. Talking about his grandmother, Arthur never spoke of her as "Grandmother." It was as if he was a reporter. On the other hand, Grandma wrote in first person. Publicly I don't believe he mentioned Douty. I could be wrong about that. However, Douty had tried to sue him, and if he had won, Arthur had a lot to lose. It wasn't until the 1990s that Adventists and formers began getting curious about Douty's books.

Steve Daily: Based on your study, your grandma's role in Adventism, and your own experience with the SDA Church, what is your opinion of Adventism, past and present?

Nancy Paige: This is a multiple answer.

My paternal grandparents' role in Adventism had a very negative effect. Before he met Grandma, Grandpa was the treasurer of the Southern Illinois Conference for two years, 1914–1915. They were training him to become a pastor. Grandma claimed that the Southern Illinois Conference's soon-to-be president chose her to be his secretary. She arrived at the Conference in Autumn of 1913 and supposedly started work in 1914.

Grandpa is noted in the 1914 and 1915 Adventist Yearbook. Grandma is not in any yearbook. But somehow, she met Grandpa there, so perhaps she was a secretary but not the Conference secretary at age 18 20. Why did Grandpa leave? Obviously, the Conference president thought he was worth training. I have very little information on Grandpa. Grandma was in charge.

My dad was born in 1919, in Kentucky, but by the 1930s they had moved to Niles, Michigan. They lived there for thirty years. They made the Niles church their home church. Somewhere between 1930 and the 1940s, they were asked to be church treasurers. At some point in the late '40s or early '50s, they stole money from a church charity. They [the church] could have had them arrested, but instead of causing front-page, embarrassing reports about the Adventist Church, they were disfellowshipped. My grandparents did not challenge it. From then on, they were never reinstated.

Grandma and Grandpa would take us kids to black camp meetings and churches several times a year, but they did not attend church regularly unless it was for promoting her book. They began to attend a church where no one knew them. But by that time, 1970 to about 1974 or 1975, Grandma's health was sporadic.

The foreword of her book sounds like Arthur. The editors could have written it, but they would have had to do some research. But since the editors admitted that they had not verified Grandma's book, I am doubtful that they would have written it. In the foreword there are nothing but lies.

My maternal grandparents were another part of the reality of the Adventist machine.

The Newbolds: Dudly Newbold (Mom's dad) became an Adventist in his early twenties. He was a pastor for many small churches, teacher at Broadview Academy, professor at EMC/Andrews University, and finally, he was a chaplain at the White Memorial. He attended Ellen White's funeral. I have a letter he sent his wife, telling her that he saw Canright at the funeral in Battle Creek.

How did my grandparents affect my opinion of Adventism? Well, for one thing, I only saw them four times in my life. They never liked me or my brothers. We rarely heard from them. Our cousins were favored because they were better than us. What caused the distance between Mom's parents and her brothers? Dudley Newbold believed sex was for procreation only. He had his own room, and Grandma Winona had her own room. All their married life there was only a little contact, just enough to have three kids.

Dudley beat his sons because he said they were stupid. Both sons were brilliant. Mom was the baby, the apple of Dudley's eye. Winona was always jealous of her little daughter. My younger brother took Mom for a weekend in Southern California. He took her to all the places she had lived, the place where Dad proposed, and he took her boating. All weekend he tried to get her to explain why she never loved us. What kind of childhood did she have? She ignored him. Mom would never answer our questions, and the fact that she was very promiscuous at age sixteen, we believe Dudley molested her.

I have hundreds of letters between my parents from 1944 through 1947. Both of them were having flings. Even when they were engaged, they continued their extracurricular pals and gals. We also know that after they were married, over the years, they were cheating on each other. It was not just them. They named names of other couples who, in their opinion, were far worse than them, which was unusual for college students.

This cheating was passed down to my older brother. At Andrews Academy he and his best friend would drive to Chicago to find sex orgies, alcohol, and drugs. His friend was the youngest son of one of the top seminary professors. In the 1960s through the 1970s, my dad belonged to an Adventist men's group who met every week or two to share the latest UFO sightings. Dad taped the meetings, and when he got home, he would play them late at night when we were supposed to be asleep. The voice of Satan was petrifying. These men would claim that they had ridden in UFOs. It affected my older brother. To this day he believes in UFOs.

While these stories are pretty wild, this is very common in Adventism. Compared with Ellen and the founding fathers, the UFOs seem to fit the narrative of the *Great Controversy*. It was the battle between Jesus and Satan, according to Ellen and others. In their minds Satan might have won the arm wrestling. No one could claim they were saved. Jesus had not finished the work of salvation. Obey Ellen or get the mark of the beast.

How does a church based on false doctrines get away with it? GOOD WORKS!! Appearances were their salvation. How often have we heard Adventists tell us that if God was not with them, how could they have members worldwide? How could they have hospitals, churches, schools, universities, missions . . . if God wasn't protecting them?

My answer is from Jesus's Sermon on the Mount:

> "Beware of false prophets. They come to you in sheep's clothing, but inwardly they are ravenous wolves. By their fruit you will recognize them. Are grapes gathered from thornbushes, or figs from thistles? Likewise, every good tree bears good fruit, but a bad tree bears bad fruit. A good tree cannot bear bad fruit, and a bad tree cannot bear good fruit. Every tree that does not bear good fruit is cut down

and thrown into the fire. So then, by their fruit you will recognize them.

"Not everyone who says to Me, 'Lord, Lord,' will enter the kingdom of heaven, but only he who does the will of My Father in heaven. Many will say to Me on that day, 'Lord, Lord, did we not prophesy in Your name, and in Your name drive out demons and perform many miracles?'

"Then I will tell them plainly, 'I never knew you; depart from Me, you workers of lawlessness!

"Therefore everyone who hears these words of Mine and acts on them is like a wise man who built his house on the rock. The rain fell, the torrents raged, and the winds blew and beat against that house; yet it did not fall, because its foundation was on the rock.

"But everyone who hears these words of Mine and does not act on them is like a foolish man who built his house on sand. The rain fell, the torrents raged, and the winds blew and beat against that house, and it fell–and great was its collapse!"

THE AUTHORITY OF JESUS

28 When Jesus had finished saying these things, the crowds were astonished at His teaching, 29 because He taught as one who had authority, and not as their scribes. (Matthew 7:15–27)

Nancy Paige
Tue, Nov 15, 2:07 PM (2022)
To me

GRANDMA

These are questions you might want to include. But I leave it to you. Do whatever you wish.

Why had she never heard of Ellen?

How could she live in Battle Creek and attend church at the Tabernacle but not heard of the Whites? or Willy?

How could she have been baptized and not have heard about Ellen?

How could she have actually seen Canright at the cafeteria, filthy and unkempt?

In her book she says that after she stopped working for Canright she worked for another man in Battle Creek. Within a few weeks she was traveling to the Southern Illinois Conference to be the new Conference president's secretary. There is no evidence that she worked for him.

If she had known Canright why didn't she have accurate information about him when she visited his family?

How could she write a book about Canright without ever reading his book? If she had, she would have known who the Whites were.

How did she find out about Canright's other books and pamphlets?—after 50 years? Maybe Arthur?

Why didn't Carrie ever talk about God or speak of the Bible?

Why didn't her siblings ever say anything about Canright's books and pamphlets? (Several of them lived in Battle Creek in 1912 and 1913.) She claimed the documents were burned up in her dad's second-story house. Wouldn't it be part of family lore?

Why did she accept the lies in the foreword on her book?

How could an eighteen-year-old girl have been so afraid of a man who was a decent, godly preacher?

There are no actual documents of Canright going crazy or being angry. In her book, Arthur supplied affidavits from his friends who claimed they knew Canright intimately, and who remembered that he had said he was a lost man. These letters were written in the 1940s and '50s. Why didn't they come forward sooner? Perhaps it was because he was too young to know them until the 1940s and 1950s?

Carrie lived in Battle Creek no more than ten months and in that time she lost her mother, she says she got a job and started education, maybe less than two months before she met D. M., and yet she was the top student?

Then she met D. M. January 2, 1913, the day his wife died. Then her teacher asked her to work for D. M. I need to see if I can find out if school started up on January 2 in 1913.

When Mom wanted to republish the book she had to proofread it. Why would it need to be proof read again? Why couldn't she just copy the first book?

The story of Canright started when Carrie was not even born yet! She could not have known the details unless Arthur gave them to her. I don't think her siblings and parents passed it down to her; however, she wrote her book as if she had been there.

It is very odd that Carrie never mentioned EGW in her book.

Ellen died in 1915. Carrie was in Battle Creek in 1912–1913. After all those people at the Tabernacle who knew the Whites, why didn't Carrie know that the church was based on EGW?

Carrie blamed Canright for treating her so badly that she was afraid he would kill her.

Appendix II

STATEMENT FROM TED JOHNSON

Friday, October 21, 2022, 11:45 a.m.

Steve, I remember Authur White coming to my grandmother's house and working on her book for hours at the kitchen table he always wore a black suit black tie white shirt drove a Lincoln and was always sweating, as you have revealed, the Whites are less than straight forward. I can only imagine what he was doing there trying to influence the content as she wrote it. The church used her book for many years until it become clear her book was just a hit job to discredit Canright.

It is clear that the foundation of the SDA church has crumbled, the book by my grandma was a hit job. When she was in Battle Creek around 1918 there were stories circulating similar to her portrayal of Canwright, he was a huge threat to the church when grandma was researching her book. I drove her to Canrights grave cleaned the weeds around it, penciled in the writing on the tombstone and took the picture of her standing by his grave. As she worked on this book it was an enterprise mentality, she viewed it as her mission to provide the church with what they needed to discredit

Canright, thus the story developed with Arthur White making sure it had the needed ingredients to do the job. This is way past anything I thought the book would come to, I didnt take it serious. And as for Douty he spent a lot of time with grandma trying to get the truth from her and almost did, but didn't come away with the one thing he needed, her admission that it was a lie. He almost got that but didn't. Steve this isn't easy to admit but you have been so relentless on your texts, I'm here to tell you I almost deleted this because it feels like I'm betraying my family but you and Nancy have this correct, Carrie Johnson's book shouldn't be taken seriously, I never have. And I helped her in her research while writing it, at the time, my belief was she took the rumors that were circulating in Battle Creek and ran with it.

Ted Johnson

Nancy Paige: **Ted Johnson** Thank you for explaining what you saw.

Our grandparents and parents were the ones who betrayed us, not the other way. It took us a long time to understand that none of their craziness, cruelty and lies, had anything to do with us.

I am so proud of you! And I love you so much!!

RESPONSE TO JONATHAN BUTLER'S REVIEW OF MY PSYCHOBIOGRAPHY

I have included this response to Jonathan Butler's review of my psychobiography, *Ellen G. White A Psychobiography,* published in *Spectrum* (vol. 49, issue 2; June 30, 2021), because two different editors of *Spectrum* refused to publish my response, claiming it was a matter of available space, but they also refused to publish it on their website, demonstrating this was only an excuse. My belief is that both of these editors were simply the sycophants of their board. I believe this because both the AAF and *Spectrum* boards include two very influential former SDA university presidents whom I worked under and who just happened to be the two most dishonest administrators I have ever known. It's not surprising to me that they have no interest in journalistic integrity, for it's my clear understanding that they've been involved in censoring my writings in the past.[1]

A Response to Jonathan Butler's Review of
My Book, *Ellen G. White: A Psychobiography*
By Steve Daily (8/18/2021; edited slightly for this book)

I want to thank my friend Jonathan for taking the time to write his lengthy review of my book, *Ellen G. White: A Psychobiography*, and to thank *Spectrum* for publishing the review. My general feeling was that Jonathan tried to be fair and balanced in his observations, and I am grateful that he found the book valuable ("I found the book well worth reading") and an important addition to his personal library ("I am pleased to add Steve Daily's biography to my bookshelf") As far as Jonathan's criticisms are concerned, they are certainly worth responding to, and I will try to do so in a systematic way, first by listing the criticism in italics, and then by providing my response.

1. An unexplained change of historical perspective: Jonathan is quick to acknowledge, in his review, the contribution that my previous historical works on Ellen White have made. However, he prefers the "old Daily" to the "new Daily," and can't resist stating that "there is no ignoring that White had her problems, while speculating, "but Daily comes across as having his own problems." In his recent letter to the editor of *Adventist Today* concerning my book, Jonathan makes the same criticism: Daily seems to do an unjustified about-face that reveals more of him than of Ellen White. I responded to Jonathan's criticism then and I will repeat it here, to explain my change in position. Jonathan implies that I basically knew everything about Ellen White 40 years ago, that I write about her in my latest book. This is certainly not the case. I learned a great deal more about Ellen in my research for this latest book than I ever knew before. I can say that each of my historical books has been focused on very specific themes. My MA thesis in history (1982) was focused on the 1919 Bible Conference as it related to the higher criticism debate in 19th century America and showed how both liberal and conservative scholars in the church colluded to hide the findings from this conference, bury the transcripts in the GC archives and see them lost and forgotten for more than 50 years. Instead of dealing with the truth about Ellen White, and sharing it with the church, both groups, for different reasons, chose their own self-benefit over truth. So, what should have been addressed more than 100 years ago remains unaddressed because of academic dishonesty.

My doctoral dissertation at Claremont (1985), *The Irony of Adventism*, explored the paradox of Ellen White's strong female leadership role in the church, compared with her opposition to women's ordination and fairly regressive attitudes and writings towards women in general. My Ph.D. dissertation (1991) focused on Adventist adolescents and addiction in the light of the Valuegenesis research. My two books on Ellen White and Adventist history, *The Prophetic Rift* I & II (2008, 2009), looked at why Adventists related to Ellen White in the context of Old Testament prophecy when they should have evaluated her as a post–New Testament professed prophet. And *Ellen White: A Psychobiography* (2020) embraces the challenge of exploring whether the repeated accusations of fraud and pathology against Ellen White leveled by various individuals during and after her lifetime stand up under historical and psychological scrutiny. As I focused on this last question, the evidence I researched forced me to conclude that Ellen was guilty of both fraud and pathology, although I am certainly not convinced that my expressed conclusions are the only legitimate explanations or interpretations for her words and actions. It is not my intention to be dogmatic, but to provide an alternative view that has not been expressed by a previous historian, psychologist, and theologian.

"He writes with a historian's version of Tourette's Syndrome:" Jonathan has a great dry wit, a fantastic sense of humor, which I have greatly appreciated over the years. My first response was to crack up when reading these words, because I enjoy laughing at myself. And I am still assuming that Jonathan is using this analogy with tongue in cheek, rather than trying to make a serious point. But, if he is actually trying to make a serious analogy between the documented arguments in my book and Tourette's Syndrome, I would have to seriously question his psychological expertise. Tourette's Syndrome is a neurological disorder that involves involuntary tics, or the blurting out of irrational random words, such as swear words. People are certainly free to disagree with my interpretation of the evidence provided in my book, which is why I included 326 extensive endnotes, so that the reader can explore the evidence and draw their own conclusions. But to mischaracterize the points I make as random or irrational, when they are

clearly reasonable and source documented, is hardly responsible or insightful. I do not lightly, or irrationally, observe that the source documentation leaves me with no choice but to conclude that Ellen was guilty at times of being a "liar, hypocrite, narcissist, con artist, fraud and yes, even demonstrating the behavior of a high functioning sociopath."

It seems to me that for Jonathan to suggest that there are not clear patterns of deception and fraud (including gross plagiarism), which he did in his letter to *AT*, "Fraud is a Bridge too far," demands the kind of questions I asked him in response to that letter and am still asking in the wake of his review. Is extensive plagiarism, stealing the works of others, and then claiming that those materials were given you by God, while you insist on the highest royalties for such books and become a millionaire (in our money today), FRAUD? Is claiming that your writings (which were not hers) were not of human origin, but only "what God has opened before me in vision" (5 T, 67), and that anyone who did not heed them would have the "Holy Spirit" "shut away" from their "soul" (1 SM, 46), FRAUD? How about attributing all kinds of false and unhealthy views that clearly came from 19th century authors to God, that involved racism, God hating various children, masturbation causing a number of serious diseases and premature death, etc., etc., FRAUD?

Is repeatedly, over many years, insisting that God gave you visions showing his coming was so soon that Adventists were to sell their homes and give the money to "the cause" (while you keep your possessions/home), and then, when the prophecy fails, and people who believed are destitute, ignoring them, while you get rich, FRAUD? Is a lifetime pattern of claiming to have visions, which demonize those who question your authority and literally see many of them lost for eternity, while you have the testimonies about them read publicly in church, and fail to follow Matthew 18 by going to the person individually, and many of these "visions" are proven to be false, FRAUD? (I lost track of how many lives she destroyed in this manner.) How about claiming to have a vision that exonerates your husband, who was guilty of embezzling at least $250,000 in our money today, from church institutions (p. 245), only to have the "vision" proven wrong, after your husband's death, and the money returned to its rightful source; is this FRAUD? I find it hard to believe that Jonathan is familiar with all this material (and much more) and still insists that none of it constitutes FRAUD! My own belief is that many Adventist historians, who have written extensively on Ellen White, have not, and do not want to fully acknowledge the dark side of the prophetess because of how it may reflect on their jobs, careers, reputations, the SDA Church, or their social relationships related to the church.

A lack of historical even-handedness: I would be the first to admit that *Ellen G. White: A Psychobiography* is not an even-handed attempt to present a balanced history of the life of the professed messenger of God, and I made this clear from the outset (as seen in my introduction). Obviously, my book was not intended to be a hagiography; way too much literature of that kind has been written about Ellen White, and I emphasized, in my book, that it was not a biography, but an attempt to do what I stated above. To see if the accusations of pathology and fraud leveled against Ellen White during and after her lifetime would stand up to historical and psychological scrutiny. There are many different kinds of psychobiographies, and I am not at all sure that Jonathan is an authority on this kind of literature. Clearly, my book is not empathetic to Ellen, because I have become convinced that she deliberately hurt a lot of people for her own benefit, largely got away with it, and has generally had the church defend and cover for her in a manner that is very wrong. My Facebook page is filled with regular testimonies of how people have had their lives damaged and negatively affected by Ellen White quotes. Jonathan compares my treatment of Mrs. White to how I might have treated his maternal grandmother (Granny), who was diagnosed with schizoid affective disorder. He notes how she had many good traits, but on occasion could also be violent, throwing a hot pie at his mother and scalding her arm, and on another occasion irrationally demolishing their new kitchen counter with an axe. Jonathan suggests with regard to his grandma that I would obsess over the negatives and ignore the positives in her life.

And this may well be, if his grandmother had founded and claimed to be the God-appointed last-day visionary of a major religious movement.

My belief is that Ellen attempted to deceive not only the acclaimed 20 million–plus SDAs living today, but two or three times that many who have left the church, to say nothing of millions more who have died, related to the faith. I don't think Jonathan's "granny" was quite this influential. A better comparison might be made to Bernie Madoff. If Bernie had died at the age of 70, before his exposure and arrest, there probably would have been many accolades given at his funeral, as there were for Sister White. He may have been remembered as a kind and sweet old man who helped many people and was a successful CEO for decades and even chairman of the NASDAQ stock exchange, a very prestigious position. All of this, before the house of cards collapsed. To treat Jonathan as he has treated me, he would want to write a psychobiography of Madoff spending much more time focusing on the positive accomplishments of this famous man that dominated the majority of his life than what was exposed in the last decade of his life. Obviously, such a book would be ridiculous, and until Ellen White is cleared of the gross deception that is source documented in my book, I am not interested in trying to make her look good or contributing to the positive myths that historians have created. No, Ellen was not a Margaret Rowan, or the author of the greatest Ponzi scheme in history, but I am convinced she could have been the most successful plagiarist of all time, and the most deceptive, fraudulent religious icon, or prophet/founder, of any major religious movement.

"Daily exaggerates her wealth": Jonathan makes this simple statement without refuting the evidence in my book. He offers no footnotes to support his position. The reader is simply expected to believe that what he says is true, because he has written it. I'm sure he would have been scathing in his criticism if I had taken the same approach in my work. One of the things I definitely learned in writing this last book on Ellen was the degree to which she and James financially exploited and took advantage of church members. I was frankly quite appalled to see the way they peddled dress patterns, Bible charts, hymnals, other books and trinkets, to the tune of making more than a million dollars in our money today, in addition to their salaries and her very generous royalties (more than 3 million in our money)

which Ellen demanded for her books. They also designed schemes to use the church to buy back old books that they personally owned to make substantial profits, and to use Ellen's "visions" to motivate believers to buy these books and to give sacrificially to "the cause" which clearly correlated with their great increase in wealth. It is no coincidence that James was accused of financial mismanagement and embezzlement throughout his years in leadership, that Ellen supported him with "visions," and that these charges were proven true after his death. Simply saying, "Daily exaggerates her wealth" without providing any evidence to substantiate this charge is neither scholarly nor convincing.

A lack of new material: Jonathan implied there was little new from a historical perspective in the book. This may have been true for Jonathan, although if that is the case, he seems to have covered well for Ellen over the years, which has been a real problem for Adventist historians. And it certainly is not true for the vast majority of Adventists. More than 99% of those I've heard from, who have read the book, have been amazed and even astounded by the revelations which were new to them. I have even had highly placed leaders in the denomination who have spent much of their lives in administrative positions, come to me confidentially and admit that they feel completely duped by what Ellen did and how the church has handled it. Largely, I have written my book for the general church membership, those who have left the church, outsiders, and people like this, more than for Adventist historians in general, who have already proven themselves to be quite untrustworthy when it really comes to telling the truth about Ellen White.

As I learned a lot that was new in researching this last book, I'm sure that others, who have not studied Ellen White much of their lives, have plenty to learn as well. What ultimately motivated me to consider writing another book about Ellen, I had no such intentions after leaving Adventism in 2010, was the hacking of the White Estate in 2012. When I saw some of the damning quotes and diary entries from Ellen that were released on to the internet in 2014 (included in my book), which were kept from me, and other scholars, when I did research in the White vaults, it certainly produced a sense of betrayal and reinforced my concerns about the dishonesty of the White Estate and the denomination in general. It didn't help that soon thereafter, the White Estate claimed that they were releasing these materials for all to see in honor of the 100th anniversary of Ellen White's death. Please don't insult our intelligence with this kind of a claim after so many years of dishonesty and cover-up.

"He often . . . does diagnose White": Jonathan accuses me of diagnosing Ellen, but anyone who reads the book carefully will note that I simply presented the historical evidence, as well as diagnostic criteria, and insisted that the readers draw their own conclusions. I specifically made it a focus in the book to point out that it is not ethical to diagnose individuals who are not your clients, dead or alive, and certainly not in a public manner without their written permission. Rather than wandering into a field where he is not trained (psychology), I would have expected Jonathan to find fault with my historical arguments or source documentation, if it was to be found. But, instead of taking issue with my specific arguments and source documentation, Jonathan makes broad generalizations without support for his claims. I know it is the Adventist way to try to discredit the messenger when anyone dares to expose the prophet, and there have already been several establishment book reviews aimed at accomplishing this purpose, but I don't see Jonathan as an apologist historian, and am frankly disappointed that his criticisms seem so unsubstantiated and, from my perspective, rather easily dismissed. This is not to say that I don't value the opinions of my friend Jonathan. I very much appreciate him serving as part of my reader's group for the book and giving me valuable input, some of which I definitely applied.

An all or nothing approach can't be justified: Jonathan finishes his piece by writing "All or nothing? Give me another choice." I want to emphasize again, as I did in the book, that I do not personally take an all-or-nothing approach to Ellen White in my thinking about her. Clearly, she did accomplish remarkable things in her lifetime, especially given her circumstances and lack of education. There is no question that many people have benefitted from the Seventh-day Adventist Church and its various institutions, and the same can be said for Mormonism. God is great at overcoming evil with good (Romans 12:21). But that does not make Joseph Smith a true prophet, and I think most Adventists would be repulsed by such a claim. Ellen's claims to being the last-day messenger of God, must be judged on their own merits or lack thereof. And her claims are about as absolute and ambitious as any person could make. I will not list them all here, but I have listed 25 of them in my presentation to the Christian Scholars Forum, May 22, 2021, available on YouTube, and on my Facebook page. Just to give a few examples:

> **5T p. 67** "In these letters which I write, in the testimonies I bear, I am presenting to you that which the Lord has presented to me. I do not write one article in the paper expressing merely my own ideas. They are what God has opened before me in vision—the precious rays of light shining from the throne."

> **1 SM p. 46** "If they [her testimonies] are not heeded, the Holy Spirit is shut away from the soul."

> **5T p. 661** "When I send you a testimony of warning and reproof, many of you declare it to be merely the opinion of Sister White. You have thereby insulted the spirit of God."

> **3 SM pp. 32, 52** "The testimonies never contradict His Word . . . There is one straight train of truth, without one heretical sentence, in that which I have written."

> **5T p. 674** "If you lose confidence in the testimonies you will drift from Bible truth."

> **4T p. 230** "God does nothing in partnership with Satan. My work for the past thirty years bears the stamp of God or the stamp of the enemy. There is no halfway in the matter."

> **2 SM p.63** "You think individuals have prejudiced my mind. If I am in this state, I am not fitted to be entrusted with the work of God."

Ellen took an all-or-nothing approach to her own writings, and if the reader is to take her claims seriously, we too, are forced to evaluate her, and investigate her claims for what she stated them to be. According to her, she either got her "visions" from God or the devil. They go hand in hand with the Bible. They are not influenced or prejudiced by human thought, and if they are not heeded, the Holy Spirit is shut away from the soul and insulted. In simple terms, this is blasphemy. And when we compare these overwhelming claims to the source-documented evidence of errors, deception, plagiarism, and fraud in the name of God, you end up with my book. All or nothing is not Jonathan's choice, it is not my choice, but it is Ellen's choice and demand, and it is left with us to deal with it.

RESPONSE TO WHITE ESTATE REVIEW OF MY PSYCHOBIOGRAPHY

The following response to Alberto Timm's review of my book *Ellen G. White: A Psychobiography* has been included as an appendix in this book because of the White Estate's refusal to publish my response on their website:

I only had the opportunity to meet and briefly chat with Arthur White once in my life, but his presentations and demeanor clearly struck me as the personification of a good Adventist Pharisee. He carried himself as the chosen one. The only living descendant of the true prophet, the last day Messenger of God, to be entrusted with overseeing her writings and her estate. He seemed to answer questions with a smug smile, which said, "If only you had known her as I did." Arthur was an expert at hagiography, although he claimed to write about his grandmother with the pure objectivity of a trained historian (the problem was, he was not at all objective, nor was he a trained historian). But when I met him, I never dreamed that I would someday have the responsibility (with Nancy Paige) of exposing him as a total fraud and a dishonest thief. I bring this up in the context of my response to Albert Timm, because he is currently a director of the White Estate, who writes with the sanctimonious air of Arthur White, but has never acknowledged the grievous sins of Arthur and the White Estate against D. M. Canright, exposed in this book, nor has he returned the stolen diary of Canright to its rightful owner, the Canright family.

Now let's consider Timm's review of my book.[1] For starters, he can't get through the first paragraph of his review without lying about me. He claims that I was fired from my Celebration Center pastorate, when the truth was that I left the Adventist ministry to pastor Kingdom Life Fellowship (DBA-Graceway Community Church) in 2010, and when the conference president, who had openly lied to our congregation about my status, confirmed that I had left, he then terminated me from employment with the SDA Church. *Fired* gives a false impression to the reader, when the truth was that I left the Adventist ministry on my own. But that is just one of many inaccuracies of which Timm is guilty.

Timm writes, "Although she had every opportunity to realize great personal gain from her prominent position, at the expense of the Adventist church, this was never a temptation for Ellen White." Again, Timm either doesn't know Adventist history, or he is deliberately lying. I would have to suspect the latter, given that Timm claims to have read the documentation in my psychobiography and never refutes it. Let the reader decide. In 1849, Ellen wrote the following words to her Adventist followers, claiming to have received them in "vision" from God. "I saw it was the will of God that the saints should cut loose from every encumbrance, dispose of their houses and lands before the time of trouble comes, and make a covenant with God by sacrifice. I saw they should sell if they laid their property on the altar and earnestly inquired for duty" (Ellen White, *To Those Who Are Receiving the Seal of the Living God*, January 31, 1849).

The "altar," or "the cause," as she put it in other "testimonies," happened to be the coffers of the movement, which were controlled by James and Ellen White at the time. And Ellen made it clear from other "visions" that the time of trouble was upon them, so they needed to act quickly. The next year she identified the time of trouble as beginning within a few months, when even the Advent believers would have their probation closed. "Some of us have had time to get the truth, and to advance step by step, and every step we have taken has given us strength to take the next. But now time is almost finished, and what we have been years learning, they will have to learn in a few months." (*Early Writings*, p. 67).

She makes it clear, in the context, that she is talking about the time of trouble starting and the probation of every Adventist closing in a few months (a false prophecy, to be sure), but also a strong motivation for believers to comply with her financial "vision" to sell their homes and properties. The evidence is strong that the Whites received these funds and misused these funds to their own benefit, and there is no evidence in any case that the Whites refunded the monies when the prophesies proved to be false.

J. B. Bezzo, a sincere follower of Ellen who had been entrusted with the responsibility of publishing these "testimonies" and sending them out to believers, became so disillusioned with what the Whites were doing that he resigned his position and quoted and applied the following words of James White to Ellen's "visions": "I must and will be free of the responsibility of publishing and sending out Ellen's visions to open the hearts of the Br'n to give, and then have that means used so that it would be better to use her own words 'Sunk in the bottom of the Ocean'" (*Messenger of Truth* 1 no. 3, October 19, 1854, p. 2). Timm knows, if he read my psychobiography, that even before the 1849 fleecing of the flock by EGW that she was guilty of several other cases of manipulation and financial exploitation, showing that this was a pattern in her early ministry that followed her the rest of her life (pp. 120–27).

He also knows that while the Whites were calling others to sacrifice their all for "the cause," they themselves were becoming wealthier by the year from the funds that were coming in. The Whites moved from total poverty when they were married in 1845, to buying their first home in 1852, during the same period when she counseled others, through her "visions" to sell theirs. It was quite a large home that had room for their printing work and for some Adventist workers to live with them. But when a larger building was purchased for publishing and the workers, the Whites kept the first home for themselves. The Whites owned at least 10 homes that we have records of, and many of them at the same time, including vacation homes. They were extremely wealthy compared to the average person in their day, and this was particularly true when compared with their fellow church members.

The Whites took denominational salaries while Ellen fought for the highest royalties she could get on her books (while other authors were reducing or donating their royalties to help the struggling Press). And more importantly they exploited church members financially in a host of different documented ways; including selling trinkets, charts, dress patterns, hymnals (they made the equivalent of a million dollars in our money today just from selling hymnals to the churches). They scammed church members into buying their old, outdated books, that they personally profited from, through "visions." They lived a lavish lifestyle that was generally unknown to most church members. And this is just the tip of the iceberg. What was most serious was that James embezzled the equivalent of $400,000–$500,000 in our money today from two different church institutions, refused to pay it back until he was on his deathbed, then paid it back but demanded the money back after he recovered (and this was supported by Ellen's "visions"). All of this was proven by Dr. J. H. Kellogg, who forced the Whites and the church to pay the money back after James was dead.

Timm knows all of this, and yet he falsely claims that Ellen was never "tempted" to use her position to exploit others or for financial gain. If he is right, it is only because Ellen did it on her own, without having to be tempted! The false image of the Whites, and especially Ellen, that Timm and so many other SDAs have perpetrated, flies in the face of the documented life patterns of dishonesty, fraud, plagiarism, false condemnation, heresy, financial exploitation, hypocrisy, alcoholism, and blasphemy, which are source documented in the psychobiography and which Timm failed to refute in his review. Timm claims that EGW did not "accumulate significant personal wealth," but that she invested the money she made in Adventism "back into the movement." This is simply false. Timm knows it is false, based on the documentation in my book, which is why they failed to print my response to his review. Ellen lived lavishly, with a huge personal staff, and even defied her own testimonies with regard to debt and how she made her will.

Timm states, "Christ was constantly uplifted in the actions and writings of Ellen White." If Christ was uplifted by the actions described above, I would hate to see what it means to betray Christ! And anyone who has the slightest knowledge of the New Covenant Gospel, and familiarity with Ellen's writings, would never make the claim that Timm does above. Much of her life Ellen generated a false religion of fear. She continued to set specific times for Christ's return for seven full years after the Millerite disappointment, and repeatedly condemned the entire world during this period, claiming they were lost, except for her small little group of approximately 150, that she also instilled with fear through her false prophecies about the terrible time of trouble. Beyond this, Ellen was responsible for the worst kind of legalism and perfectionism in Adventist theology, attributing all of it to "visions" from God.

Again, Timm is either grossly ignorant of Adventist history, or he is deliberately lying. For the first forty-four years of her prophetic ministry in Adventism, Ellen emphasized a religion of fear, guilt, legalism, and perfectionism which she claimed was based on "visions" from God. Again, from these false "visions," which she asserted would be fulfilled in the near future, she wrote that once "God ceases his work in the heavenly sanctuary" for us, we will have to live with "no mediator between God and man (*Early Writings*, 48; see also 279–85). She warned of a "terrible time of trouble" that would follow this judgment and that "every sin must be overcome before it starts" (*Testimonies for the Church*, vol. 2, pp. 430–31). I sat in SDA classes in Sabbath School and church school, which emphasized these points, and saw the fear, guilt, and hopelessness that resulted from these false teachings in my own life and the lives of my fellow students. For years as a psychologist in Adventism, I had adult clients who suffered from these false teachings from their youth. It is tragic to see how many suicides have been traced to her teachings.

To say that Ellen "constantly" uplifted Christ is a joke. She uplifted the "Shut Door" close of probation, the Sabbath, the law, and the false SDA

Remnant doctrine, but not Christ. In fact, she argued against the assurance of salvation in Christ, and this was well after she supposedly found the gospel for herself in 1888. Notice the following two quotes from *Christ's Object Lessons*, published in 1900: "Those who accept the Saviour, however sincere their conversion, should never be taught to say or to feel that they are saved" (*Christ's Object Lessons*, 155). The White Estate to this day tries to say she was only speaking against "once saved always saved," but this isn't true. And the way they define this term is "believing you are saved if you don't keep the law." This of course would disqualify everyone from salvation.

Ellen also continued to emphasize perfectionism, long after the 1888 Conference on righteousness by faith. She claimed that perfectionism was necessary in order for Christ to return. "When the character of Christ shall be perfectly reproduced in His people, then He will come to claim them as His own" (*COL* p. 69). Ellen showed complete confusion about these matters while attributing contradictory "visions" to God. It is Ellen who writes on the one hand, based on "visions," that "true Christians will never indulge the thought that they are sinless" (*Sanctified Life*, 7), while, on the other hand, insisting that "sinlessness" is a state that God expects us to attain in this life (*SDA Bible Commentary* 6:1118). Moreover, Ellen demonstrates a tragic misunderstanding of the character of God in the way she raised her own children and wrote about children in general.

To her own son, Willie, she wrote, "You must not get angry, but remember the Lord could not love you if you should be naughty." And "The Lord loves those little children who try to do right and he has promised that they shall be in his kingdom, but wicked, naughty children, God does not love" (EGW to Willie White, Letter 10, 1859; Letter 3, 1860). She was even more specific and condemning (as well as blasphemous) in the general "testimony" she directed at the children of the Church. "God hates unruly children who manifest passion and evil tempers, etc. He cannot save them in the time of trouble" (EGW *Manuscript 1:* 1854). For a "prophet" to claim that God hates children of any kind, when Jesus said, "Suffer the little children to come unto me, and forbid them not, for such is the kingdom of heaven" (Matthew 19:14), is hardly what I would call "lifting up Jesus," much less "constantly uplifting Jesus."

Then, Timm quotes EGW's 1901 statement to the General Conference, asking them to use the Bible as their authority, rather than her writings or prophetic writings. What he doesn't say is that she made these comments at a time when Anna Rice Phillips was getting a significant following among SDA leadership as a true prophet, and Ellen had done everything possible to put Phillips down, so now she de-emphasizes the prophetic, in contrast to what she had done with her own writings her entire life. (See the following quotes)

Ellen White's Claims for Her Writings

5T p. 67 "In these letters which I write, in the testimonies I bear, I am presenting to you that which the Lord has presented to me. I do not write one article in the paper expressing merely my own ideas. They are what God has opened before me in vision—the precious rays of light shining from the throne."

1 SM p. 46 "If they [her testimonies] are not heeded, the Holy Spirit is shut away from the soul."

5t p. 661 "When I send you a testimony of warning and reproof, many of you declare it to be merely the opinion of Sister White. You have thereby insulted the spirit of God."

3 SM pp. 32, 52 "The testimonies never contradict His Word . . . There is one straight train of truth, without one heretical sentence, in that which I have written."

5T p. 674 "If you lose confidence in the testimonies you will drift from Bible truth."

4T p. 230 "God does nothing in partnership with Satan. My work for the past thirty years bears the stamp of God or the stamp of the enemy. There is no halfway in the matter."

2 SM p.63 "You think individuals have prejudiced my mind. If I am in this state, I am not fitted to be entrusted with the work of God."

8T, p. 298 "We must follow the directions given through the Spirit of Prophecy [Mrs. White's writings]. . . . God has spoken to us through His Word. He has spoken to us through the Testimonies to the church and through the books that have helped to make plain our present duty and the position that we should now occupy."

3 SM, p. 30 "The Holy Ghost is the Author of the Scriptures and of the Spirit of Prophecy."

Battle Creek Letters, p. 74 "God has outlined His plan in His Word, and in the Testimonies He has sent to His people."

5T, p. 217 "The testimonies are unread and unappreciated. God has spoken to you. Light has been shining from His word and from the testimonies, and both have been slighted and disregarded.

Vol. 5T, p. 66 "If you lessen the confidence of God's people in the testimonies he has sent them, you are rebelling against God as certainly as were Korah, Dathan and Abirum."

5T, p. 98 "If you lose confidence in the testimonies you will drift away from Bible truth."

Letter H-339, Dec. 26, 1904 "These books contain clear, straight, unalterable truth and they should certainly be appreciated. The instruction they contain is not of human production."

1 SM, p. 35, 1906 "These books, giving the instruction that the Lord has given me during the last sixty years, contain light from heaven, and will bear the test of investigation."

5T, p. 63 "When I went to Colorado, I wrote many pages to be read at your camp meeting . . . God was speaking through clay. You might say this communication was only a letter. Yes, it was a letter, but prompted by the Spirit of God, to bring before your minds things that had been shown me.

Letter 90, 1906 "How many have read carefully *Patriarchs and Prophets*, *The Great Controversy*, and *The Desire of Ages*? I wish all to understand that my confidence in the light that God has given stands firm, because I know that the Holy Spirit's power magnified the truth, and made it honorable, saying: 'This is the way, walk ye in it.' In my books, the truth is stated, barricaded by a 'Thus saith the Lord.' The Holy Spirit traced these truths upon my heart and mind as indelibly as the law was traced by the finger of God, upon the tables of stone."

Letter 50, 1906 "I am thankful that the instruction contained in my books establishes present truth for this time. These books were written under the demonstration of the Holy Spirit."

***Review and Herald*, May 25, 1905** "After the passing of the time in 1844 we searched for the truth as for hidden treasure. I met with the brethren, and we studied and prayed earnestly . . . When they came to the point in their study where they said, 'We can do nothing more,' the Spirit of the Lord would come upon me. I would be taken off in vision, and a clear explanation of the passages we had been studying would be given me, with instruction as to how we were to labor and teach effectively. Thus light was given that helped us to understand the scriptures in regard to Christ, his mission, and his priesthood. A line of truth extending from that time to the time when we shall enter the city of God, was made plain to me, and I gave to others the instruction that the Lord had given me."

Ms. 22, 1890. (VSS 398.2) "In the night season the Lord gives me instruction in symbols, and then explains their meaning. He gives me the word, and I dare not refuse to give it to the people."

Letter 280, 1906, p. 4 "It has been presented to me that, so far as possible, I am to impart instruction in the language of the Scriptures; for there are those whose spiritual discernment is confused, and when their errors are reproved, they will misinterpret and misapply what I might write, and thus make of none-effect the words of warning that the Lord sends. He desires that the messages He sends shall be recognized as the words of eternal truth."

Letter 25b, 1895, pp. 1-3, to Brother and Sister Hare, April 1895 "I beg of you for Christ's sake to consider what I say; for I say it not of myself. It is the word of God to you."

Spiritual Gifts, **vol. 2, pp. 292, 293** "At times I am carried far ahead into the future and shown what is to take place. Then again, I am shown things as they have occurred in the past. After I come out of vision I do not at once remember all that I have seen, and the matter is not so clear before me until I write, then the scene rises before me as was presented in vision, and I can write with freedom. Sometimes the things which I have seen are hid from me after I come out of vision, and I cannot call them to mind until I am brought before a company where that vision applies, then the things which I have seen come to my mind with force. I am just as dependent upon the Spirit of the Lord in relating or writing a vision, as in having the vision. It is impossible for me to call up things which have been shown me unless the Lord brings them before me at the time that He is pleased to have me relate or write them."

2 SM, p. 388 "I testify the things which I have seen, the things which I have heard, the things which my hands have handled of the Word of life. And this testimony I know to be of the Father and the Son. We have seen and do testify that the power of the Holy Ghost has accompanied the presentation of the truth, warning with pen and voice, and giving the messages in their order. To deny this work would be to deny the Holy Ghost, and would place us in that company who have departed from the faith, giving heed to seducing spirits."

4T pp.147-148 (1876) 5T 661 "In ancient times God spoke to men by the mouth of prophets and apostles. In these days He speaks to them by the testimonies of His Spirit. There was never a time when God instructed His people more earnestly than He instructs them now concerning His will and the course that He would have them pursue."

Does Timm really want us to take him seriously when he ignores these kinds of claims attributed to God? He makes a big deal of the fact that I changed my views of Ellen White over the years. But this is easily explained: the more I learned about her, the less inclined I was to believe the false things I was taught about her in Adventism. Timm quotes a number of my statements in his review, but he never comments on the strong source documentation that they were based on, much less refutes that source documentation. He takes me to task for not quoting SDA apologists, and thereby providing a more balanced picture of White. But my psychobiography was focused on one question that I emphasized from the beginning.

My research question was, "Will the abundant accusations of fraud and pathology leveled against EGW, both during and after her lifetime, stand up to historical and psychological scrutiny." And I had to conclude, after doing my research, that they clearly did! Timm makes some nitpicky points about certain inaccuracies in my book, at the end of his review, but none of these address the major thesis of the psychobiography that he totally fails to refute, based on the extensive source documentation that it contains. He suggests that I wrote out of frustration and bitterness, though I stated the opposite, and then warned against ascribing false motives to people. He wrote about a population positively affected by EGW's writings, while making no mention of the many more who have suffered both psychologically and theologically from her false claims and teachings attributed to God.

Timm closes, with these words:

> Since we cannot read the heart of another, let us beware of ascribing wrong motives to any man, lest we find ourselves involved in guilt similar to that of Miriam—condemning those whom the Lord is teaching and guiding—and thus bring upon ourselves the rebuke of God.

> Throughout the book there is a pervasive negative and even destructive spirit toward White that is voiced in a rather tendentious and biased manner. Even conflicting ideas and concepts should be discussed without becoming so judgmental. Unfortunately, this is not the case in this book. Furthermore, there is a repeated pattern discernable where historical evidence is not accurately dealt with or opposing opinions and alternative interpretations are not fairly presented or even listed. This is not good scholarship and puts a dark shadow over the credibility of the entire book. In this sense the book by Steve Daily reflects not the truth about Ellen White, but rather the truthiness of his thinking.

> I have spent my life trying to seek the truth and to speak the truth, as I am led by God's Spirit, and this has stepped on SDA toes many times throughout my career in Adventism, and after. I have seen a great deal of corruption and dishon-

esty in Adventist leadership, and that applies to the White Estate as well. I am not at all impressed with Timm's sanctimonious tone in his review, nor with his failure to address the overwhelming source documentation in my book, which clearly demonstrates that Ellen White had a major problem with dishonesty, fraud, and pathology. This current book on the White Estate demonstrates that her grandson Arthur did not fall far from the tree. What Arthur and the White Estate did to D. M. Canright was completely immoral and inexcusable. If Timm is not willing to admit that, and to try to make it right, I think that speaks for itself, regardless of his pious and Pharisaical words!

NOTES

PREFACE

1. Arthur L. White, *Ellen G. White: The Early Years: 1827–1862*, vol. 1 (n.p.: Ellen G. White Estate, 1985), xiv. This book is available for online view on the Ellen G. White Estate website, at https://ellenwhite.org/publications/13313.

INTRODUCTION: THE GOD FRAUD

1. Carrie Johnson, *I Was Canright's Secretary* (Washington, DC: Review and Herald, 1971), 7.
2. Ellen Harmon's first vision (in the Adventist movement) occurred in December of 1844, it was initially published by Enoch Jacobs in the Cincinnati Day-Star on January 24, 1846, then republished by James White on April 6, 1846, in the broadside "To the Little Remnant Scattered Abroad." On May 30, 1847, it was published yet again by James White in the pamphlet A Word to the Little Flock (available in facsimile form at any Adventist Book Center).

CHAPTER 1: THE BIG LIE

1. Adolf Hitler, *Mein Kampf* (1939), trans. James Murphy, chap. 2, available online at Project Gutenberg Australia, https://gutenberg.net.au/ebooks02/0200601h.html, updated February 2016.
2. Edwin L. James, Hitler's Biggest Lie," *New York Times*, April 11, 1943, available online at https://www.nytimes.com/1943/04/11/archives/hitlers-biggest-lie-the-fuehrers-lies-are-legion-and-colossal-his.html. James wrote, "The Fuehrer's lies are legion and colossal; his biggest is that Germany was not beaten in 1918. Hitler may be planning to use that lie again. Whatever Hitler's purpose in taking up the lie of an undefeated Germany, the record of the col-

lapse is clear.' See also Jeffrey Herf, *The Jewish Enemy: Nazi Propaganda During World War II and the Holocaust* (Cambridge, MA: Harvard University Press, 2006), 211; and Jeffrey Herf "The Jewish War: Goebbels and the Antisemitic Campaigns of the Nazi Propaganda Ministry," *Holocaust and Genocide Studies* 19 (2005): 51–80.

3. Ashe Schow, "Harry Reid Is Proud He Lied About Mitt Romney's Taxes," *Washington Examiner*, March 31, 2015. https://www.washingtonexaminer.com/harry-reid-is-proud-he-lied-about-mitt-romneys-taxes.

4. See Nia Prater and Benjamin Hart, "A Newly Elected Congressman Seems to Have Made Up His Whole Life Story," *Intelligencer* (blog), December 20, 2022, https://nymag.com/intelligencer/2022/12/congressman-george-santos-seems-to-have-invented-life-story.html.

5. *Testimonies* 5:67.

6. *SM* 1:46.

7. *SM* 1:27.

8. *SM* 3:32, 52.

9. Following is a list of works debunking and exposing the errors of Ellen G. White. This list is not at all exhaustive but represents a good sample of some of the most notable works over a significant span, twenty works selected over eighteen decades of Adventism.

   Miles Grant, *An Examination of Mrs. Ellen White's Visions* (Boston: Advent Christian Publication Society, 1877). Although this book was not published until the 1870s, it documents a good deal of the dishonesty and fraud perpetrated by Ellen White and her claimed "visions" from the very beginning of the Seventh-day Adventist movement, including the accusations of Ellen's best friend at the time, Lucinda Burdick.

   H. S. Case and C. P. Russell, *The Messenger of Truth*, first published in June 1853. This periodical documents both the visionary fraud and the financial fraud perpetrated by the Whites from the 1840s on. The two major reasons given why these ministers left the church in 1853 were the fraudulent visions of Ellen White and the financial embezzlement of James White, supported by his wife.

   B. F. Snook and Wm. H. Brinkerhoff, *The Visions of E. G. White Not of God* (Cedar Rapids, IA: Cedar Valley Times Book and Job Printers, 1866), available online from the Internet Archive at archive.org.

   Sydney Cleveland, *White Washed: Uncovering the Myths of Ellen G. White*, originally published in 1868, republished with a foreword by Dale Ratzlaff (Glendale, AZ: Life Assurance Ministries, 2000).

   D. M. Canright, *Seventh-day Adventism Renounced* (Cincinnati: Standard, 1889).

   Dr. Charles Stewart, Charles E. Stewart to Ellen White, May 8, 1907, published as *A Response to an Urgent Testimony from Mrs. Ellen G. White.* Also known in Adventist history as "The Blue Book," It is available online at https://ellenwhite.org/media/document/1023.

   Albion Fox Ballenger, *Cast Out for the Cross of Christ* (1909) (available for free and published in full on the internet; see the Ellen White Investigation website at https://nonsda.org/egw/ballenger/castout.htm.

Aaron Nyman, Astounding Errors: The Prophetic Message of the Seventh-day Adventists and the Chronology of Pastor Charles T. Russell in the Light of History and Bible Knowledge (Chicago: Nyo Vecko-Posten, 1914). The book is available for free online; it was republished in 2014. See the Ellen White Investigation website, https://www.nonsda.org/egw/ae/index.html.

D. M. Canright, *Life of Mrs. E. G. White, Seventh-day Adventist Prophet: Her False Claims Refuted* (Cincinnati: Standard, 1919). Transcripts of the 1919 Bible Conference revealed the major doubts and concerns that SDA Church leaders had about Ellen White's claims and how the church had understood her inspiration. Their conclusions were so controversial that the transcripts were buried in the General Conference archives, forgotten, lost, and not rediscovered until 1974.

R. A Greive, *In Chains to Seventh-day Adventism* (Brisbane, AU: Gospel Book Depot, 1958).

W. W. Fletcher, *The Reasons for My Faith* (Sydney: William Brooks, 1932).

Ronald Numbers, PhD, *Prophetess of Health: Ellen G. White and the Origins of Adventist Health Reform* (Knoxville: University of Tennessee Press, 1976, 1992; Grand Rapids: Eerdmans, 2008).

Desmond Ford, PhD, *Daniel 8:14, The Day of Atonement, and the Investigative Judgment* (Casselberry, FL: Evangelion, 1980). Ford demonstrated in this work that the SDA doctrine of the Heavenly Sanctuary and the Investigative Judgment were unbiblical and based on Ellen White rather than on Scripture. He was defrocked and fired by the church for providing this revelation.

Robert Brinsmead, *Judged by the Gospel* (Fallbrook, CA: Verdict, 1980).

Walter Rea, *The White Lie* (Turlock, CA: M&R, 1982).

Fred Veltman PhD, *The Desire of Ages Project* (summary available in *Ministry* magazine, December 1990, available online at https://www.ministrymagazine.org/archive/1990/12/). This work found that 31 percent of White's writing were plagiarized and that her content in general was derived rather than original.

Dirk Anderson, *White Out* (Glendale, AZ: Life Assurance Ministries, 2001); and *More Than a Profit, Less Than a Prophet* (n.p.: 2008; ISBN-10: 0981860621); see also his *Prophet or Pretender? Does Ellen White Pass the Biblical Tests of a Prophet?* (n.p.: 2021) (available online along with the rest of his amazing online ministry at www.ellenwhite.info).

Dale Ratzlaff, *The Cultic Doctrine of Seventh-day Adventism* (Glendale, AZ: Life Assurance Ministries, 2003).

Dr. Jack Gent, *The Desirer of Wages* (2010), Published by Robert Sanders and available on the website Truth or Fables (http://www.truthorfables.com/The_Desirer_of_Wages.htm) and referenced in Dirk Anderson, "Ellen G. White: Prophet or Profit?," Ellen White Investigation, last updated January 222, https://nonsda.org/egw/egw25.shtml.

Steve Daily PhD, *Ellen G. White A Psychobiography* (Conneaut Lake, PA: Page, 2020). This is the most comprehensive and highly documented work that exposes the fraud and dishonesty of Ellen G. White.

10. Don Neufeld, ed. *Seventh-day Adventist Encyclopedia* (Washington DC: Review & Herald, 1966), s.v. "Ellen G. White Estate Incorporated," 373.

11. William C. White and Dores E. Robinson, *The Work of Mrs. E. G. White's Editors* (St. Helena, CA: Elmshaven Office, August 30, 1933), 3. Other claims for her writings made by Ellen White, in addition to those given in the text, include the following:

"If you lose confidence in the testimonies, you will drift away from Bible truth." *Testimonies* 5:674.

"God does nothing in partnership with Satan. My work for the past thirty years bears the stamp of God or the stamp of the enemy. There is no halfway in the matter." *Testimonies* 4:230

"You think individuals have prejudiced my mind. If I am in this state, I am not fitted to be entrusted with the work of God." *SM* 2:63.

"We must follow the directions given through the Spirit of Prophecy [Mrs. White's writings]. . . . God has spoken to us through His Word. He has spoken to us through the Testimonies to the church and through the books that have helped to make plain our present duty and the position that we should now occupy." *Testimonies* 8:298.

"The Holy Ghost is the Author of the Scriptures and of the Spirit of Prophecy." *SM* 3:30.

"God has outlined His plan in His Word, and in the Testimonies He has sent to His people." Ellen White, Battle Creek Letters (Loma Linda University Library: Heritage Research Center), 74.

"The testimonies are unread and unappreciated. God has spoken to you. Light has been shining from His word and from the testimonies, and both have been slighted and disregarded. *Testimonies* 5:217.

"If you lessen the confidence of God's people in the testimonies he has sent them, you are rebelling against God as certainly as were Korah, Dathan and Abirum." *Testimonies* 5:66.

"These books contain clear, straight, unalterable truth and they should certainly be appreciated. The instruction they contain is not of human production." Letter H-339, December 26, 1904 (Loma Linda University Library: Heritage Research Center)

"These books, giving the instruction that the Lord has given me during the last sixty years, contain light from heaven, and will bear the test of investigation." *SM* 1:35.

"When I went to Colorado, I wrote many pages to be read at your camp meeting . . . God was speaking through clay. You might say this communication was only a letter. Yes, it was a letter, but prompted by the Spirit of God, to bring before your minds things that had been shown me. *Testimonies* 5:63

"How many have read carefully *Patriarchs and Prophets*, *The Great Controversy*, and *The Desire of Ages*? I wish all to understand that my confidence in the light that God has given stands firm, because I know that the Holy Spirit's power magnified the truth, and made it honorable, saying: 'This is the way, walk ye in it.' In my books, the truth is stated, barricaded by a 'Thus saith the Lord.' The Holy Spirit traced these truths upon my heart and mind as indelibly as the law was traced by the finger of God, upon the tables of stone." Letter 90, 1906

"I am thankful that the instruction contained in my books establishes present truth for this time. These books were written under the demonstration of the Holy Spirit." Letter to evangelist W. W. Simpson, 1906.

"After the passing of the time in 1844 we searched for the truth as for hidden treasure. I met with the brethren, and we studied and prayed earnestly." *Review and Herald*, May 25, 1905.

"When they came to the point in their study where they said, 'We can do nothing more,' the Spirit of the Lord would come upon me. I would be taken off in vision, and a clear explanation of the passages we had been studying would be given me, with instruction as to how we were to labor and teach effectively. Thus light was given that helped us to understand the scriptures in regard to Christ, his mission, and his priesthood. A line of truth extending from that time to the time when we shall enter the city of God, was made plain to me, and I gave to others the instruction that the Lord had given me." Letter 50, 1906.

"In the night season the Lord gives me instruction in symbols, and then explains their meaning. He gives me the word, and I dare not refuse to give it to the people." Ellen White, Manuscript 22, 1890 (vss 398.2); (Loma Linda University Library: Heritage Research Center).

"It has been presented to me that, so far as possible, I am to impart instruction in the language of the Scriptures; for there are those whose spiritual discernment is confused, and when their errors are reproved, they will misinterpret and misapply what I might write, and thus make of none-effect the words of warning that the Lord sends. He desires that the messages He sends shall be recognized as the words of eternal truth." Letter 280, 1906, p. 4.

"I beg of you for Christ's sake to consider what I say; for I say it not of myself. It is the word of God to you." Letter 25b, to Brother and Sister Hare, April, 1895, pp. 1–3.

"At times I am carried far ahead into the future and shown what is to take place. Then again I am shown things as they have occurred in the past. After I come out of vision I do not at once remember all that I have seen, and the matter is not so clear before me until I write, then the scene rises before me as was presented in vision, and I can write with freedom. Sometimes the things which I have seen are hid from me after I come out of vision, and I cannot call them to mind until I am brought before a company where that vision applies, then the things which I have seen come to my mind with force. I am just as dependent upon the Spirit of the Lord in relating or writing a vision, as in having the vision. It is impossible for me to call up things which have been shown me unless the Lord brings them before me at the time that He is pleased to have me relate or write them." *Ellen White, Spiritual Gifts, volume 2 (Washington D. C.: Review and Herald Publishing Association, 1945). Pp. 292-293.*

"I testify the things which I have seen, the things which I have heard, the things which my hands have handled of the Word of life. And this testimony I know to be of the Father and the Son. We have seen and do testify that the power of the Holy Ghost has accompanied the presentation of the truth, warning with pen and voice, and giving the messages in their order. To deny this work would be to deny the Holy Ghost, and would place us in that company who have departed from the faith, giving heed to seducing spirits." *SM* 2:388.

"In ancient times God spoke to men by the mouth of prophets and apostles. In these days He speaks to them by the testimonies of His Spirit. There was never a time when God instructed His people more earnestly than He instructs them now concerning His will and the course that He would have them pursue." *Testimonies* 4:147–48; 5:661.

12. With regard to her being expelled from the Methodist Church, see Steve Daily, *Ellen G. White: A Psychobiography* (Conneaut Lake, PA: Page 2020), 20–23; with regard to her injury at the age of nine, see 37–39. With regard to her being rejected by Israel Dammon, whom she worked with, for fraudulent "visions," see Dirk Anderson, "Why Did Israel Dammon Reject Ellen White?," Ellen White Investigation, last edited July 5, 20233, https://nonsda.org/egw/egw44.shtml. With regard to her "visions" in the Millerite Movement, see Donald Edward Casebolt, *Child of the Apocalypse: Ellen G. White* (n.p.: Wipf & Stock, 2021); and Casebolt, *Father Miller's Daughter: Ellen G. White* (n.p.: Wipf & Stock, 2022).

13. Ellen White, relating her conversation with Joseph Turner in a letter she wrote in 1847, quoted in A. L. White, Ellen G. White and the Shut Door Question, Letter 3, Loma Linda University SDA Heritage Room, pp. 49–51.

14. James White documented that he and their entire small group, which included Ellen Harmon, opposed and condemned marriage in a letter he wrote to Enoch Jacobs that was published in their newspaper, the *Day Star Extra*, in 1845. This letter included condemnation of a specific couple who chose to be married against the group's advice and called marriage "a wile of the devil." James White, "Letter to Brother Jacobs," published in the *Day Star Extra*, October 11, 1845, available from Loma Linda University Library SDA Heritage Room. Regarding the strange circumstances of James and Ellen getting married despite their previous condemnation of marriage, see Ellen White's Manuscript Releases, 5:208; and Ellen White's Manuscript 131 (1906), Loma Linda University Library: Heritage Research Center.

15. L. S. Burdick letter, quoted in Miles Grant, "An Examination of Mrs. Ellen White's Visions," published by the Advent Christian Publication Society, Boston, Massachusetts, 1877, online at Ellen White Investigation, https://www.nonsda.org/egw/miles_grant.shtml.

16. Burdick, quoted in Grant.

17. Ellen White Manuscript 11 (1850), Loma Linda University Library Heritage Room, 3–4.

18. Ellen G. White, *Early Writings of Ellen G. White*, 2nd ed., ed. Gerald E. Green (n.p.: CreateSpace, 2013), 64, 67.

19. Ellen White's Camden, New York, vision on June 21, 1851, quoted in D. M. Canwright, *Life of Ellen White*, rev. ed. (n.p.: Lulu Enterprises, 2005), 66–67

20. Examples of Ellen's denials that she had ever had a vision teaching the shut door, include the following references:

    Ellen White, "I never have stated or written that the world was doomed or damned. I never have under any circumstances used this language to anyone, however sinful. I have ever had messages of reproof for those who used these harsh expressions."–Letter 2, 1874. Quoted in Selected Messages, book 1, p. 74.

    R&H Aug 19,1851 p.13 Door now opened. When Ellen saw that her Time of Trouble prophecy had failed by the summer of 1851 she attempted to deny the repeated shut door claims she had attributed to God.

    "With my brethren and sisters, after the time passed in 1844, I did believe that no more sinners would be converted. But I never had a vision that no more sinners would be converted." *SM* 1:74 (1874).

"For a time after the disappointment in 1844, I did hold, in common with the advent body, that the door of mercy was then forever closed to the world. This position was taken before my first vision was given me. It was the light given me of God that corrected our error, and enabled us to see the true position." Ellen White 1883 statement, quoted in Arthur L White, *Ellen White and the Shut Door Question* (White Estate 1982, revised),.13

These denials clearly conflicted with the actual "visions" of the shut door that she claimed to have received from God between 1844 and 1851.

21. Two of the most racist testimonies Ellen attributed to God were the following:

"But if there was one sin above another which called for the destruction of the race by the flood, it was the base crime of amalgamation of man and beast which defaced the image of GOD, and caused confusion everywhere." Ellen G. White, *Spiritual Gifts*, vols. 3 and 4 (Hagerstown, MD: Review and Herald, 1945), 3:64.

"Every species of animal which GOD had created were preserved in the ark. The confused species which GOD did not create, which were the result of amalgamation, were destroyed by the flood. Since the flood there has been amalgamation of man and beast, as may be seen in the almost endless varieties of species of animals, and in certain races of men." White, 3:75).

In Ellen's day, it was commonly believed that it was possible for a human and certain animals to sexually produce offspring. This can be found in various sources, including the book of Jasher (published in 1840), which falsely claimed to be a lost book of the Bible, and from which Ellen was known to have plagiarized. These "testimonies" caused both vindication and outrage in the church of Ellen's day. They were presumed vindication for the overt racists in Adventism, who believed that the "negro" race was somehow less than human. And they caused outrage for those who were sure that God would reveal nothing of the kind to the "prophetess." We need to re-member that these supposed revelations were written during the time of the Civil War, when pas-sions about the "negro" race were at a pinnacle. The ongoing controversy over these published statements escalated to the point where the Whites and other leaders recognized that something had to be done to save the "prophet's" status. So, in 1868, Uriah Smith, the *Review* editor, took it upon himself to write a booklet attempting to defend Ellen and defuse the situation. It was titled *The Visions of Mrs. E. G. White, A Manifestation of Spiritual Gifts According to the Scripture*. In it, Smith presumed to answer the critical question, Which races are the product of amalgamation between man and beast? To cleverly protect Ellen from the growing charges of "racism against negroes," Smith claimed that the races Ellen was referring to as having come from the union of man and beast were "such cases as the wild Bushmen of Africa, some tribes of the Hottentots, and perhaps the Digger Indians of our own country." How Smith thought he could isolate such a practice to such groups over centuries is purely laughable; and the practice itself, is laughable to those who have any knowledge of genetics today. Both Ellen, and Smith were ignorantly trying to defend something that was a genetic impossibility. If Ellen had truly seen these things in vision, she could have spoken for herself, but because the position she had taken was really impossible to justify, the Whites were glad for Uriah Smith to try to bail them out of their bind. James White carefully examined Smith's proposed solution and then embraced it by taking two thousand of Smith's books to sell at camp meeting as a solution to their problem. He promoted the sale of the books in advance in the church paper, the *Review & Herald*:

The Association has just published a pamphlet entitled, "The Visions of Mrs. E.G. White, A Manifestation of Spiritual Gifts According to the Scriptures." It is written by the editor of the *Review*. While carefully reading the manuscript, I felt grateful to God that our people could have this able defense of those views they so much love and prize, which others despise and oppose. (James White, *Review & Herald,* August 15, 1868)

James and Ellen, along with Uriah Smith, W. C. White (Ellen's son), and D. D. Robinson (Ellen's secretary), all were fully convinced that Ellen's statements described the interbreeding of human beings with animals or beasts. It was not until 1947, after Dr. Frank Marsh tried to convince an Adventist panel exploring these statements that such an interpretation was impossible based on biological science, that the church and the White Estate, along with apologists such as Francis Nichol, tried to deny the obvious meaning of what Ellen had written. Marsh and Nichol claimed that Ellen had been referring to interbreeding between various species of animals, and between various races of humans. This interpretation clearly did not fit with the context of her statements and failed the test of Occam's razor—whatever defies the straightforward meaning and demands far-reaching assumptions is to be rejected. The idea that Ellen had been referring to interracial marriage in these statements is certainly wrong, since she had condemned such relationships: "There should be no intermarriage between white and the colored race" (*SM* 2:343), but never suggested that such an act brought on the flood or resulted in distinctive or subhuman races.

Ellen's writings about blacks were racist from our perspective today, but her views were shared by many in her culture. It is the claim that she was given these views in visions from God that makes them so revoltingly offensive. It is ironic that Ellen insisted she had received revelations from God about the black race that directly contradicted the Bible. In Scripture we are told that the saved will consist of people from every kindred, tribe and nation; all racial and ethnic groups will be represented. But Ellen saw that God would turn everyone "white" in heaven. Compare these two statements:

After this I looked, and there before me was a great multitude that no one could count, from every nation, tribe, people and language, standing before the throne and before the Lamb. They were wearing white robes and were holding palm branches in their hands. (Rev. 7:9 NIV)

You are the children of God. He has adopted you, and He desires you to form characters here that will give you entrance into the heavenly family. Remembering this, you will be able to bear the trials which you meet here. *In heaven there will be no color line; for all will be as white as Christ himself.* Let us thank God that we can be members of the royal family. (Ellen White, *The Gospel Herald*, March 1, 1901, par. 20; italics added)

First, Jesus wasn't "white." He was a Palestinian Jew. So evidently, Ellen saw that Jesus was whitewashed too. Second, the Word says the nations have "white robes," not white skin. Somehow, the "prophet" confused these two things. Third, Ellen refers to this whitewashed multitude as the "royal family," as if whiteness and royalty go together. I highly doubt, and indeed deny, that God showed Ellen any of this. But there is much more.

While the Bible teaches that every human being will be judged and either rewarded with heaven or punished by hell, Ellen's "testimonies" insist that the slave of her day would not be allowed into heaven or be subject to hell. Instead, it would be as though they had never existed. Again, compare and contrast:

And I saw a great white throne . . . and I saw the dead, small and great, stand before God . . . They were judged *every man* according to their works . . . and *whosoever was not found written in the book of life was cast into the lake of fire.* (Rev. 20:11–15 KJV; italics added)

GOD cannot take the slave to heaven, who has been kept in ignorance and degradation, knowing nothing of GOD, or the Bible, fearing nothing but his master's lash, and not holding so elevated a position as his master's brute beasts. But he does the best thing for him that a compassionate GOD can do. *He lets him be as though he had not been.* Ellen White, *Spiritual Gifts,* vol. 1 (Battle Creek, MI: James White, 1858), 193 (italics added).

Ellen also prophesied, falsely, that slavery would reemerge after the Civil War. Because she believed that the slave could not be saved, she urged that the truth of the gospel not be preached openly to the "colored people: "*Slavery will again be revived in the Southern States,* for the spirit of slavery still lives. Therefore, it will not do for those who labor among the *colored people* to *preach the truth* as boldly and openly as they would be free to do in other places. Even Christ clothed His lessons in figures and parables to avoid the opposition of the Pharisees." Ellen White, *Spalding, Magan Collection,* 21; and 2 Manuscript Release#153, page 300 (italics provided).

Other "testimonies" by Ellen White about blacks, include the following and again demonstrate that her views concerning the "negro race" were drawn from the culture of her day and not from "visions" given to her by God.

The Colored People should not urge that they be placed on an equality with White People. *Testimonies* 9:214, par. 3.

We cannot expect that they . . . [Colored People] will be as firm and clear in their ideas of morality. *Testimonies* 9:223, par. 3.

No one is capable of clearly defining the proper position of the colored people. *Testimonies* 9:213. par. 4.

The work of proclaiming the truth for this time is not to be hindered by an effort to adjust the position of the Negro race. *Testimonies* 9:214, par. 4.

22. As a child, Ellen was filled with fear about God and overwhelmed with dread that she was lost and rejected by God. She did not understand that God loves all His children with an unconditional love. So, as an adult, she taught her own kids, as well as the children in her church, that God hated them when they were bad. To her own son Willie, she wrote, "You must not get angry, but remember the Lord could not love you if you should be naughty," and, "The Lord loves those little children who try to do right and He has promised that they shall be in His kingdom, but wicked, naughty children, God does not love." Ellen White to Willie White, Letter 10, 1859; Letter 3, 1860. These letters were not released by the White Estate until after 2014, when they had been hacked. To children in the church in general, Ellen wrote, "God hates unruly children who manifest passion and evil tempers, etc. He cannot save them in the time of trouble." Ellen

White, Manuscript 1, 1854, not released until 2014. Again, it is bad enough that Ellen believed these things herself, but attributing them to God is a despicable sin.

23. The following are just a few examples from Ellen's pen of "inspiration":

> In many cases I have advised out-of-door work for piano tuners, telling them that unless they changed their business, they would have to deal with insanity. We are made up of nerves and senses, as well as conscience and affections. All parts of the living machinery are to be wisely cared for and considerately treated. (Letter 104, 1901)

I have known several long-term piano tuners, and none of them ever showed the slightest indications of insanity.

> I was shown that the people of God should not imitate the fashions of the world. Some have done this and are fast losing the peculiar, holy character which should distinguish them as God's people. I was pointed back to God's Ancient People, and was led to compare their apparel with the mode of dress in these last days. What a difference! What a change! Then the women were not so bold as now. When they went in public, they covered their faces with a vail. In these last days, fashions are shameful and immodest . . . The small bonnets, exposing the face and head, show a lack of modesty . . . The inhabitants are growing more and more corrupt. (*Testimonies* 1:188–89)

Talk about sexist! How much more "corrupt" can you get than showing your face in public? Ironically, Ellen failed to observe her own counsel.

> A large share of the youth now living are worthless. . . . Many professed Christians are more animal than divine. They are, in fact, about all animal. *Ellen White, A Solemn Appeal Relative to the Solitary Vice and Abuses and Excesses of the Marriage Relation (Battle Creek: Steam Press, 1870) pp. 62, 173.*

The only ones who didn't fall into this category were non-masturbaters.

> Never can the proper education be given to the youth in this country, or any other country, unless they are separated a wide distance from the cities. The customs and practices in the cities unfit the minds of the youth for the entrance of truth. . . .
> The very atmosphere of these cities is full of poisonous malaria. (*Special Testimonies On Education*, 1897, pp. 87–88)

Again, Ellen's words reflect the cultural urbanophobia that was common in her day. Adventists have conveniently ignored this admonition.

> Now hear her warnings against marriage, being a woman, observing holidays, drinking tea, singing, and laughing:
> There are many who are losing their souls in this age of the world, by becoming absorbed in the thoughts of marriage, and in the marriage relation itself. (*Advent Review and Sabbath Herald*, September 25, 1888)
> Thus Satan used an unconsecrated woman [Jezebel] to sway the heart of the king, and through the king to cause all Israel to sin. It is a terrible thing to be an instrument in the hands of Satan. Satan chooses women, for he can use them more

successfully than he can men. (*Manuscript Releases*, vol. 10 p. 76, Ms. 29, 1911, p. 13. Released by the White Estate, Washington, DC July 16, 1980)

The many holidays have had a baleful influence upon the minds of the youth; their effect is demoralizing to the government, and they are entirely contrary to the will of God. . . . These holidays, with all their train of evil, result in twentyfold more misery than good. . , . Through the observance of holidays the people both of the world and of the churches have been educated to believe that these lazy days are essential to health and happiness, but the results reveal that they are full of evil, which is ruining the health and the morals, and demoralizing the country. . . . But from their youth up they have been educated to the popular idea that the appointed holidays must be treated with respect and be observed. From the light that the Lord has given me, these days have no more influence for good than would the worship of heathen deities; for this is really nothing less. These days are Satan's special harvest seasons." (*Manuscript Release* no. 941, "Depressed Conditions in Australia and the Remedy"; *Special Testimonies on Education*, 86, 87, 92, 93, 97)

The practice of using liquor, tobacco, tea, and coffee must be overcome by the converting power of God. There shall nothing enter into the kingdom of God that defileth. (MR vol. 20, p. 6)

I beseech my brethren and sisters to lay aside their darling luxury of tea and coffee, the use of which creates an unnatural state of mind and body. "Thou hast a few names even in Sardis which have not defiled their garments" [Rev. 3:4]. How are their garments defiled? By eating of that which brings disease and infirmity. (MR Vol. 20, p. 6)

Singing should not be allowed to divert the mind from the hours of devotion. If one must be neglected, let it be the singing. It is one of the great temptations of the present age to carry the practice of music to extremes, to make a great deal more of music than of prayer. Many souls have been ruined here. When the Spirit of God is arousing the conscience and convicting of sin, Satan suggests a singing exercise or a singing school, which, being conducted in a light and trifling manner, results in banishing seriousness, and quenching all desire for the Spirit of God. Thus the door of the heart, which was about to be opened to Jesus, is closed and barricaded with pride and stubbornness, in many cases never again to be opened. By the temptations attending these singing exercises, many who were once really converted to the truth have been led to separate themselves from God. They have chosen singing before prayer, attending singing schools in preference to religious meetings, until the truth no longer exerts its sanctifying power upon their souls. Such singing is an offense to God. (*Review and Herald*, July 24, 1883)

You sport and joke and enter into hilarity and glee. Does the Word of God sustain you in this? It does not. Christ is our example. Do you imitate the great Exemplar? Christ often wept but never was known to laugh. I do not say it is a sin to laugh on any occasion. But we cannot go astray if we imitate the divine, unerring

> Pattern. We are living in a sad age of this world's history. (*Manuscript Releases* Vol. 6, pp. 90–91)

There is no end to such statements. Ellen even warns that those who take drugs and medications to treat problems that arise from their "intemperate" lives, will not be healed by God and their prayers will not be answered. This is particularly ironic, given SDA medical practice today. The point is that Ellen reflected the thinking of her day, much of it absurd, and attributed these beliefs to God. In the process she did a lot of harm. I can still remember my SDA grandmother, who was a big EGW fan, strongly reprimanding me for laughing over something that was completely innocent when I was a small child. She told me that the prophet condemned such behavior. Thankfully, her rebukes did not take with me; I still love to laugh today. But it is not surprising that SDAs ("Sadventists") test out to be much more sober and serious than the general population. When you are taught that all these condemnations were given by God, it puts you in a difficult spot.

24. J. N. Anderson, "Inspiration of the Spirit of Prophecy," *Stenographic Report of the 1919 Bible Conference* (Loma Linda University Library, SDA Heritage Room).

25. The 1919 Bible Conference was called in the summer of 1919 by top Adventist leaders who felt the need to address the major problems that had been left for the Church to deal with from the ministry of Ellen White. It is not really a surprise that the leaders of the 1919 Bible Conference decided not to publish the minutes from this important meeting. Rather, it was decided that these 2,400 pages of typewritten transcripts should be buried deep in the archives of the General Conference vault—so deep, in fact, that they would become lost and forgotten for more than fifty-five years. The 1919 Bible Conference became the incredible disappearing conference, and one of the best-kept secrets in Adventist denominational history, until it came to light, almost by accident, on December 6, 1974. The materials were discovered by G. C. archivist Dr. Donald Yost, who stumbled on these packaged documents while responding to a research request made by Donald Mansell, the assistant secretary of the White Estate. He had found a reference that mentioned a significant Bible Conference held in Takoma Park, Maryland, in July 1919, and despite his attempts to gain information from "old timers" in the church, had learned nothing. After examining the transcripts, Mansell quickly realized that he had found much more than he had ever expected. Ironically, it was the White Estate that was ultimately responsible for uncovering these documents, which revealed how aware church leadership was of the deceptions and plagiarisms of Ellen White right after her death.

26. See John Ankerberg shows, "Christianity versus Seventh-day Adventism." Walter Martin's debates against William Johnson (editor of R&H) over the prophetic standing of Ellen White. Martin concludes that EGW is a false prophet and that Adventism is a cult in its relationship to her. Available on YouTube – SkySplash (October 19, 2007).

27. The major document that was used to purge Daniells and his colleagues from their positions was J. S. Washburn, *The Startling Omega and Its True Geneology* (Philadelphia: 5318 Chancellor Street, 1920). Washburn had attended the 1919 conference.

28. See Maynard Shipley, Alonzo L. Baker, and Francis Nichol, *The San Francisco Debates on Evolution* (Mountain View, CA: Pacific Press, 1925).

29. See Francis D. Nichol, *Ellen G. White and Her Critics: An Answer to the Major Charges That Critics Have Brought Against Mrs. Ellen G. White* (Washington, DC: Review & Herald, 1951). See also Nichol, *Answers to Objections: An Examination of the Major Objections Raised Against the Teachings of Seventh-day Adventists* (Washington DC: Review & Herald, 1952).

30. Nichol only mentions the following EGW quotes on the shut door that were given between 1844 and 1851:

> Ellen's first Adventist "vision" (December 1844): "The light behind them went out, leaving their feet in perfect darkness, and they stumbled and lost sight of the mark and of Jesus, and fell off the path down into the dark and wicked world below. It was just as impossible for them to get on the path again and go to the City, as all the wicked world which God had rejected." Nichol, *Ellen G. White and Her Critics*, 204.
>
> "I was shown that the commandments of God, and the testimony of Jesus Christ, relating to the shut door, could not be separated . . . My accompanying angel bade me look for the travail of soul for sinners as used to be. I looked, but could not see it, for the time of their salvation is past." EGW 1849, Manuscript Releases, 5:93; *Present Truth*, August 1849, LLU Library Heritage Room:
>
> Nichol only quotes two of the nine major testimonies where Ellen White strongly teaches the shut door from visions between 1844 and 1851, and tries to dismiss these statements, based on her later denials, cited above, in 1874 and 1883. This is blatant dishonesty and fails to deal with any of Ellen's crucial shut-door testimonies.

31. *SM* 1:74 (1874).

32. Ellen White, 1883 statement, quoted in Arthur L White, *Ellen White and the Shut Door Question*, rev. (White Estate, 1982), 13.

33. See Nichol, *Ellen G. White and Her Critics*, 306–22, 334–41. Nichol completely ignores the fact that both Ellen White and James White endorsed the book written by Uriah Smith, promoted it, and sold it at camp meetings to try to relieve the heat that Ellen was experiencing for her racist testimonies about amalgamation between man and beast, but Uriah's explanation still conceded that certain races and tribes were the product of sex between humans and animals.

34. Nichol failed to even address many of the most ridiculous statements of Ellen White, completely ignoring them. What he did address concerning her bizarre health reform statements (362–402), dress reform (136–60), plagiarism (403–515); financial affairs (516–30), and so on, was purely apologetic in nature, and like the shut door and the racist comments, always failed to get at the true issues, demonstrating that she had not gotten these teachings and practices from God-given visions.

CHAPTER 2: THE THREAT OF DUDLEY CANRIGHT

1. Walter Rea, "Ellen White, Prophet or Plagiarist," excerpts from his book *The White Lie*.
    1. The *Great Controversy* contains the pillars and foundation of Adventist theology.

2. White copied these key doctrines in the Great Controversy from books written by James White.
3. James White copied his books from books written by J. N. Andrews.
4. Thus, the ultimate source of Seventh-day Adventist theology is not God inspiring new truths to White but plagiarizing (copying) J. N. Andrews.
5. We suggest that White step down and let Andrews take her place as the single most influential source of doctrine in the SDA Church. (Just a few of the many examples are provided below)

The Great Controversy	Life Incidents
E. G. White 1888 (1911 ed.)	James White 1868 [page]
Page 317: "He [William Miller] had a sound physical constitution, and . . . more than ordinary intellectual strength. As he grew older, this became more marked. . . . He did not enjoy the advantages of a collegiate education. . . . He possessed an irreproachable moral character."	[28] "In his [William Miller's] early childhood, marks of more than ordinary intellectual strength and activity were manifested. A few years made these marks more noticeable. . . . He possessed a strong physical condition . . . and an Irreproachable moral character. . . . He had enjoyed the limited advantages of the district school."
Pag 318: "He was thrown into the society of deists . . . mostly good citizens and men of humane and benevolent disposition	[30] "But the men with whom he associated . . . were deeply affected with . . . deistical theories. good citizens . . . humane and benevolent."
Page 318: He continued to hold these views . . . about twelve years."	[30] "He has stated the period of his deistical life to have been twelve years."
Page 318: "He found in his former belief no assurance of happiness beyond the grave. The future was dark and gloomy."	[30] "He found that his former views gave no assurance of happiness beyond the present life. Beyond the grave all was dark and gloomy."
Page 318: "Annihilation was a cold and chilling thought, and accountability was sure destruction to all. The heavens were as brass over my head, and the earth as iron under my feet. Eternity—what was it? And death—why was it? The more I reasoned, the further I was from demonstration. The more I thought, the more scattered were my conclusions. I tried to stop thinking, but my thoughts would not be controlled. I was truly wretched, but did not understand the cause. I murmured and complained, but knew not of whom. I knew that there was a wrong, but knew not how or where to find the right. I mourned, but without hope."	[31] "'Annihilation was a cold and chilling thought, and accountability was sure destruction to all. The heavens were as brass over my head, and the earth as iron under my feet. Eternity! what was it? And death why was it? The more I reasoned, the further I was from demonstration. The more I thought, the more scattered were my conclusions . . . but my thoughts would not be controlled. I was truly wretched, but did not understand the cause. I murmured and complained, but knew not of whom. I knew that there was a wrong, but knew not how or where to find the right. I mourned, but without hope."

[319] "'Suddenly,' he says, 'the character of a Saviour was vividly impressed upon my mind. It seemed that there might be a being so good and compassionate as to himself atone for our transgressions, and thereby save us from suffering the penalty of sin. I immediately felt how lovely such a being must be, and imagined that I could cast my self into the arms of, and trust in the mercy of, such a one. But the question arose, How can it be proved that such a being does exist? Aside from the Bible, I found that I could get no evidence of the existence of such a Saviour, or even of a future state.'"	[31] "'Suddenly,' he says, 'the character of a Saviour was vividly impressed upon my mind. It seemed that there might be a being so good and compassionate as to himself atone for our transgressions, and thereby save us from suffering the penalty of sin. I immediately felt how lovely such a being must be; and imagined that I could cast my-self into the arms of, and trust in the mercy of, such an one. . . . But the question arose, How can it be proved that such a being does exist? Aside from the Bible, I found that I could get no evidence of the existence of such a Saviour, or even of a future state.'"
[319] "I saw that the Bible did bring to view just such a Saviour as I needed; and I was perplexed to find how an uninspired book should develop principles so perfectly adapted to the wants of a fallen world. I was constrained to admit that the Scriptures must be a revelation from God. They became my delight; and in Jesus I found a friend. The Saviour became to me the chiefest among ten thousand; and the Scriptures, which before were dark and contradictory, now became the lamp to my feet and light to my path. My mind became settled and satisfied. I found the Lord God to be a Rock in the midst of the ocean of life. The Bible now became my chief study, and I can truly say, I searched it with great delight. I found the half was never told me. I wondered why I had not seen its beauty and glory before, and marveled that I could have ever rejected it. I found everything revealed that my heart could desire, and a remedy for every disease of the soul. I lost all taste for other reading, and applied my heart to get wisdom from God." –S. Bliss, Memoirs of Wm. Miller, pages 65–67.	[32] "'I saw that the Bible did bring to view just such a Saviour as I needed; and I was perplexed to find how an uninspired book should develop principles so perfectly adapted to the wants of a fallen world. I was constrained to admit that the Scriptures must be a revelation from God. They became my delight; and in Jesus I found a friend. The Saviour became to me the chiefest among ten thousand; and the Scriptures, which before were dark and contradictory, now became the lamp to my feet and light to my path. My mind became settled and satisfied. I found the Lord God to be a Rock in the midst of the ocean of life. The Bible now became my chief study, and I can truly say, I searched it with great delight. I found the half was never told me. I wondered why I had not seen its beauty and glory before, and marveled that I could have ever rejected it. I found everything revealed that my heart could desire, and a remedy for every disease of the soul. I lost all taste for other reading, and applied my heart to get wisdom from God.

[319] "But he reasoned that if the Bible is a revelation from God, it must be consistent with itself; and that as it was given for man's instruction, it must be adapted to his understanding. He determined to . . . ascertain if every apparent contradiction could not be harmonized."	[33] "If the Bible is a revelation of God, it must be consistent with itself; all its parts must harmonize, must have been given for man's instruction, and, consequently, must be adapted to his understanding. He said . . .'I will harmonize all those apparent contradictions to my own satisfaction.'"

2. Ellen White, *Last Day Events,* chap. 9, "Sunday Laws," 128–34.

3. *Testimonies* 5:621, 625.

4. *COMDC*, quoting the *Review and Herald*, extra ed., November 1887, 1; italics in the original.

5. Ellen had warned Adventists that "many a star that we have admired for its brilliancy" and bright lights in the movement will "go out," thereby preparing church members to reject intelligent people who questioned her writings and claimed authority. *Testimonies for the Church* 5:80–81.

6. Douty, *The Case of D. M. Canright*, 94–95.

7. Douty, 94.

8. Douty, quoting Canright, 96. This quote appeared in the November 1887 *Review and Herald* (p. 2) in an article wherein Butler quoted Canright and accused him of being hypersensitive.

9. For the pages of testimonials on behalf of Canright's character and integrity, see Douty, 42–48, including the account of the the main street of Canright's hometown being named after him (168). With regard to James White being an authoritarian and dictatorial leader who exercised near-absolute power in Adventism for years, this was not only the testimony of Canright (*Seventh-day Adventism Renounced,* p.42*)*, documented by Douty (*The Case of D. M. Canright*, 61–62), but has even been confirmed by SDA historian Gilbert M. Valentine. See his lengthy book, *J. N. Andrews* (Nampa, ID: Pacific Press, 2019). Valentine documents the very mean-spirited public rebukes that James leveled against leading SDA pioneers, such as Andrews, Waggoner, Smith, Butler, and others, which were backed up by Ellen's "visions." Valentine, 473–500. Even the public press, wrote of James, "Elder White lays down the laws for them all [SDAs]; the people look to him as their chief counselor in all matters of importance. . . . [He] wields so strong an influence—amounting to almost unbounded power." *Detroit Post & Tribune*, June 16, 1878. See also Steve Daily, *Ellen G. White: A Psychobiography*, for many more examples of Ellen confirming wrong or evil things James did by her "visions."

10. James and Ellen lived on opposite coasts for many years of their marriage and clearly had a very rocky marital relationship during these years (see Daily, *Ellen G. White*, 126–36). James even specifically told Ellen in one of his letters to "quit lecturing him about matters of mere opinion," along with some very choice words, which revealed that he wasn't about to be manipulated by her alleged visions in their personal relationship. James White to Ellen White letter, quoted in Ellen White, *Daughters of God* (E. G White Estate: 1998), 270.

11. D. M. Canright, *Seventh-day Adventism Renounced* (Chicao: Fleming H. Revell, 1889), 42.

12. For a litany of sources that document the abuses of James and Ellen White, see chap. 1 n. 9, and for a current SDA historian who does so, see Valentine, *J. N. Andrews*.

13. *Testimonies* 3:304–29.

14. *Testimonies* 3:304.

15. *Testimonies* 3:308.

16. The most highly documented book on this topic, with extensive historical evidence and source documentation, is Daily, *Ellen G. White: A Psychobiography*.

17. Following are some of the "testimonies" in which Ellen called the saints to sell their homes and possessions and give the money to "the cause," or to at least downsize their homes and do the same:

    I saw it was the will of God that the saints should cut loose from every encumbrance, dispose of their houses and lands before the time of trouble comes, and make a covenant with God by sacrifice. I saw they should sell if they laid their property on the altar and earnestly inquired for duty. Ellen White, To Those Who Are Receiving the Seal of the Living God (January 31, 1849), https://media4.egwwritings.org/pdf/en_Broadside2.pdf.

    More than eight years later, Ellen was still pushing this same agenda even though neither the time of trouble nor Christ's coming had ever occurred (nor did she refund the sacrifices of those who made them). But now she was writing that people could just downsize rather than giving up their homes completely:

    I saw that at present God did not call for the houses his people need to live in, unless expensive houses are exchanged for cheaper ones . . . But if those who have of their abundance do not hear his voice, and cut loose from the world, and dispose of a portion of their property and lands, and sacrifice for God, he will pass them by, and call for those who are willing to do anything for Jesus, even to sell their homes to meet the wants of the cause. Ellen White, *Review & Herald*, November 26, 1857.

    During this eight-year-plus period, the Whites saw their net worth dramatically increase, and they never donated money from any of their homes to the church.

18. The historical evidence that Ellen was a narcissist is quite overwhelming when one compares this evidence to the characteristics of narcissistic personality disorder. see Daily, *Ellen G. White*, 247–51.

19. *Testimonies* 3:311–12.

20. *Testimonies* 3:311.

21. For Ellen's hypocritical dietary practices, see Ronald Numbers, *Prophetess of Health: A Study of Ellen G. White* (New York: Harper & Row, 1976), 42–43, 83, 164, 170–71, 194. Comparing her strong dietary condemnations based on supposed visions with her own dietary practices is striking. Not only did she eat countless foods that she forbade to church members, but she even indulged in what she considered "unclean meats and foods" that were most taboo, such as pork and oysters. As Numbers points out, James White scribbled on one of Ellen's letters regarding swine's flesh, "That you may know how we stand on this question, I would say that we have just put down a two-hundred-pound porker." Numbers, 43.

22. *Testimonies* 3:314.

23. *Testimonies* 3:314

24. *Testimonies* 3:316, 321, 325.

25. *Testimonies* 3:313, 317.

26. *Testimonies* 3:324.

27. *Testimonies* 3:325.

28. *Testimonies* 3:305.

29. Ellen's overwhelming hypocrisy is most thoroughly documented in Daily, *Ellen G. White*.

30. *Testimonies* 3:318–19.

31. For documentation of James White's financial fraud and Ellen's failed attempt to cover it over with a professed "vision" from God, see, J. H. Kellogg, *An Authentic Interview with E. W. Amadon and A. C. Bordeau*, stenographic report by J. T. Casco (October 7, 1907), section titled "The $5,000."

32. *SM* 2:162–63.

CHAPTER 3: THE DISHONEST OPPORTUNIST

1. Nancy Paige, interview by Steve Daily (September 24, 2021, 1:56 p.m.), included as appendix 1 at the end of this book).

2. Nancy Paige interview. See appendix 1.

3. Johnson, *IWCS*, back cover.

4. The publishers, "Foreword," in Johnson, 7.

5. Johnson, 5.

6. Amazing, isn't it, that a such a poverty-stricken man could have his own secretary?

7. Willard Santee, "Historical Interview of Carrie Johnson (Adventist History Concerning Elder DM Canright)," recorded September 15, 1971, and sponsored by the Post Falls SDA Church. 34:21 minutes. Copyright ©2009 Post Falls SDA Church. Available online at https://www.audioverse.org/en/teachings/1782/historical-interview-of-carrie-johnson-adventist-history-concerning-elder-dm-canright.

8. Carrie Johnson claims that there were conflicting reports concerning whether Canright had a funeral but mentions a niece who was not close to Canright, who, nine years after his death, said he had no funeral service at all. Johnson, *IWCS*, 166. Carrie tries to present this as offsetting evidence against Canright's son and the various newspaper accounts that documented a well-attended funeral, with many ministers and an abundance of residents from Grand Rapids who honored Canright. (Again, he was so well thought that a main street of town was named after him.) Carrie had to ignore or belittle the legitimate historical sources to support her false claim that Canright died in obscurity. See Douty, *The Case of D. M. Canright*, 135. Douty quotes a letter from Jesse Canright, who attended the funeral and testified that the church was "crowded" (letter dated August 18, 1960). Douty also quotes the newspaper accounts of the *Ostego Union* (May 22, 1919) and the *Grand Rapids Herald* (135–36), but these are all to be doubted compared to the memory of a niece who didn't like Canright, nine years after his death.

9. Nancy Paige interview; see appendix 1.

10. Page interview.

11. The proof that this book was a total fabrication will be provided in chapter 5 of this volume.

12. Douty, *The Case of D. M. Canright*, 171.
13. See appendix 1.

Chapter 4: The Diary Theft

1. Cathy Scott, "The Art of the Con and Why People Fall for It," *Psychology Today*, September 26, 2019, https://www.psychologytoday.com/us/blog/crime-she-writes/201909/the-art-the-con-and-why-people-fall-it.
2. Johnson, *IWCS*, 6.
3. See Douty, *CODMC*, 159–66.
4. See appendix 1.
5. Nancy Paige, describing her grandma Carrie, in a comment on my Facebook thread.
6. It is clear from both the writing style in Carrie's book and much of the material it contains that Arthur White was secretly guiding and directing her.
7. Douty, *CODMC*, 170.
8. Douty, 171.
9. Douty, 171.
10. Douty, 170.
11. The testimonies of both Nancy Paige and Ted Johnson, contained in appendices 1 and 2 of this book, make it clear that Arthur White and Carrie Johnson started secretly meeting in 1950, and continued meeting regularly until Carrie's book was published in 1971.

    Under normal circumstances, it would never take more than twenty years to write a 191-page book like *I Was Canright's Secretary*. But we have documented throughout this book that Carrie, along with Arthur White, were making it up as they went; that Carrie had numerous false accusations that were exposed in the process; and that she wasn't a writer of any expertise. The entire book was a fabrication, and given what was at stake, it is not surprising that the process dragged on for as long as it did.
12. See again Douty, *CODMC*, 159–66.
13. The fact that so many of the false claims Carrie made to Canright's family and to Norman Douty and his wife, were excluded by Arthur White from the book, and that White and the SDA Church threatened to sue Douty for the damning evidence in his book, forcing him to hire attorneys or to take it off the market, shows that Carrie was not a credible witness and that Adventism was threatened by the well-documented material contained in Douty's book.
14. For the actual correspondence, see Douty, *CODMC*, 167–69.
15. Douty, 167–69.
16. Douty, 169.
17. Douty, 169.
18. See appendix 1.
19. Douty, *CODMC*, 169–71.

20. On July 17, 1962, Carrie Johnson declared in writing that she no longer had control over the Canright diary because she had "turned over the diary to the Board of Trustees of the White Publications," and therefore could not return it to the Canright family. After an eighty-day delay, Arthur White finally responded to the requests to have the diary returned to the family by claiming that the "diary is not our property" and that it could only be given to the one who had submitted it to the White Estate. See Douty, 171. So, both Johnson and Arthur White claimed they had no ability to return the diary to its rightful owners. They covered each other with lies to protect their theft, and the White Estate has never returned the diary to this day. This kind of dishonesty is the legacy of EGW and Arthur White in Adventism.

21. Douty, 170.
22. Douty, 171.
23. Douty, 170.
24. Douty, 170.
25. Douty, 170.

CHAPTER 5: THE NORMAN DOUTY CONNECTION

1. The book was Norman Douty, *Another Look at Seventh-day Adventism* (Grand Rapids: Baker Book House, 1962). His description of this is found in Douty, *CODMC*, 9, 12. The SDA leader was Arthur White, but Douty does not identify Arthur by name, nor did he identify Carrie Johnson by name in *CODMC* because they both tried to intimidate him by threatening lawsuits. He could not afford to hire attorneys to fight the denominational attorneys on consignment, so he even took his book off the market for a time in response to their threats. This is what White and Johnson wanted, because Douty's book did a great deal to document their fraud.

2. Quoted in Douty, *CODMC*, 12. Footnote 12 on that page refers the reader to chapter 13 of his book, which fully refutes these charges against Canright.

3. Douty, 159.

4. Douty, 160. It is notable that Douty was so careful and precise about documenting everything with dates and places, while Johnson ran around like a chicken with her head cut off, and then tried to make up for her many mistakes, usually after consulting with Arthur White, by taking actions such as this one. She is the one who showed up at Douty's house and took their entire day spouting foolishness. Now she is going to forbid them to use their notes for any purpose?

5. This claim was made in her first letter to Clifton Dey (Canright's grandson), dated May 31, 1960. See Douty, *CODMC*, 160.

6. Douty, 160.

7. Johnson, *IWCS*, 6.

8. Douty, *CODMC*, 161.

9. Douty, 161.

10. Douty, 161.

11. Douty, 161.

12. Douty, 161.
13. See Nancy Paige interview, appendix 1.
14. See Brian E. Strayer, " Cornell, Merritt Eaton," in *SDA Encyclopedia of Seventh-day Adventists*, ed. D. J. B. Trim (Silver Springs, MD: General Conference of Seventh-day Adventists, 2020), https://encyclopedia.adventist.org/article?id=4962&highlight=Merritt|Eaton|Cornell. See also Merritt's brother Myron from Battle Creek-Convergence: *Family Archivist*, March 18, 2016.
15. Douty, *CODMC*, 159.
16. Douty, 165.
17. See appendix 2.

CHAPTER 6: DESPERATE COLLUDERS

1. William Shakespeare, *The Tempest*, 2.2.40–41. References are to act, scene, and line.
2. These are the motivations Nancy Paige attributed to her grandmother in her interview. See appendix 1.
3. Oxford Online Dictionary, s.v. "psychopathology."
4. *Merriam-Webster.com Dictionary*, s.v. "sociopathic," accessed July 13, 2023, https://www.merriam-webster.com/dictionary/sociopathic.
5. See *Collins Dictionary*, s.v. "expediency," accessed July 13, 2023, https://www.collinsdictionary.com/us/dictionary/english/expediency.
6. See the Nancy Paige interview, appendix 1.
7. See, William C. White and Dores E. Robinson, *The Work of Mrs. E. G. White's Editors* (St. Helena, CA: Elmshaven Office, 1933), 3.
8. See Karl Menninger, *Whatever Became of Sin* (n.p.: Hawthorn, 1973); M. Scott Peck, *People of the Lie* (Touchstone Books: 1985).
9. See appendix 1.
10. Nancy Paige documents that her grandmother was frustrated and annoyed with how Arthur White treated her. See appendix 1.
11. Johnson, *IWCS*, 9. Nancy Paige raises major questions about whether Carrie even attended this school, and also raises significant questions about Carrie misrepresenting it as a college. See the Paige interview in appendix 1.
12. See appendix 1.
13. Read her claims for yourself:
    "In these letters which I write, in the testimonies I bear, I am presenting to you that which the Lord has presented to me. I do not write one article in the paper expressing merely my own ideas. They are what God has opened before me in vision—the precious rays of light shining from the throne." *Testimonies* 5:67.
    "If they [her testimonies] are not heeded, the Holy Spirit is shut away from the soul." *SM* 1:46.

"When I send you a testimony of warning and reproof, many of you declare it to be merely the opinion of Sister White. You have thereby insulted the spirit of God." *Testimonies* 5:661.

"The testimonies never contradict His Word. . . . There is one straight train of truth, without one heretical sentence, in that which I have written." *SM* 3:32, 52.

"If you lose confidence in the testimonies you will drift from Bible truth." *Testimonies* 5:674.

"God does nothing in partnership with Satan. My work for the past thirty years bears the stamp of God or the stamp of the enemy. There is no halfway in the matter." *Testimonies* 4:230.

"You think individuals have prejudiced my mind. If I am in this state, I am not fitted to be entrusted with the work of God." *SM* 2:63.

"We must follow the directions given through the Spirit of Prophecy [Mrs. White's writings]. . . . God has spoken to us through His Word. He has spoken to us through the Testimonies to the church and through the books that have helped to make plain our present duty and the position that we should now occupy." *Testimonies* 8:298,

"The Holy Ghost is the Author of the Scriptures and of the Spirit of Prophecy." *SM* 3:30.

"God has outlined His plan in His Word, and in the Testimonies He has sent to His people." Ellen G. White, *Battle Creek Letters* (n.p.: Leaves-of-Autumn Books, 1975), 74.

"The testimonies are unread and unappreciated. God has spoken to you. Light has been shining from His word and from the testimonies, and both have been slighted and disregarded. *Testimonies* 5:217.

"If you lessen the confidence of God's people in the testimonies he has sent them, you are rebelling against God as certainly as were Korah, Dathan and Abirum." *Testimonies* 5:66.

"If you lose confidence in the testimonies you will drift away from Bible truth." *Testimonies* 5:98.

"These books contain clear, straight, unalterable truth and they should certainly be appreciated. The instruction they contain is not of human production." "Lt 339, 1904," EGW Writings, https://m.egwwritings.org/en/book/10576.1#7.

"These books, giving the instruction that the Lord has given me during the last sixty years, contain light from heaven, and will bear the test of investigation." *SM* 1:35.

"When I went to Colorado, I wrote many pages to be read at your camp meeting . . . God was speaking through clay. You might say this communication was only a letter. Yes, it was a letter, but prompted by the Spirit of God, to bring before your minds things that had been shown me." *Testimonies* 5:63.

"How many have read carefully *Patriarchs and Prophets*, *Great Controversy*, and *Desire of Ages*? I wish all to understand that my confidence in the light that God has given stands firm, because I know that the Holy Spirit's power magnified the truth, and made it honorable, saying, 'This is the way, walk ye in it.' In my books, the truth is stated, barricaded by a 'Thus saith the Lord.' The Holy Spirit traced these truths upon my heart and mind as indelibly as the law was traced by the finger of God upon the tables of stone." "Lt 90, 1906," EGW Writings, https://m.egwwritings.org/en/book/14071.7783001#7783001.

"I am thankful that the instruction contained in my books establishes present truth for this time. These books were written under the demonstration of the Holy Spirit." "Lt 50, 1906," EGW Writings, https://m.egwwritings.org/en/book/14071.8472001?

"After the passing of the time in 1844 we searched for the truth as for hidden treasure. I met with the brethren, and we studied and prayed earnestly . . . When they came to the point in their study where they said, 'We can do nothing more,' the Spirit of the Lord would come upon me. I would be taken off in vision, and a clear explanation of the passages we had been studying would be given me, with instruction as to how we were to labor and teach effectively. Thus light was given that helped us to understand the scriptures in regard to Christ, his mission, and his priesthood. A line of truth extending from that time to the time when we shall enter the city of God, was made plain to me, and I gave to others the instruction that the Lord had given me." *Review and Herald*, May 25, 1905.

"In the night season the Lord gives me instruction in symbols, and then explains their meaning. He gives me the word, and I dare not refuse to give it to the people." "Ms 22, 1890," EGW Writings, https://m.egwwritings.org/es/book/5727.1#1.

"It has been presented to me that, so far as possible, I am to impart instruction in the language of the Scriptures; for there are those whose spiritual discernment is confused, and when their errors are reproved, they will misinterpret and misapply what I might write, and thus make of none-effect the words of warning that the Lord sends. He desires that the messages He sends shall be recognized as the words of eternal truth." "Lt 280, 1906," EGW Writings, https://m.egwwritings.org/en/book/8193.1.

"I beg of you for Christ's sake to consider what I say; for I say it not of myself. It is the word of God to you." " Lt 25b, 1895,"

"At times I am carried far ahead into the future and shown what is to take place. Then again I am shown things as they have occurred in the past. After I come out of vision I do not at once remember all that I have seen, and the matter is not so clear before me until I write, then the scene rises before me as was presented in vision, and I can write with freedom. Sometimes the things which I have seen are hid from me after I come out of vision, and I cannot call them to mind until I am brought before a company where that vision applies, then the things which I have seen come to my mind with force. I am just as dependent upon the Spirit of the Lord in relating or writing a vision, as in having the vision. It is impossible for me to call up things which have been shown me unless the Lord brings them before me at the time that He is pleased to have me relate or write them." *Spiritual Gifts*, 2:292–93

"I testify the things which I have seen, the things which I have heard, the things which my hands have handled of the Word of life. And this testimony I know to be of the Father and the Son. We have seen and do testify that the power of the Holy Ghost has accompanied the presentation of the truth, warning with pen and voice, and giving the messages in their order. To deny this work would be to deny the Holy Ghost, and would place us in that company who have departed from the faith, giving heed to seducing spirits." *SM* 2:388.

"In ancient times God spoke to men by the mouth of prophets and apostles. In these days He speaks to them by the testimonies of His Spirit. There was never a time when God instructed His people more earnestly than He instructs them now concerning His will and the course that He would have them pursue." *Testimonies* 4:147–48; 5:661.

14. See Nancy Paige interview, appendix 1.

15. Arthur White's biography of Ellen White is considered the official biography by the church because of Arthur's longtime position as director of the White Estate and the fact that he was commissioned by the Church to write these volumes at their request.

16. A thorough look at the kind of man Canright was will be presented in chapter 11.

17. For an example of how Carrie was used by SDA leaders on the camp meeting circuit to destroy Canright's reputation, see Santee, "Historical Interview of Carrie Johnson (Adventist History Concerning Elder DM Canright)" (see chap. 3, n. 7). Why would she feel any obligation of loyalty to him, especially for more than thirty years? It makes no sense because it was not true.

CHAPTER 7: PUBLISHING A TOTAL FABRICATION

1. See "Pacific Press Lawsuit: The Other Side of the Story," *Ministry* magazine, February 1989), https://www.ministrymagazine.org/archive/1989/02/pacific-press-lawsuit-the-other-side-of-the-story.

2. Nancy Paige discusses this intimidation in her interview, see Appendix I, p. 139. E. S. Ballenger's role is discussed in Douty, p. 139.

3. Ellen White's documented dishonesty was demonstrated by numerous lifetime patterns that dominated her entire life, not by occasional or isolated incidents, See Daily, *Ellen G. White: A Psychobiography*.

4. See White and Robinson, *The Work of Mrs. E. G. White's Editors* (see chap. 6, n. 7).

5. See White and Robinson, 3.

6. Virtually all the content of the "visions" that Ellen attributed to God can now be traced to sources that she plagiarized from other authors. As SDA researcher Fred Veltman concluded, her claimed writings were "derived," not original.

7. As a researcher I have personally examined the works of Francis Nichol (the most famous SDA apologist), particularly his books, *Ellen G. White and Her Critics,* and *Answer to Objections,* and found them to be intentionally dishonest. He deliberately excluded from both books many historical documents and materials that he had access to.

8. Albert Timm, "A Book Review of Steven Daily's book: *Ellen G. White A Psychobiography,*" Ellen G. White Estate website, accessed July 17, 2023, https://ellenwhite.org/articles/130. Timm quotes Ellen G. White, "'Judge Not,'" *Signs of the Times*, March 14, 1892, 294.

9. See Ted Johnson statement, appendix 2.

10. See Nancy Paige interview, appendix 1.

CHAPTER 8: THE WILLINGLY DECEIVED

1. This was true when I wrote my book *Adventism for a New Generation*, and it is even truer today. See Steve Daily, *Adventism for a New Generation* (Portland: Better Living, 1993), 6–16, 246;

and Errol Webster, "Why Are So Many Leaving the Church" *Adventist Review*, February 22, 2020, https://adventistreview.org/why-are-so-many-leaving-the-church/.

2. Ellen White's first "vision" in Adventism (December 1844), first published by Enoch Jacobs, *Cincinnati Day-Star,* January 24, 1846; republished by James White, *To the Little Remnant Scattered Abroad* (May 30, 1847); now available in all SDA bookstores under the title *A Word to the Little Flock.*

3. Both these concepts are strongly taught in Ellen White's well-known book *The Great Controversy,* of which SDAs have recently decided to have up to one billion copies distributed to the world.

4. See Ron Graybill, "Millenarians and Money: Adventism Wealth and Adventist Beliefs," *Spectrum* 10, no. 2 (August 1979); Paul Richardson, writing in *Adventist Baby Boom Awareness,* (July-August 1990) 1, p. 12; Peter Bath, "Profit or Prophets?" *Spectrum*, 21, no. 2 (1991): 35–40; Daily, *Adventism for a New Generation*, 252–61; Malcolm Bull and Keith Lockhart, *Seeking a Sanctuary: Seventh-day Adventism and the American Dream*, 2nd ed, (Indiana University Press, 2007), 350–56.

5. "*Prophetess of Health* Reappears" (interview with Ron Numbers), *Spectrum,* August 10, 2008, https://spectrummagazine.org/article/interviews/2008/08/10/prophetess-health-reappears.

6. "*Prophetess of Health* Reappears." I wish I could say that my experience with Ron Graybill has shown him to be more honest, but unfortunately, I can't. When I asked Graybill to be part of the reading group for my psychobiography he gave me an enthusiastic yes. But despite my repeated attempts to get feedback from him, before the book was published, he failed to do so. Then when his friend Alden Thompson was preparing to write a letter to the editor at *Adventist Today,* lambasting them for interviewing me regarding the book (a letter I took him to task for), Graybill, trying to dig up dirt on me for his friend, suddenly started bombarding me with emails that contained all kinds of ridiculous accusations and questions. He claimed I didn't have a master's degree in history, or a PhD, or my other doctorate from Claremont; that I didn't work for UCLA, and so on. This was information that anyone could easily find, much more a historian, scholar, or researcher. I found his inquiries and assertions to be quite laughable, and extremely embarrassing to him. But what made it even worse, and humiliating for him, is that he began to contact present and former faculty at La Sierra to share these claims. Some of them called me and said, "What is wrong with Ron Graybill?" One said, "I told him I personally attended your graduation at Loma Linda, saw you get your degree, and read your excellent thesis." Ron also made some historical claims about my book that I found very disappointing for one who had been a secretary at the White Estate, and when I emailed him the references showing him that he was wrong, his response was simply, "Fair enough!" I'm not big on people who pretend to be your friend and then attempt to stab you in the back! The only other member of my reading group who really disappointed me was Gil Valentine (the other nineteen were great). Along with Graybill, Gil gladly agreed to be part of the group and never resigned but also failed to give me the valuable input I expected (based on his impressive historical works). I took his silence to be valuable feedback itself, assuming he was concerned about keeping his job. But like Graybill, he attacked me right after my book was published. At least he had the guts to sign his name to the 1 out of 5 review

he gave my book on Amazon (the lowest possible score), but the two 1s were strongly offset by a host of 5s from other readers. The last time I checked, my overall average score was 4.5, and 70 percent of the reviews have been 5s. Valentine also accused me in his review of making a "disingenuous claim" because I offered a general word of thanks to my reading group in the introduction for their feedback. I found that pretty rich and extremely petty, that a person who agreed to be part of the group but failed to say his piece before publication would then unethically attack the book after publication and self-righteously claim I was being disingenuous for thanking the group! Let me just say, Ron and Gil have both done some valuable work in history, but I have lost a great deal of respect for them as human beings.

7. "*Prophetess of Health* Reappears."

8. Loren Seibold, "Who Speaks for the Hoi Polloi?," *Adventist Today* September 14, 2018, https://atoday.org/50-years-of-the-adventist-forum/. In this article Loren comes across as a great supporter of Ron Numbers, now that Adventist academia is no longer attacking him. But Loren has recently shown himself to be very much a part of the old guard and the establishment by the way he responded to my psychobiography. When I was contacted to be interviewed by the new board chair of *Adventist Today,* Tim Ruybalid (who was brought in to help reach the younger generation), I was very much impressed with both Tim and Paul Richardson, who was the *AT* CEO. The hour-long interview went very well, and I was getting a lot of good feedback about it, but then Alden Thompson and his friend Loren Seibold (editor of *AT)* got involved. Thompson wrote a self-humiliating letter to the editor at *AT,* showing dismay that my interview was posted on the *AT* website, calling for it to be removed and my work to be censored, and lamenting that this incident somehow besmirched his reputation as a writer for *AT.* Evidently, he feels that he can only write for journals or magazines where everyone agrees with him (the anti-academic). Seibold, who claimed ignorance about the interview, quickly sided with Thompson and tried to talk me out of having my response to Thompson's ridiculous letter published, knowing it would make Thompson look like a fool (both letters are available online). But that was not the end of it. The next thing I knew, Ruybalid was leaving *AT* as board chair despite his very brief span of service, and shortly thereafter Richardson left as CEO. Seibold tries to present himself as the great progressive, but don't be fooled. *AT* has shown its true colors once again through this whole incident.

9. Gillian Ford, "The Soteriological Implications of the Human Nature of Christ" (unpublished research paper, Avondale College, Cooranbong, Australia, 1975).

10. See Robert Brinsmead, *Judged by the Gospel* (n.p.: Verdict Publications, 1980); Throughout the 1970s Brinsmead also published *Present Truth* magazine, and *Verdict* magazine, which clearly taught the new covenant gospel and rejected the false substitute of Ellen White and Adventism.

11. Bull and Lockhart, *Seeking a Sanctuary*, 88.

12. See Fred Veltman "Desire of Ages Project Parts I & II," *Ministry* magazine, October 1990, and December 1990. The "derived versus original" conclusion is the second conclusion listed in the December article.

13. Walter Rea, *Pirates of Privilege* (1984), ed. Kerry Wynn July 2, 2009, available online at https://www.nonsda.org/egw/rea/pirates-of-privilege.htm.

14. See Daily, *Adventism for a New Generation*, chap. 19.

15. Daily, 198.

16. Lord Acton in Acton Research, "Power and Authority," Lord Acton Quote Archive, accessed July 18, 2023, https://www.acton.org/research/lord-acton-quote-archive.

17. See Jack Patt, "Living in a Time of Trouble: German Adventists Under Nazi Rule," *Spectrum* 8, no. 3 (1977): 2–10; Erwin Sicher, "SDA Publications and the Nazi Temptation" *Spectrum* 8, no. 3 (1977): 11–24.

18. Roy Branson, "Bleeding Silently–Adventists in South Africa," *Spectrum* 17, no. 2 (1986): 2–13; see also Oxana Antic, "More Persecution of Soviet Adventists," *Spectrum* 16, no.2 (1985): 39–41.

CHAPTER 9: WHO WAS CARRIE JOHNSON?

1. Nancy Paige interview, appendix 1.

2. See appendix 1.

3. Douty was amazed that Johnson would consistently lie and misrepresent things "even when there is nothing to gain by doing so." *CODMC*, 165.

4. Nancy Paige interview, appendix 1.

5. See appendix 1.

6. See appendix 1.

7. See appendix 1.

8. DSM IV Narcissistic Personality Disorder

9. See appendix 1.

CHAPTER 10: ARTHUR L. WHITE: A PSYCHOBIOGRAPHY

1. If you google "books about Ellen White," you will quickly be directed to fourteen of what are considered the best books about Ellen White, which include, of course, what Arthur wrote about her. I have read all these books, and I can assure you that none of them come remotely close to being honest considering the overwhelming historical evidence and source documentation that demonstrates that she was clearly a false prophet. In fact, all of these books seem to be deliberate hagiographies.

2. *Oxford Dictionary of the English Language*, s.v. "confirmation bias," **[[GIVE ACCESS DATE AND URL"**

3. Wikipedia, s.v. "Arthur L. White," accessed July 18, 2023.

4. William C. White and Dores E. Robinson, *The Work of Mrs. E. G. White's Editors* -St. Helena: Elmshaven Office, August 30, 1933, p.3.

5. J. H. Kellogg, "An Authentic Interview with E. W. Amadon and A. C. Bordeau," stenographic report by J. T. Casco (October 7, 1907), 58.

6. See Wikipedia, s.v. Arthur L. White. See also *Spectrum* 10, no. 1 (May 1979), https://www.andrews.edu/library/car/cardigital/Periodicals/Spectrum/1979-1980_Vol_10/1_May_1979.pdf; and Ronald Graybill, *Visions & Revisions: A Textual History of Ellen G. White's Writings* (Westlake Village, CA: Oak & Acorn, 2019), 70, 154, 211; and Jonathan Butler, "Wrestling with the Angel at Bull Run: The Story of Adventist History," *Spectrum*, July 30, 2022).

7. Kimberly Holland, "What is a High-Functioning Sociopath," Healthline, May 28, 2019.

Chapter 11: Who Was D. M. Canright?

1. This warning and rebuke from Ellen White (which she claimed to be a testimony from God) was originally sent in a personal letter to D. M. Canright in the fall of 1880 and later published in her book *Selected Messages*, vol. 2 (p. 169). Ellen's prophecy that Canright would amount to nothing and die in obscurity can be found in other places in her writings too, and has often been quoted by SDA authors as well as by Carrie Johnson; see *SM* 2, p. 163. Ellen Gould White: ". . . to be too much, and make a show and noise in the world, and as the result your sun will surely set in obscurity." *Notebook Leaflets from the Elmshaven Library*, vol. 1, p. 73.; Ellen Gould White: ". . . to be too much, and make a show and noise in the world, and as the result your sun will surely set in obscurity." Letters and Manuscripts, vol. 3 (1876– 1882), Lt 1, 1880, par. 4 ". . . to be too much, and make a show and noise in the world, and as the result your sun will surely set in obscurity." See also Herbert Douglass, *Messenger of the Lord* (p. 153) who states that this prophecy was tragically fulfilled in the case of D. M. Canright; and Arthur L. White, *The Ellen G. White Writings*, 94.

2. Douty strongly documents, from their own church paper, Adventists's repeated criticisms of Canright, using false and disparaging language, well before Canright could attempt to defend himself from these false charges. See *CODMC*, 93–98.

3. Douty, *CODMC*, 98.

4. Canright, *Seventh-day Adventism Renounced*, 55–56.

5. The two most influential SDA leaders who castigated and condemned Canright after he left Adventism were Ellen White herself (*SM* 2, pp. 162–70) and G. I. Butler, president of the General Conference. (Butler attacked Canright in many ways, but his most outrageous claim was that Canright was possessed by an evil spirit. *Review & Herald Extra*, December 1887, p. 2, col. 2). Other well-known SDA leaders who attacked Canright and made false claims against him in the church's public papers were Uriah Smith, *Review & Herald* editor (*Review & Herald Extra*, December 1887); W. A. Spicer, "Moments with Old-time Volumes" R&H (1926); J. L. McElhany, F. M. Wilcox, F. D. Nichol, R. R. Figuhr, W. H. Branson, and many others. See Douty, *CODMC*, 10–11, 96–116.

6. Canright, *Seventh-day Adventism Renounced*, 4th ed., 55; for full context read 40–55.

7. Concerning Canright's integrity, Douty (*CODMC*) does a tremendous job in his book of demon-strating that Canright was a man of remarkable integrity and that this was revealed through abundant testimonies from those who knew him well, as well as by his correspondence while he was within the SDA Church. See the following chapters in his book: chapter 4, "Canright's Integrity"; chapter 7, "Some Correspondence"; chapter 11, "Among the Baptists"; chapter 12, "Personal History: Part II" and chapter 13, "Post-Mortem Developments."

8. Douty did a lot of great research in his book *The Case of D. M. Canright*, including more than a dozen pages of annotated research on Canright's family background, which I have no intention of duplicating. Hiis quote above is from page 31 of his book, and the research is contained in chapter 1, pages 15–31. He also did extensive research into Canright's actual birth date (see chapter 2, "Canright's Beginnings"), which Carrie Johnson failed to understand. The difference in research between Douty's book on Canright, and Johnson's book is absolutely astounding. Douty did outstanding work. Carrie Johnson and Arthur White not only made up the stories in their book, but did a very poor job with the research they attempted to include in it.

9. Canright describes his upbringing in an article in the R&H, March 28, 1882, and his son Jess also spoke of his father's memories growing up on their farm in a letter he wrote to Norman Douty, dated July 16, 1962.

10. Although the records of all students at Coldwater High School during the time Canright attend-ed there were lost in a fire, Dudley was listed as a student there in *Who's Who in America*, vol. 1 (1897–1942), 190. See also D. M. Canright, *SDAR*, 37.

11. Canright, *SDAR*, 37.

12. Canright, 37.

13. This information was provided in a letter from Canright's son, Jess, to Norman Douty, dated October 4, 1962; "My father lived with the Whites for some time . . . he was acting as secretary for them." See Douty, *CODMC*, 138.

14. Just a few examples of how the Whites mixed personal and church finances, beyond boarding members in their home and using church funds to help with the costs: (1) In 1849 Ellen White claimed to have a vision in which God showed her that church members were to sell their homes, properties, and possessions and give the money to "the cause" because time was so short. Ellen White, *To Those Who Are Receiving the Seal of the Living God*, January 31, 1849). The Whites themselves did nothing of the kind, and from the available evidence, used some of that money to buy their first home. (2) In 1852 Ellen and James bought their first home, which doubled as a church publishing house, but when a new publishing house was purchased in 1855, they kept the deed to the first house for themselves. See Anderson, "Ellen G. White: Prophet or Profit?," https://nonsda.org/egw/egw25.shtml; Daily, *Ellen G. White: A Psychobiography*, 280–82; see also Dirk Anderson, *More Than a Profit: Less than a Prophet* (2008), available by title and author online); Dirk Anderson, *White Out* (Life Assurance Ministries, 2001), for many more ex-amples of how the Whites defrauded the Adventist Church. (3) These financial practices caused a great uproar with many in Adventism and was listed as the major reason the whole Messenger Party left the church in 1853, along with their belief that Ellen White's "visions" were not from God. C. P. Russell, *Messenger of Truth*, November 2, 1854, p. 2. (4) The worst example is the

grand larceny that J. H. Kellogg proved against James White, supported by his wife's "visions" to justify the theft, which the church was forced to pay back after James died. J. H. Kellogg, *An Authentic Interview with E. W. Amadon and A. C. Bordeau*, stenographic report by J. T. Casco, October 7, 1907, section titled "The $5,000.".

15. Douty, *CODMC*, 38–39.

16. "General Conference in session is God's highest authority on earth and is not to be opposed"–when her husband was GC president. Testimonies 3:492–93; "General Conference in session is not the voice of God or God's highest authority on earth"–when her husband was no longer GC president. *Testimonies* 9:260–61.

17. The secular press noted that James White was a man of unrivaled power. Referring to him as the founder of the SDA Church, it wrote, "There is probably no other man in the country who wields so strong an influence–amounting to almost unbounded power–over so many people as he does." *Detroit Post & Tribune*, June 16, 1878.

18. In fact, Canright was chosen to debate Miles Grant, author of the strongest book against EGW and Adventism before Canright turned away from the church himself. See Canright, *SDAR*, 42, 45.

19. James's abuse, short-tempered fits, and mean-spirited mistreatment of people in general were documented by his wife, Ellen, in confidential letters in which she questioned his sanity. See Ellen White, "Letters to Lucinda Hall" in *Daughters of God*, 266–72), They were also documented by Canright and other church leaders who repeatedly gave in to his tantrums (Canright, *SDAR*, 38–43) and by Adventist historians. See Gilbert Valentine, *J. N. Andrews* (Nampa, ID: Pacific Press, 2019). Valentine documents in this volume the mean-spirited public rebukes that James White published against Andrews, J. H. Waggoner, G. I. Butler, J. N Loughborough, S. N. Haskell, Uriah Smith,and others, in every case backed up by the "visions" of Ellen White. Finally, they were documented by non-Adventist historians. See Douty, *CODMC*, 59–62.

20. D. M. Canright, *The Life of Mrs. E. G. White: Her Claims Refuted* (1919), public domain; digital edition (Jawbone Digital, 2013) pp. 65–66.

21. For the full context of these concerns, see, D. M. Canright, *The Life of Mrs. E. G. White*, chapter 11, esp. 115–17.

22. White, *Testimonies* 3:304.

23. *Testimonies*, 3:304.

24. *Testimonies*, 3:4–25.

25. *Testimonies*, 4:96, 648–53.

26. Canright, *Seventh-day Adventism Renounced*, 10–15, 55.

27. Canright, 45.

28. Canright, 47.

29. Canright, 47.

30. Canright, 49.

31. Canright, preface, 56; see also Douty, *CODMC*, 108–9.

32. EGW, *Testimonies*, 5:621, 625.

33. *Testimonies*, 5:571–73.

34. *Testimonies*, 5:621–28.

35. The term cognitive dissonance was coined by Leon Festinger, in his books, *When Prophecy Fails: A Social and Psychological Study of a Modern Group That Predicted the Destruction of the World* (1956) and *A Theory of Cognitive Dissonance* (1957). Festinger believed that people strive for internal psychological consistency to effectively function mentally in the real world. A person who experiences internal inconsistency tends to become psychologically uncomfortable and is motivated to reduce that discomfort or cognitive dissonance.

36. "**Emotional blackmail** and **FOG** are terms popularized by psychotherapist Susan Forward about controlling people in relationships and the theory that fear, obligation and guilt (FOG) are the transactional dynamics at play between the controller and the person being controlled. Understanding these dynamics is useful to anyone trying to extricate themself from the controlling behavior of another person and deal with their own compulsions to do things that are uncomfortable, undesirable, burdensome, or self-sacrificing for others." Wikipedia, s.v. "emotional blackmail," accessed July 18, 2023, https://en.wikipedia.org/wiki/Emotional_blackmail. See also Susan Forward and Donna Frazier, *Emotional Blackmail: When the People in Your Life Use Fear, Obligation, and Guilt to Manipulate You* (London: HarperCollins, 1997), 28, 82, 145, 169.

37. See, as prime examples, Ellen's paranoid responses to William Gage and others, Fannie Bolton, and John Harvey Kellogg in my book *Ellen G. White: A Psychobiography*, 144–55, 191–213, 242–50.

38. There are three main types of paranoia: paranoid personality disorder, delusional (formerly paranoid) disorder, and paranoid schizophrenia. The historical evidence seems to indicate that's Ellen's paranoia would fit best with the first two categories.

39. Daily, *Ellen G. White: A Psychobiography,* 207–11.

CHAPTER 12: WHY IS THIS BOOK IMPORTANT?

1. Steven Hassan, generally considered the leading cult expert in the world today, now considers Seventh-day Adventism to be a cult. See Steve Hassan, "Concerns with The Seventh Day Adventist Church with Dr. Steve Daily," Freedom of Mind Resource Center, May 11, 2023, https://freedomofmind.com/concerns-with-the-seventh-day-adventist-church-with-dr-steve-daily/. In the 1950s SDAs conducted a major, deceitful campaign to convince cult expert Walter Martin that they were not a cult, through a number of lies. But Martin discovered their deception and reversed his position.

2. A good book on Ellen White's role in the Millerite movement is Donald Edward Casebolt, *Father Miller's Daughter: Ellen Harmon White* (Eugene, OR: Wipf & Stock, 2022).

3. How this pattern continues to the present is seen in this volume's appendixes.

Appendix III

1. The two *Spectrum* editors who demonstrated a total lack of journalistic integrity by refusing to allow my response to Butler's review of my psychobiography to even be posted on their website were Bonnie Casey and Alexander Carpenter. I see both as simply the sycophants of two *Spectrum/*AAF board members who seem to have a real vendetta against me. I served under both of these men and found them to be tragically dishonest. The one was Fritz Guy, the first president of La Sierra University (once it separated from LLU). Shortly after he became president, he called me into his office and was very affirming about my many contributions to the university. I was the founder of the annual Resurrection Pageant, which brought thousands of visitors to our campus, was the biggest PR event for the university, and was featured on the front page of the local newspapers each year. He also affirmed me for being the founder of the Riverside Community Service Day, where the university dismissed classes for an entire day to provide between thirty and thirty-five major service projects to needy people throughout the city. Two different mayors had given us awards for this community service. I was also the only faculty member who had received the Faculty of the Year Award at the university who was not a full-time teacher. At that time, I was also preparing to publish a book that would become highly influential in SDA circles and be used as a textbook at many Adventist colleges, *Adventism for a New Generation.* Finally, at this same time I was making plans to start the LSU soup kitchen, which would feed between 60 and 120 homeless and needy people near the university two full meals every day (this would occur for seven years), as well as receiving various other honors as a university chaplain. Guy's compliments took me by surprise, because I had never felt that he liked me, even as a student, but I figured it was the presidential thing to do. The next time he called me into his office, many months later, he abruptly said, "We are letting you go!" Surprised, knowing there were no moral or competence concerns, I inquired as to the reason. He said, "I don't have to give you a reason!" That was the dishonesty and disrespect I got after more than a decade of highly committed service. Thankfully, before he could implement his plan, the board asked Guy to step down as president; evidently, he had mistreated several other people with similar unfairness and insensitivity. This is just the tip of the iceberg where Guy is concerned.

   But by far my greatest disappointment with any SDA leader I have worked with came from Larry Geraty. This is because I considered Larry a good friend and really liked him (some of you who know him may feel the same way). I first got to know Larry back at AUC when he was president there and I conducted a week of prayer for him. He was a great host and seemed to be a well-liked and gifted president. When Guy was removed, I stuck my neck out on the search committee to push for Geraty's name and was very pleased when he got the call. We worked together well our first several years, and I considered him a good friend.

   But in the fall of 1997 a new academic administration on campus brought in what they called the CORE Curriculum from Washington, DC, an academic program that was popular with many of the liberal universities in America at that time. Right off the bat I heard a lot of negative things about the program from the students, not just incidentally, but visiting them from room to room in their dorms. They hated the team teaching and found it ambiguous and unfair, they felt the grading was highly subjective, they resented the political and religious agenda built into the program, and over the first two years there were many complaints about the credits not transferring to other schools as they had been promised they would, and enrollment drastically dropped as a result. But as campus chaplain, I was most disturbed by the number of students who came to my office devastated by what they were being taught about God. This was not a conservative student body, but large numbers were angry, frustrated, or even in tears over required freshman courses that taught that Jesus was not God, God is not a personal being, monotheism is the worst form of religion, etc., etc., while the students' parents were being told that their kids were being given a good Adventist education. When I passed on these student concerns to Geraty, he pretended he wasn't totally sold on the CORE program either but said we need to give it a chance. The next thing I knew, he was part of secret meetings plotting to push me out of my position. This really disturbed me, because I had been at the university more than eighteen years at this point, and I had received three very attractive calls in the previous two years. In each case I asked Geraty if I should consider the call, and in each case he begged me to stay. But the worst was yet to come.

While Geraty was plotting against me, he continued to treat me as if he were my close friend. He finally informed me that political forces were against me but that he was now going to try to find me a position, when in reality, he was blackballing me throughout Adventist academia. As the year drew to a close, he tried to make me the scapegoat for the whole CORE fiasco and the huge drop in enrollment that had accompanied it. Worst of all, behind my back Geraty made all kinds of false accusations against me and tried to play amateur psychologist, claiming, both privately and publicly (confirmed by close friends of both of us), that I had experienced a mental breakdown. I found this so despicable that I lost all respect for the man. At the same time, being on the editorial board of *Adventist Today* for years, I was asked to write three separate articles about the CORE situation at La Sierra. In every case, I carefully researched the articles, interviewed student leaders, and carefully documented student surveys and concerns. At that time, *AT* was housed on the La Sierra campus. In each case my articles were accepted for publication, and in each case, they were censored "from the top" by "university administration" at the last minute. In the final case, the article was pulled so late that it remained in the table of contents when the magazine was published. At this point I realized that there was simply no freedom of speech, even at *AT.* The university board did move in and end the CORE program at the close of the year, and all the academic administrators were demoted back to their teaching tenured positions. But Geraty stayed on as president; evidently, he was able to BS the board as well. One leader at the university who was part of all the plotting against me, came to me after I left, fully confessed what was done, and asked forgiveness. I have great respect for that man to this day. As for Geraty and Guy, I have forgiven them based on God's Word, but will never trust or respect either of them until they acknowledge their dishonesty and ask for forgiveness. I should also say that the way I was mistreated in Adventism was no motivation at all for writing my last two books, I owe those who drove me out of the SDA Church a major thank-you from the standpoint that the last fourteen years of my life have been by far the happiest and most fulfilling I have experienced. Some will surely question why I have been this candid in an endnote, but it has been my observation that Adventism silences its victims, and that terrible leadership rarely is held accountable for their failures and evil deeds.

This is not a good pattern, to say the least. Maybe next time *Spectrum, AT,* and men like Guy and Geraty will think twice before they censor or engage in other unethical activity.

Appendix IV

1. Quotations from this review are from Albert Timm, "A Book Review of Steven Daily's Book: *Ellen G. White A Psychobiography,*" Ellen G. White Estate website, accessed July 19, 2023, https://ellenwhite.org/articles/130.
2. Here Timm has a footnote number, with the note itself citing Ellen G. White, "'Judge Not,'" *Signs of the Times,* March 14, 1892, 294.
3. Here, too, Timm has a footnote number. The footnote reads, "Truthiness" is the "truthful or seemingly truthful quality that is claimed for something not because of supporting facts or evidence but because of a feeling that it is true or a desire for it to be true" (Merriam-Webster. com Dictionary, s.v. "truthiness," https://www.merriam-webster.com/dictionary/truthiness [accessed April 25, 2021]).

ABOUT THE WRITERS

Steve Daily Ph.D. (Author) Is the award-winning author of Ellen G. White a Psychobiography, and the author of 27other books. He is a licensed psychologist, church historian, theologian and pastor. He taught in all three fields at Loma Linda University/La Sierra University for 24 years, before leaving Adventism in 2010 to work as a psychologist for UCLA. In this book he uncovers what has never been exposed before, the fraud perpetrated by Arthur White, the White Estate, the Seventh-day Adventist Church, and Carrie Johnson, in an attempt to destroy the reputation of D. M. Canright -Ellen White's most effective critic. Daily has been married to his fine wife Erlys for nearly 50 years, has 3 great children (Lindsay, Justin, Stevanie) & 6 super grandkids (Aubrey, Cadence, Peter, Wesley, Lucy, Ruth)

Nancy Paige (Contributer): Nancy is the granddaughter of Carrie Johnson and without her powerful testimony and eye-witness accounts, this book would not have been possible. She has also researched the story of her grandma meticulously!

www.ingramcontent.com/pod-product-compliance
Lightning Source LLC
Chambersburg PA
CBHW031456120626
46545CB00005B/1626